T4-ABL-710

DISCARDED

Corporate Staying Power

How America's most consistently successful corporations maintain exceptional performance

James B. Hobbs
Lehigh University

Lexington Books
D.C. Heath and Company/Lexington, Massachusetts/Toronto

Library of Congress Cataloging-in-Publication Data

Hobbs, James B.
  Corporate staying power.

  Includes index.
  1. Organizational effectiveness. 2. Industrial organization—United
States. 3. Organizational effectiveness—Case studies. 4. Industrial organization—United
States—Case studies. I. Title.
HD58.9.H62   1987   338.7′4′0973   85-45096
ISBN 0-669-11153-8 (alk. paper)

Copyright © 1987 by D.C. Heath and Company

All rights reserved. No part of this publication may be reproduced or transmitted in any form or by any means, electronic or mechanical, including photocopy, recording, or any information storage or retrieval system, without permission in writing from the publisher.

Published simultaneously in Canada
Printed in the United States of America
International Standard Book Number: 0-669-11153-8
Library of Congress Catalog Card Number: 85-45096

The paper used in this publication meets the minimum requirements of American National Standard for Information Sciences—Permanence of Paper for Printed Library Materials, ANSI Z39.48-1984. ∞™

88 89 90 8 7 6 5 4 3 2

*To vacations
foregone and forthcoming,
particularly
for Peg*

Contents

Figures and Tables   ix

Preface   xi

1. The Crème de la Crème of American Business   1

   Beginnings of the Project   2
   The Selection Criteria   3
   The Fourteen Corporations   7
   Some Observations on the Fourteen   7
   Sources of Information   15
   Some Comparisons with *In Search of Excellence*   16
   A Glance Ahead   18

2. A Crystal-Clear Mission and Focused Central Thrust   21

   Clarity of Mission   22
   Well-Defined Acquisition Strategy   32
   A Long-Run Perspective and Patience   41

3. Internal Operating Procedures: Planning and Monitoring Activities   45

   Extensive Planning Activity   45
   Financial Objectives Established and Performance Results   50
   Intensive Monitoring Activity   55

4. The Top Echelon and the Front Office   61

   Visionary Founder and Influential CEOs   62
   Planning Managerial Succession into Top Management   73
   Promotion from Within   76
   Routes to the Top   77
   Lean Headquarters and Central Staff   78
   Degree of Centralization and Decentralization   79
   Transition from Entrepreneurial to Professional Management   81
   Control of the Corporation   84
   Summary   86

5. **Cultural Characteristics of the Organization** 87
    Cultivation of a Culture 88
    Esprit de Corps 95
    A Give-a-Damn Attitude 97
    Concern for Employees and Degree of Unionization 99

6. **The External Community: Customers and Competitors** 103
    Obsession with Top Quality, Superior Performance, and Outstanding Service 104
    The Critical Role of Innovation and R&D Activity 106
    Selected Marketing, Promotional, and Advertising Strategies 114
    Attitudes toward the Competition 122
    Forcing Competitive Advantages to Occur 127
    Being in the Right Place at the Right Time—and Luck 130

7. **Some Overall Perceptions and Insights** 133
    Composite Portrait of the Fourteen Organizations 133
    Some Caveats 139
    Stock Market Performance 141
    Some Predictions of Future Arrivals and Departures 143
    An Ending Note 145

Appendix A: ROS and ROI of Firms in the *Fortune* 500   147

Appendix B: Financial Statement Analysis of Profitability, Liquidity, Leverage   149

Appendix C: Interview Schedule Outline   161

Appendix D: International Involvement   163

Bibliography 165

Index 173

About the Author 179

Figures and Tables

Figures

1–1 ROS and ROI: Average of *Fortune*'s Top 500 and Top 20% Cutoff, 1954–1985   5

1–2 Return on Sales and Return on Owners' Investment by Three Categories, 1975–1985   12

6–1 Effective Patent Life of Pharmaceutical Product   108

Tables

1–1 Overview of the Fourteen   8

7–1 Individual Stock Performance Compared to the Standard and Poor 500 Index, 1 January 1976 through 31 December 1985   142

7–2 Past Members of the Most Consistently Highly Successful Companies   144

Preface

The United States is favored with some fifteen million business establishments, of which approximately 2.5 million are organized as corporations, either publicly or privately held. Of the publicly held organizations, perhaps 2,500 (or .1 percent of the total incorporated firms) have found their way onto the *Fortune* 500, second 500, and service 500 lists during the past decade. Now, for a rather intriguing question: Of those in the *Fortune* directories, which are the *consistently* top-performing companies? One director of the McKinsey and Company consulting firm recently asserted that "even the best companies, by anyone's definition of excellence, retain their superior competitive performance for only three to four years." Going one step further, he maintains that "only one manufacturing company in the U.S. during the last 20 years, Xerox, has been able to sustain a position of financial leadership in its industry for ten years."[1] I think additional homework needs to be done.

This book summarizes the results of a six-year investigation of identifying attributes and characteristics associated with the fourteen most consistently, most highly successful large publicly held U.S. corporations during the last ten or more years. In fact, five of these firms have generated return on both sales and owners' investment that place them in the top 20 percent of the *Fortune* directory organizations continuously, without interruption, for almost a quarter century. In short, consistent outstanding performance by major U.S. corporations is a fact! And here are some insights and observations of the inner workings of those organizations that may, at least in part, account for their extraordinarily superb records of accomplishment.

Some are less than household names. A few may even have escaped your attention completely. Others will be as familiar as your breakfast, checkbook, beverage, or favorite over-the-counter pain remedy. At least two keep such low public profiles that many may be surprised to discover that they actually exist. But each of these fourteen comprise an elite group of corporations that have demonstrated a stamina for superb achievement that is probably unexcelled in corporate United States, perhaps the world.

One must be somewhat cautious, however, not to get overly carried away with this group's impressive records, for not included in this investigation are the large number of privately held corporations that rarely release any financial or operating information for public consumption. Such large privately held firms as the Bechtel Group (mega-large energy and construction projects), Cargill (commodities trading), Hallmark Cards, S.C. Johnson and Sons (wax and household products), and Mars (confectionery goods) are believed to generate extremely handsome records of business efficiency and effectiveness consistently, very likely surpassing even those among our distinguished group.

Again, stamina is the hallmark of members of this elite group. Each organization belongs in a class with such outstanding individual performers as Isaac Asimov, George Burns, Benny Goodman, Vladimir Horowitz, and Charles Schulz. These firms, like their individual counterparts, are in the public's eye constantly, evoking admiration as entities that reflect perseverance, endurance, and a "class" act. Discovering some ingredients of what it is that makes such human organizations tick is most exciting and rewarding, even to the point of providing an educational experience.

But we must also proceed somewhat warily because one or more of these fourteen competitors could experience circumstances that would cause them to "fall from grace" and membership on this list. One such enterprise, Dover, has recently faltered falling, in 1985, just slightly below one criterion that was established for presence in this group. However, I elected to retain that corporation in the study in the belief that its inclusion would not severely damage the insights uncovered during this investigation, and also that its perhaps temporary demise might lend credence to the obvious fact that consistent success rarely lasts forever.

One criticism of this study for which I was frankly unprepared arose during a presentation of preliminary findings to a group of faculty and graduate students at the University of Edinburgh (Scotland) in May 1984. In that seminar were two visiting faculty members from a university in New Zealand (where I had taught during 1976) who could not understand why I had elected to include in my study so many corporations that produced and sold products of "questionable social value and unredeeming qualities," such as over-the-counter placebo-like medications, tobacco goods, scent and taste enhancers, and alcoholic beverages. My off-the-top response was two-pronged. First, the criteria were not designed to include or exclude any specific company, product, or service. The firms included simply satisfied preset standards without preconceived prejudice toward particular product or service exclusions or inclusions. Second, in the United States (and a large part of the world), it is the market's response to products and services that, for the most part, determines the success or failure of specific business enterprises. Each organization in this study must be doing "something right" to survive for so long, so well—at least the public believes so. And for the reader who wishes to catch a glimpse of how well those in the investment community appraise members of this particular group, your attention is invited at this juncture to the exhibit in the concluding chapter which summarizes how this portfolio of fourteen stocks performed in comparison to the Standard and Poor's 500 over a recent ten-year period.

These prefacing remarks must not close without noting particular individuals who made enormous contributions to this six-year project. First and foremost are the many individuals that I interviewed among these fourteen firms, who (because of a personal commitment to them I am honor-bound to abide by) must remain unnamed. Nonetheless, for their insights, comments, charity, and patience, I am most grateful. The two hours in the spring of 1982 that I was privileged to spend with Reginald Jones (General Electric's immediate past chairman of the board and CEO) provided me with several penetrating observations from one of the outstanding business leaders in the United States. I am also deeply indebted to several colleagues in various universities for their constructive criticisms and suggestions of avenues to explore that otherwise might have been overlooked: Dr. James E. Boyce of Michigan Technological University; Dr. Val F. Ridgway at Colorado State University; and those at Lehigh University—Professors Alden Bean, Carl Beidleman, John Bonge, James Greenleaf, John Guerard, Michael Kolchin, Benjamin Litt, James Maskulka, Robert Mills, Vince Munley, and Steven Thode. At least three members of Lehigh's administration afforded me some released time from teaching responsibilities to bring this research to closure—namely Provost Arthur Humphrey, Dean Richard Barsness, and Chairman Bruce Smackey—thank you. I am also deeply indebted to all those individuals who contributed both time and financial resources to establish the professorship that I hold, which was created in honor of Frank L. Magee, retired chairman of the executive committee of the Aluminum Company of America. Without the support of that chair's funding, this investigation might never have progressed beyond the idea stage. And much of the work required to bring the entire work to press could hardly have been accomplished without the dedicated assistance of William Fincke, of Lehigh's library system, and the following for secretarial and editorial assistance: Alice Boyce, Joyce Chiz, Renee Hollinger, Diane Oechsler, and Janice Schaeffer. Finally, my wife's eagle eyes detected errors both in substance and style that warranted numerous corrections. Thank you to all.

Note

1. Richard Foster, *Innovation* (New York: Summit Books, 1986), p. 29.

1
The Crème de la Crème of American Business

> He would not claim to know what all these principles are but he is groping toward them, convinced from the outset that they exist.
> —C. Northcote Parkinson
> *Drucker: The Man Who Invented Corporate Society*

Only a handful of the relatively large publicly held corporations in the United States consistently outdistance their peers in profitable performance. American Home Products and SmithKline Beckman have done it for at least thirty consecutive years, including 1985, and Merck's record runs a close twenty-nine. Eleven others have been outperforming the field over ten or more successive years. To surpass one's competition once, twice, or even five years in succession is a notable achievement, but to maintain that supremacy continuously for one, two, even three decades is nothing short of phenomenal. It is indeed a phenomenon that compels investigation.

What accounts for such exceptional performance? Do these firms have any discernible characteristics that distinguish them from the rest of the field? What combinations of factors generate such continuity of outstanding performance? What can we learn from their experience?

Three of the most pervasive common characteristics that this study was able to identify among this august group of fourteen are:

A crystal-clear idea of what the organization is about—its central mission and overriding thrust—and a religious adherence to it.

Adherence to a long-run perspective—as opposed to the quick-fix or short-term payoff so currently in vogue.

A sincere "give-a-damn" attitude on the part of employees—from production floor and delivery dock to front office—to generate products and services of outstanding quality.

Stamina, perseverance, and a knack for making a competitive advantage happen—as opposed to waiting for it to occur—are additional hallmarks of these enterprises.

What corporations comprise this elite group, and what products and services do they provide? Who are the individuals that lead these firms? And, perhaps most important, what specific attributes or characteristics are discernible among these fourteen companies that may, in part, account for their records of consistently extraordinary performance?

These questions, together with some of the answers, are what this book is about—the results of a six-year investigation into fourteen organizations that comprise the crème de la crème of American business.

Beginnings of the Project

In truth, this project began in July 1955, after I had received the first *Fortune* directory of the 500 largest U.S. industrial corporations—a roster that, in subsequent annual editions, became better known as the *Fortune 500*. While immersed in pursing an MBA at a midwestern university, I became intrigued with identifying business organizations that were at or near the pinnacle, whether in terms of greatest dollar sales, largest total assets, most sales per employee, or highest profitability: dollar profits, return on sales, or return on owners' investment. Once the best had been pinpointed from among the 500, I assumed that the task of parlaying the savings accumulated during my Korean tour of duty into a magnificent nest egg would be achieved automatically if I invested in a portfolio of these best securities and let the mechanism of the surging stock market of the fifties do the rest. As events turned out, expectations far surpassed the amassing of monetary wealth.

This exercise whetted my curiosity over the next several years. I began to wonder about what, if any, components might be required to assist an organization in becoming extraordinarily successful in terms of long-term profitability. As Parkinson's quote (which refers to Peter Drucker's quest for "principles of management") suggests, the more I looked, the more I became convinced that certain attributes, traits, or characteristics must underlie such outstanding long-run performances.[1]

In about 1980, after I had had some twenty-three years of experience in industry, university teaching and administration, and corporate consulting, a meaningful project began to emerge. It seemed an undertaking that might hold considerably greater promise of providing benefits to a larger business community than did my earlier personal investment portfolio pursuit. The essence of the question on which the investigation finally focused was—once several of the most consistently successful business organizations in the United States were identified (success being measured by return on sales *and* return on owners' investment), might it be possible to detect and uncover attributes and characteristics among them that would—at least partially—account for their consistent records of success? If such traits exist and are identifiable, the larger business community could benefit from those findings in at least two ways. First, characteristics associated with such an elite group of outstanding performers might prove useful and possibly even transferable to other organizations—both profit-seeking and not-for-profit. Second, tangible specific examples of brilliant performances would help assuage and refurbish the tarnished self-confidence in America's business system that has been generated by the intimidating onslaught from overseas and offshore competitors.

This book, then, focuses on identifying and examining attributes found to be generally common among the most consistently profitable, relatively large, publicly held U.S. corporations.

We will begin by nailing down the specific criteria that were used to select the organizations in this study and follow with the identification of the fourteen corporations that comprise the backbone of this report. Then, to help satisfy the curiosity of those who feel the need for this type of data, there is a summary of the sources of information used in the study, plus a few words concerning methodology. Next, some preliminary remarks comparing the sixty-two firms in Peters' and Waterman's *In Search of Excellence* with my list, which involves fourteen organizations, might prove instructive.[2] Finally, a quick review of some highlights of this report, along with a brief outline of the content of subsequent chapters, will prepare the way for an in-depth look at specific findings, beginning in chapter 2.

The Selection Criteria

Success, for purposes of this study, is defined in terms of two key and widely accepted measures of profitability:

>Return on sales (net profit after taxes divided by total sales), hereafter identified as ROS.

>Return on owners' investment (net profit after taxes divided by total owners' investment), hereafter identified as ROI.

Included in this study is every firm that has been in the top 20 percent of all firms in *Fortune's* top 500 from 1956 to 1985, the second 500 from 1969 to 1981, and the top 50 categories of commerical banks, life insurance, diversified financial, retailing, transportation, and utility companies from 1957 to 1985 in both of the return ratios for a minimum of ten consecutive years, including the 1985 fiscal year. The minimum acceptable ROS and ROI cutoff points for 1956 to 1985 were established with reference to the respective returns experienced by firms in the top 500 group.

The ROS reflects the *efficiency* with which a business enterprise carries out a particular sales volume of business. Since after-tax profit equals revenue (or sales) less total expenses, ROS measures the ability of the organization to maintain control over its total expenses. Generally, the higher a firm's ROS, the better. The average ROS experienced by all United States enterprises hovers around 3 percent to 5 percent, and the average of the 500 during the thirty-two–year period, 1954 to 1985, was 5.1 percent—ranging from 3.7 percent (in 1982) to 6.9 percent (in 1955). However, the minimum ROS reflected by any of our fourteen firms was 6.6 percent (1983), up to a maximum of 25.0 percent (1971)—a rather impressive ceiling above a relatively high floor.

The ROI measures the *effectiveness* with which the capital that is invested by the owners is used in the enterprise. In general, owners' investment represents the total monies invested in the corporation by all types of stockholders (less any stock held in the treasury), plus the earnings that are retained in the business. The average ROI of the top 500 ranged from 9.5 percent (in 1958 and 1970) to 16.1 percent (1979); whereas the minimum return achieved by any of our fourteen firms was 13.5 percent (1963) to a maximum of 63.1 percent (1980). Again, an extremely impressive distance above a relatively high floor. For the statistically inclined, appendix A at the end of this book displays the ROS and ROI ratios for each of the years 1954 to 1985 that were generated by the top 500, along with the minimum cutoff returns required for any firm to be included in the top twentieth percentile group.

A graphic depiction of those ratios is reflected in Figure 1–1.

Two well-known indicators of business performance were rejected as auxiliary measures of success in this study: return on total assets and earnings per share (EPS). Return on total assets (net profit after taxes divided by total assets) was rejected because the ratio focuses on the total financial resources that are committed to the business regardless of whether those resources were contributed by equity investors or outside creditors. One of management's prime responsibilities is to maximize (or at least optimize) the return to ownership interests—not necessarily the return to the creditors. (In most cases, creditors expect and are entitled to receive only the contractual interest specified in the loan or debt agreement).

One method of enhancing ROI is through an astute use of leverage—the employment of a prudent level of debtor-furnished capital in lieu of equity capital. It is true that some degree of risk is inherent in the use of leverage because the contractual interest must be paid whether or not the enterprise is profitable, but, management's overall task centers on continuously undertaking various types of risk while attempting to generate lucrative returns for the owners.

EPS was rejected for two reasons. First, the number of common shares

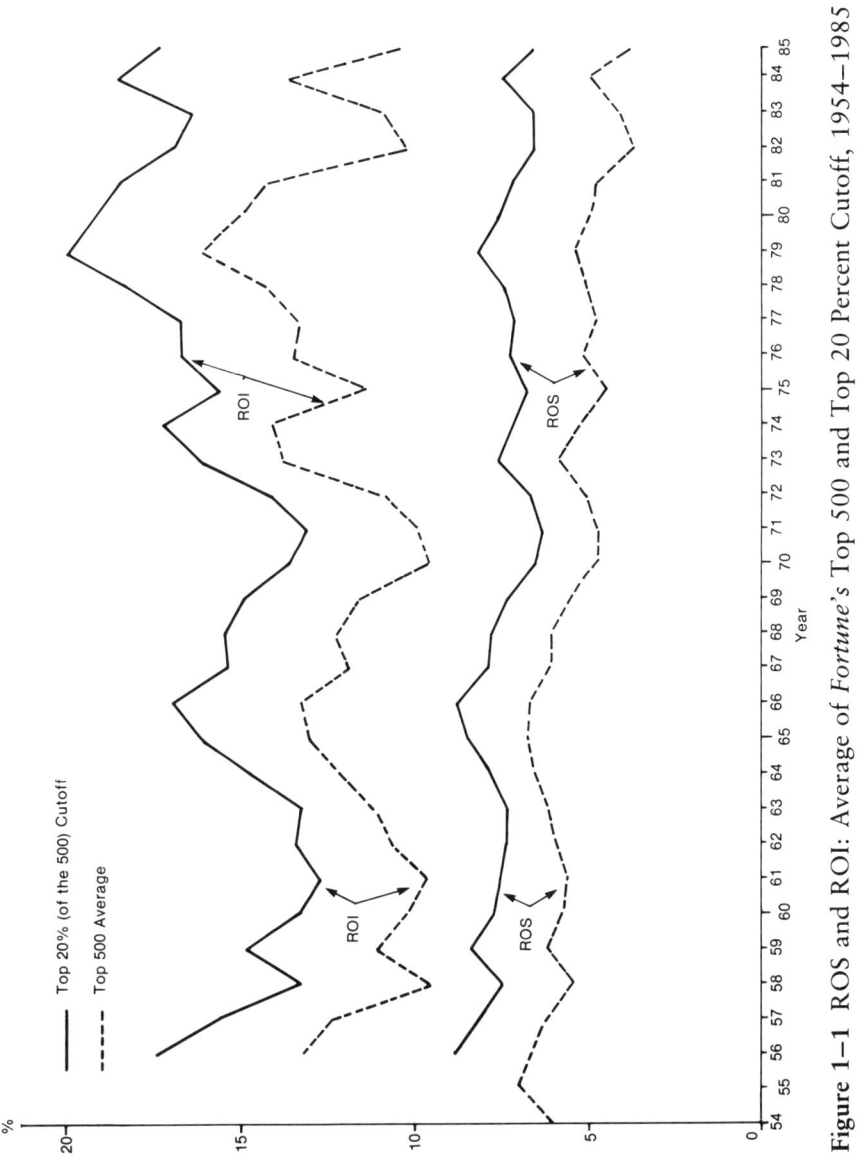

Figure 1–1 ROS and ROI: Average of *Fortune*'s Top 500 and Top 20 Percent Cutoff, 1954–1985

issued and outstanding reflects a considerably narrower base of owner investment than does total contributed equity capital (net of any treasury stock) plus retained earnings. Furthermore, the number of common shares issued and outstanding (the denominator in the ratio) can be markedly altered through significant repurchases of those shares. Also, useful comparisons of EPS among various firms in any single year become difficult because of the wide variability among corporations in the number of shares issued and outstanding. In addition, any calculations of EPS growth over a particular time frame depend on the particular base-year selected.

There is one additional observation on the criteria selected in this study. Bruce Johnson and two of his colleagues at Northwestern University argued, in the fall 1985 issue of the *Journal of Business Strategy*, that "shareholder wealth creation is the most appropriate criterion for evaluating corporate economic performance."[3] The specific measure of performance they suggest is "dividends plus the appreciation in price per share" of a particular stock over a prescribed period, divided by the owner's investment in the company's stock. In short:

$$\frac{\text{Dividends + Price appreciation}}{\text{Original cost of the stock to the investor}}$$

I disagree with the applicability of their suggested criterion to our "staying power" study for several reasons.

First, this "shareholder wealth creation" measure does not necessarily indicate how effectively the corporation is using investor-contributed capital within the firm—something that ROI does reflect. For example, financial resources that are distributed to shareholders in the form of taxable cash dividends might better be deployed within the organization. Many highly profitable growth companies pay remarkably low or zero cash dividends—and not to the long-run detriment of their stockholder group. Second, the price of a particular stock can be influenced by a variety of noneconomic factors over which a corporation may be able to exert very little direct control—such as political, sociological, psychological, and even occasionally whimsical factors.

Third, different investors will experience different percentages of "shareholder wealth creation," depending on the price at which respective shares of stock were purchased. Hence, any calculation of an aggregate "wealth creation" percentage is dependent on the price per share that is selected at a specific time. In other words, the base year chosen can be crucial. Finally, Cynthia Hutton reported an interesting finding in the January 6, 1986 issue of *Fortune* in the article, "America's Most Admired Corporations." She discovered that, over the past ten years (1975 to 1984), the ten least admired corporations reflected a median total return to investors (dividends plus stock price appreciation) of 4.6 percent—well below the 18.7 percent median for the *Fortune* 500. But more interesting, the 14.9 percent ten-year median total return experienced by the ten most admired corporations was also considerably below the 500's median.

In short, the two measures of profitability that were selected for the present study—ROS and ROI—seem to me to be reasonable, useful, and comprehensive indicators of business success.

The Fourteen Corporations

The fourteen corporations identified in table 1–1 are those that were in the top 20 percent of all firms in *Fortune's* top 500, second 500, and top 50 categories in both ROS and ROI at least ten consecutive years, including fiscal 1985. Included in this organizational overview are the location of headquarters, the number of consecutive years in this select group as of 1985, the 1985-dollar sales volume, ROS, and ROI (the return on *average* owner's investment in this case), and each firm's principal products and services.

Some Observations on the Fourteen

These enterprises are relatively large in terms of dollar sales volume, which range from Tambrands' low of $68.1 million in 1969, to Philip Morris's $12.1 billion in 1985. And they are growth-oriented, at least in terms of sales volume. Except for six instances (out of a possible 261 aggregate years), each of these firms generated dollar sales growth in every year it has been a member of this elite group. (Dover incurred a $25 million—2.5 percent—sales decline in 1983; Dow Jones, $7 million—4.9 percent—in 1970; International Flavors and Fragrances, $3.4 million—1.5 percent—in 1975 and $3.2 million—.7 percent—in 1982; Merck, $12.2 million—.1 percent—in 1985; and U.S. Tobacco, $.4 million—.4 percent—in 1972).

Each corporation is publicly held and therefore is subject to various Securities and Exchange Commission regulations. The capital stock of all but two of the enterprises is traded on the New York Stock Exchange, with accompanying specific exchange requirements that must be met. (Betz Labs and Commerce Clearing House are traded over the counter).

It is noteworthy that only those companies that are broadly classified as manufacturing industrials were able to satisfy the criteria used in this study. No publicly held bank, stock life insurance, agricultural, mining, construction, diversified financial, retailing, transportation, or utility enterprise achieved, much less exceeded, the ROS and ROI cutoff points for ten or

8 • Corporate Staying Power

Table 1–1
Overview of the Fourteen

Company and Headquarters	Continuous Years Meeting Criteria	Sales Volume ($-billion)	ROS[a]	ROI[b]	Principal Products or Services
American Home Products Corporation New York, New York	30	$ 4.7	15.3%	32.7%	Ethical drugs, medical supplies, packaged medicines, foods, household products, and housewares.
Betz Laboratories, Inc. Trevose (near Philadelphia), Penna.	12	.3	11.5	20.1	Specialty chemicals plus technical and laboratory services for treatment of water, waste water, and process systems in chemical, petroleum refining, paper, and steel industries.
Commerce Clearing House, Inc. Chicago, Illinois	11	.5	9.9	36.6	Publisher of topical law, tax, and government regulatory reports; computerized processing of income tax returns.
Deluxe Check Printers Inc. St. Paul, Minnesota	17	.8	13.6	31.9	Produces and markets preprinted checks, deposit tickets, and related business forms.
Dover Corporation New York, New York	11	1.4	6.9	16.8	Elevators; petroleum extraction devices and specialized high technology equipment.
Dow Jones & Co., Inc. New York, New York	17	1.0	13.3	25.1	Publishes *The Wall Street Journal* and *Barron's*; operates Ottaway newspapers, and R.D. Irwin, book publisher.
International Flavors & Fragrances, Inc. New York, New York	17	.5	13.9	17.9	Produces flavor and fragrance ingredients and markets them to other manufacturers as additives to various consumer and industrial products.

Kellogg Company Battle Creek, Michigan	26	2.9	9.6	48.0	Ready-to-eat cereals and various convenience foods.
Eli Lilly & Company Indianapolis, Indiana	24	3.3	15.8	22.5	Human and animal medicines, electronic medical instruments, agricultural products, and cosmetics.
Merck & Co., Inc. Rahway, New Jersey	29	3.5	15.2	20.9	Human and animal medicines and health products, specialty chemicals, and water purification products.
Philip Morris Incorporated New York, New York	17	12.1[c]	10.3	28.4	Cigarettes, beer, and carbonated beverages. General Foods added in 1985.
SmithKline Beckman Corporation Philadelphia, Pennsylvania	30	3.3	15.8	23.7	Human and animal medicines, and medical instruments; provides data management systems for hospitals and chemical laboratories.
Tambrands Inc. Lake Success, New York	17	.4	13.8	27.3	Feminine tampon and external menstrual napkins.
United States Tobacco Company Greenwich, Connecticut	17	.5	19.5	30.9	Moist and dry smokeless tobacco, cigars, pipes, wine, and various writing instruments.

[a] Return on sales
[b] Return on average owners' investment
[c] Excluding excise taxes

more consecutive years (including fiscal 1985). The rather narrow spectrum of manufacturing sectors that is represented among the principal products of the fourteen follows. Three of the companies are listed under two sectors because of their product mix.

Chemicals and allied products	American Home Products
	Betz Laboratories
	International Flavors and Fragrances
	Lilly
	Merck
	SmithKline Beckman
Food and kindred products	American Home Products
	Kellogg
	Philip Morris
Printing and publishing	Commerce Clearing House
	Deluxe Check Printers
	Dow Jones
Tobacco	Philip Morris
	U.S. Tobacco
Paper and allied products	Tambrands
Machinery	Dover
Measuring, analyzing, and controlling instruments	Betz Laboratories

Except for Dover and Betz Laboratories, the principal product lines of the remaining twelve could be broadly classified as consumer nondurables.

Industrial segments that are notably absent from these groupings are petroleum, automotive, the "smokestack" industries, heavy manufacturing (except Dover), and data processing equipment—although IBM could be a prime candidate for future membership in this group. Several companies in these excluded segments have reflected excellent profitability from time to time, particularly some petroleum pipeline firms in recent years, but they have been unable to sustain continuously high profitability for a decade or longer. Another notable absence from the fourteen is the conglomerate enterprise—such as Gulf and Western, ITT, and Textron. One explanation that might account for this fact would be the tendency of conglomerates to spread themselves over an excessively wide variety of product lines, industrial segments, or channels of distribution. Several implications of this point will be developed more emphatically in chapter 2, when we discuss the presence of a crystal-clear mission and the relatively few product lines that exist in each of the fourteen.

Reginald Jones, former chief executive officer of General Electric, noted, during an early stage of this investigation, the relatively large number of pharmaceuticals, four, among the fourteen. He believed that patentability of ethical drugs and the general rise in the public's concern over and expenditures for health care in this country partially account for the high percentage of drug manufacturers among this group. This observation has validity, to be sure; however, a considerable number of well-known ethical drug manufacturers are absent from the list—such as Pfizer, Schering-Plough, G.D. Searle, Sterling Drug, and Warner-Lambert. Apparently, patentability of product and escalating health care costs alone are not sufficient to assure sustained ROS and ROI of the magnitude reflected in these fourteen.

A vice-president of one of the pharmaceutical firms represented in the study made a somewhat startling statement that his organization probably should *not* be among the fourteen most highly and most consistently profitable U.S. corporations. He argued that "if our enormous R&D expenditures were capitalized, instead of being expensed as they now are in the period of their cash outflow, our ROS and ROI would be considerably lower. If accountants capitalized these outlays, we probably wouldn't make your list." This argument is one that occasionally arose before the Kefauver Committee hearings into the ethical drug industry during the early 1960s by defenders and proponents of the industry. However, if research and development (R&D) expenditures were capitalized, rather than immediately expensed, both ROS and ROI would increase—not decrease—at least during the early portion of their capitalization period, and particularly so if the level of R&D outlays remains constant or increases. In general, R&D expenditures have reflected significant increases among the major U.S. ethical drug manufacturers during the last fifteen to twenty years. In short, the four pharmaceuticals that are members of this elite group belong in it, regardless of whether their R&D expenditures are capitalized or immediately expensed.

The ROS and ROI that each of these firms, alone and collectively, has generated during the period it was in this group are extremely impressive. Appendix B provides data for those readers who wish to review the entire array of "financials" for each of the fourteen organizations during its membership on this list. That appendix reflects the ROS, ROI, current ratio, cash cycle, degree of overall leverage, and interest-bearing debt as a percentage of total assets for each firm for each year it has appeared on this list. Frequent reference will be made to that data during the course of this book, particularly in chapter 2. At this point, it is enough to focus on one particular aspect of that financial information.

Displayed in figure 1–2 are four graphs covering the eleven-year period 1975 through 1985, during which the fourteen met the highly selective cri-

12 • *Corporate Staying Power*

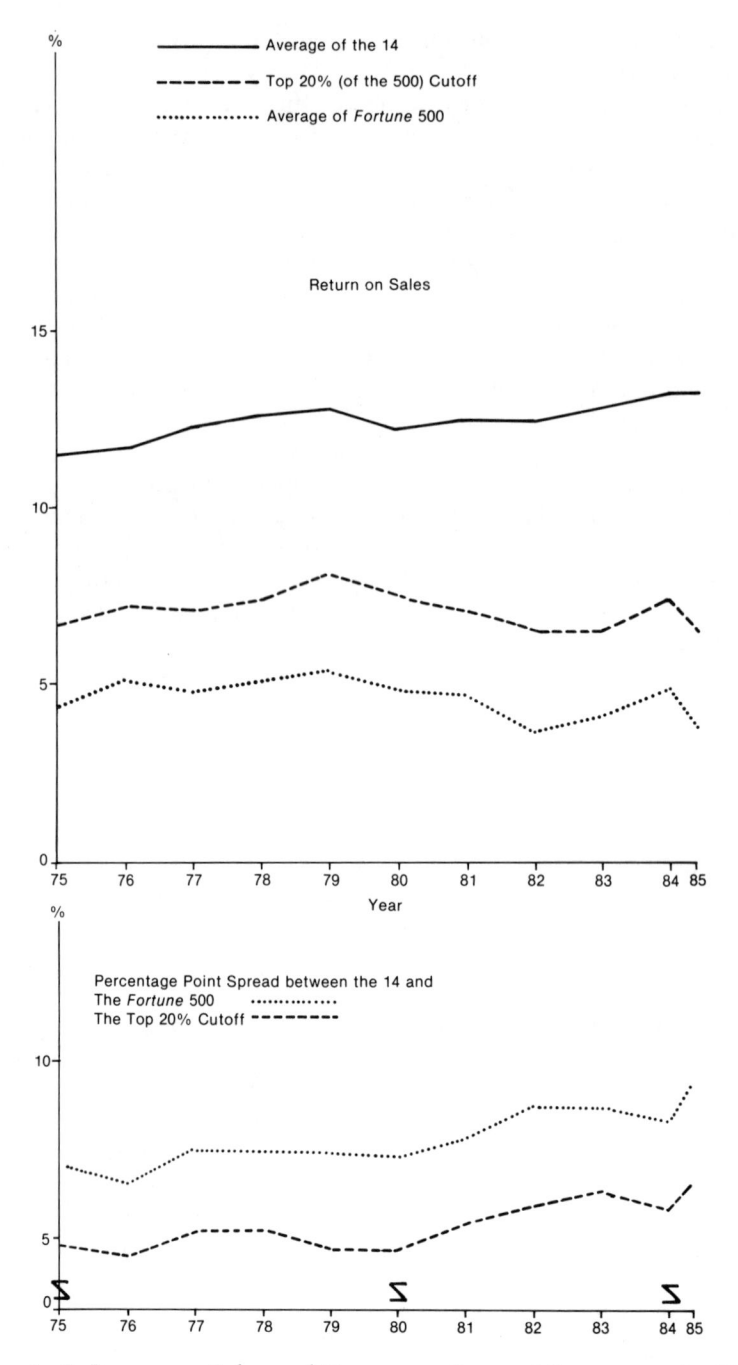

Figure 1–2 Return on Sales and Return on Owners' Investment by Three Categories, 1975–1985

Return on Owners' Investment

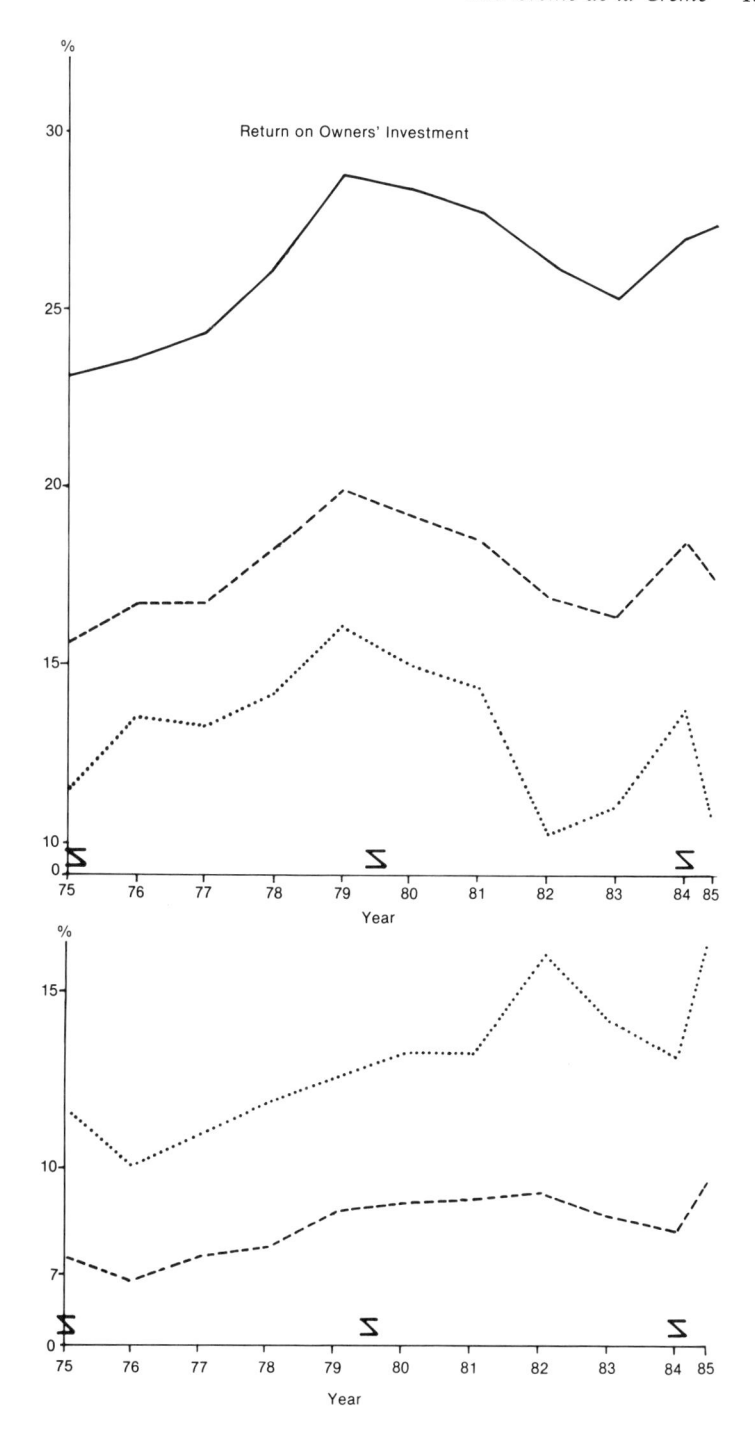

teria used in this study. The upper two graphs reflect: (1) the average ROS and ROI generated by all *Fortune* 500 firms during that decade (dotted line); (2) the minimum ROS and ROI cutoff points of the top 20 percent of the 500 (dashed line); and (3) the average ROS and ROI generated in each of those years by our fourteen as a group (solid line). Note that the dashed and dotted lines in both graphs present moving targets that each of the fourteen companies might have aimed for in each of those years—had their objective been to attain membership among the fourteen. However, the exact placement of those particular lines were not known until after the close of each fiscal year.

The bottom two graphs reveal the percentage-point spread between our fourteen and (1) the 500 and (2) the top twentieth percentile during the ten-year period. Observe that these respective point spreads range within a relatively narrow band.

A few moments spent in absorbing and digesting the magnitude and significance of what this series of financial graphs depict should prove extremely revealing of the caliber of corporations included in this study. What is most impressive is that the average ROS and ROI experienced by our fourteen in each and every year from 1975 through 1985 is *considerably* and *consistently* higher than those necessary for inclusion among the top 20 percent. Without belaboring the point, these fourteen exhibited absolutely superb performances during this eleven-year period—a historical period that encompassed a broad spectrum of economic and political climates. And five of the fourteen enterprises appear among the elite in excess of two decades—a period that was affected by considerable technological change.

My contention here is that there must be reasons for such extraordinary records of accomplishment. Although I seriously doubt I have been able to pinpoint *all* of those reasons, an honest effort was made to identify several of those that appear to be the most significant.

There are two minor points regarding the financial criteria. First, recall that *Fortune* discontinued publishing the second 500 industrial category after 1981. In addition, Betz Laboratories, Commerce Clearing House, Tambrands, and U.S. Tobacco were not always included among the top 500 category in each of the years 1982 through 1985. In order to determine if these four companies would have ranked among the second 500 (with respect to sales volume, had that category been published), an alternative was developed. I assumed that, if the percentage of increase in dollar sales volume experienced by each of these four firms in each of the respective years equaled or exceeded the percentage of increases in the total sales volume of *all* firms in the top 500, each of the four probably would have remained on a second 500 listing. In each of the relevant years, the percentage of increase in dollar sales volume that each of these four firms generated substantially exceeded the percentage of increase experienced by the total of all firms in the top 500.

Second, close inspection of the data in appendix B reveals that two corporations failed to equal or exceed the ROI criteria in three instances. Dover slipped .1 and .6 percentage points below the 1983 and 1985 cutoffs, respectively; and International Flavors and Fragrances fell .4 of a percentage point below the 1975 cutoff. However, because the ROI generated by each of these firms in two subsequent periods exceed the minimum ROI cutoffs, I decided to retain them in the study. I do not believe the investigation suffered from their inclusion.

Sources of Information

Considerable information was gathered from annual reports to stockholders for each year that each of the fourteen firms met the criteria. Sprinkled among these 275 reports were data on areas such as new products and services offered, corporate restructuring (for example, acquisitions and divestitures), major policy changes, and strategic reconfigurations. For example, the substantial repurchase of over 3.5 million shares of common stock on the open market and from the estate of Oakleigh L. Thorne was noted in Commerce Clearing House's 1978 and 1979 annual reports, the result of which almost tripled its already substantial ROI from 21.8 percent, in 1977, to 63.1 percent, in 1980 (see appendix B). Dow Jones's proposal to create a new Class B stock was revealed in its 1984 annual report; its purpose to preserve the future editorial independence of the firm's publications by facilitating retention of voting control of the corporation among members of the Bancroft family. International Flavors and Fragrances disclosed, in its 1982 annual report, its intention to stress research activity into subliminal odor alertness signals for potential use in home and work environments—a "far-out" concept in the minds of many industrial experts. And Tambrands announced, in its 1982 report, a substantial strategic policy shift—diversifying beyond its traditionally strong expertise in the catamenial tampon field by developing other packaged goods to be distributed through its strong food and drug retailing network.

Numerous articles and books were examined to ferret out additional information on each company and to cross-validate some data that were acquired during the interview process. A fairly exhaustive compilation of these sources is reflected in the bibliography of this book. Those references are segregated into two groups: (1) articles and books of general interest and (2) those that are specific to each company, arranged in alphabetical order by company name. An assortment of in-house publications was also obtained, but they were not included among the references.

Probably the most rewarding and intriguing information obtained during the course of this study was from personal interviews conducted with several executives in these corporations during the early part of 1984. A substantial number of top managers—ranging from president and chief executive officer to various vice-presidents and corporate economists—were interviewed at their offices with the use of a detailed interview schedule. The essential ingredients of that schedule are reflected in the Interview Outline, appendix C.

Only three of the fourteen organizations declined to be intensively interviewed—in two instances because of long-standing corporate policies not to participate in such endeavors; in the third case because of a recent unsettling corporatewide reorganization. In my judgment, their reluctance to participate in the interview process probably did not materially alter the overall outcome and conclusions of this report.

Findings presented in this book are derived from three basic perspectives: (1) intensive investigations of each of the fourteen corporations—using the previously noted sources of information; (2) insights gleaned from analyzing problems and challenges associated with some eighty case histories of business and not-for-profit organizations that have been integral parts of executive, graduate, and undergraduate seminars I have conducted over the past twenty years; and (3) a few personal convictions and prejudices that I have developed during twenty-four years of industrial, university administration, teaching, and consulting experiences.

Some Comparisons with *In Search of Excellence*

A few similarities and differences can be pointed out between this study and Peters and Waterman's best-selling 1982 book, *In Search of Excellence*. Both are exploratory studies that seek insights into some factors that may, at least in part, account for or explain the successful performance of a select group of U.S. corporations. They are exploratory in the sense that neither study can be called an experimental or scientific exercise that sought cause and effect answers to corporate success and failure by examining a large population of organizations under controlled, laboratorylike conditions, using elaborately constructed control groups. Although several insights are gleaned by identifying factors that help account for well-known failures that have occurred on the U.S. corporate scene, the focus of both studies is on examples of success: most consistently highly profitable corporations in this book, and "best-run" companies in *In Search of Excellence*. I believe that greater strides can probably be taken in the practice of management by examining in detail hale and hearty enterprises rather than dwelling on those nearing or passing beyond insolvency.

In Search of Excellence grew from a project that Thomas Peters and Robert Waterman were pursuing for the large German electronic company, Siemens AG, and the numerous examples presented in their book draw heavily upon their experiences gained while employed as principal and director, respectively, of the consulting firm McKinsey and Company. As was revealed earlier in this chapter, this study saw its genesis in 1955—a seed that slowly germinated during the next twenty-five years, pending construction of a more focused interest in 1980.

In Search of Excellence involved sixty-two U.S. corporations (fifty-eight publicly held or their subsidiaries and four privately held), compared to fourteen (all publicly held) in this book. Whereas *In Search of Excellence* involved a wider spectrum of organizations, its selection criteria were considerably less restrictive. To be included in their sample, a company had to be in the top half of its industrial grouping in at least *four of the following six measures over the twenty-year period,* 1961 to 1980:

Compound asset growth.

Compound equity growth.

Average ratio of market value (closing share price times common shares outstanding) to book value (common book-value equity).

Average return on total capital (net income divided by total long-term debt, non-redeemable preferred stock, common equity, plus minority interests).

Average return on equity.

Average return on sales.

Again, recall that *Staying Power's* criteria require qualifying firms to be in the *top twenty percent on both ROS and ROI* (the last two measures above) of *Fortune's* 500, second 500, and top 50 categories each year for a minimum of *ten consecutive years,* including 1985.

Only one corporation, Merck, is common to both studies, having satisfied the selection criteria of each project. It is referred to only once (on page 20) in Peters' and Waterman's work—by name only—without further comment in their study. Allowing a one-to-two year grace period (since their study bears a 1982 publication date), only one other corporation cited in their study approaches meeting this book's criteria. Avon Products satisfied the criteria for ten consecutive years as of both 1980 and 1981. However, Avon was excluded from my study since it failed to satisfy the ROS and ROI cutoffs for 1982 to 1985.

Note that a firm could meet the first four *In Search of Excellence* criteria and yet reflect a substantially subpar performance on two of the most critical financial measures: ROI (which measures the effectiveness with which owners' capital is being used) and ROS (which measures the efficiency with which a particular volume of sales is undertaken). The Peters and Waterman criterion of "compound asset growth" merely means the firm is growing with respect to the book value of assets that are reflected on the balance sheet—without any reference to how effectively those assets are being used. By the same token, "compound equity growth" indicates that the owners' investment is increasing, again without reference to how effectively management is using that investment. The ratio of "market value" to book value stresses how the investment community values the firm's stock—for a wide variety of financial, noneconomic, and frequently fickle reasons—with respect to the book value of the stock as reflected by the historical cost conventions still required by generally accepted accounting principles. Finally, the fourth measure—return on capital—includes long-term debt in its denominator, even though management (as pointed out previously) usually has a contractual obligation merely to generate sufficient cash flow to pay annual interest payments on that debt and retire the debt instruments at their maturity date. In short, a firm could stand in the upper half of its industry on each of those first four measures and hence qualify for membership in the *In Search of Excellence* study without attaining any notable distinction in the critical ROI and ROS areas.

A Glance Ahead

A quick overview of several of the key common areas that were discovered among the fourteen companies may provide a bit of perspective as we proceed through the remainder of this book. The critical nature of a crystal-clear definition of the organization's mission and central thrust is addressed in the first part of chapter 2. Also probed in that chapter is the relevance of two other closely related issues: (1) a well-defined acquisition strategy for those firms that engage in growth and diversification using this vehicle; and (2) the nurturing of a long-run perspective, as opposed to the quick-fix syndrome that has today become so pervasive in U.S. business.

Chapter 3 dwells on three internal operating procedures:

The importance of extensive planning activity as it impinges on several functional areas of the firm, including R&D, territorial expansion, and financial forecasting.

Establishing various financial objectives and the extent to which they are specific and detailed. Also highlighted is a brief look at selected performance measures for these organizations during the period they have been among this elite group.

The role and extent of control and monitoring mechanisms in these fourteen enterprises.

Facets of the organizational structure comprise the content of chapter 4. The criticalness of visionary founders and some very influential chief executive officers in several of our fourteen are pinpointed, along with their respective contributions to each organization. The long-term durability of several of their key ideas is interwoven with the long-term perspective philosophy that is introduced in chapter 2. Precisely how these enterprises anticipate and plan for managerial succession into their top managerial positions is also examined in some detail. Of particular interest is the presence in many of our fourteen organizations of an extremely lean headquarters and central staff—despite the relative large dollar-sales volume generated by several of these organizations.

Those particularly interested in behavioral aspects may wish to direct their attention to chapter 5. Of some interest is the degree to which these organizations consciously cultivate and nurture a corporate culture—some quite actively and explicitly while others witness a common culture developing and flourishing despite almost zero conscious attention being directed toward its cultivation. The overriding importance of a high esprit de corps and a pervasive "give-a-damn" attitude comes through quite clearly in the vast majority of these enterprises. Supplementing the various cultures is the effort these organizations direct toward developing executive and employee compensation and fringe benefit programs.

In chapter 6, attention moves toward the external environment. Customer client relations from the product-planning stage through servicing warranties are addressed. The importance of innovation, R&D activity, marketing research, and promotional programs are probed in considerable detail. Three aspects that are not commonly touched on in other management studies are examined near the close of this chapter: (1) forcing a competitive advantage to occur, as opposed to waiting for it to happen; (2) the fortuitous happenstance of being in the right place at the right time; and (3) the possibility that luck might play a significant role in the successful performance of several of our fourteen organizations.

Two precautions, however, before we delve deeply into these commonalities. First, most of the attributes and traits discussed in subsequent chapters were identified in each of the fourteen to some degree, but not always to the same extent or depth. Second and far more important, I discovered that the continued success of a business enterprise probably results from a mixture of various attributes and factors that are combined in complex clusters in enormously subtle ways, rather than from the simple addition of one attribute after another until some magic number of items, say eight or twelve, have been implemented. Whatever "magic" is involved may lie in the way in which attributes are combined within the organization. The following chapters examine some of these specific attributes and commonalities more closely.

Notes

1. In John J. Tarrant, *Drucker: The Man Who Invented Corporate Society* (Boston: Cahners Books, 1976), p. xi.

2. Thomas J. Peters and Robert H. Waterman, *In Search of Excellence: Lessons from America's Best-Run Companies* (New York: Harper & Row, 1982).

3. W. Bruce Johnson, Ashok Natarajan, and Alfred Rappaport, "Shareholder Returns and Corporate Excellence," *Journal of Business Strategy* (Fall 1985), p. 53.

2
A Crystal-Clear Mission and Focused Central Thrust

> Wherever we find a business that is outstandingly successful, we will find that it has thought through the concentration alternatives and has made a concentration decision.
> —Peter F. Drucker
> *Management: Tasks, Responsibilities, Practices*

> Now, in America some companies certainly do have constancy of purpose, but most do not. Most have a president who was brought in to improve the quarterly dividend. . . . There is no quick road.
> —W. Edwards Deming

Probably the most crucial dimension in any organization is the mission for which it is created. Only after the central thrust and focal point of a business enterprise becomes clearly delineated, can all other aspects of the corporation begin to fall into a coherent framework. Unless the central purpose of the organization is clearly understood by its members, particularly those in key positions, the business may flounder and proceed in a haphazard fashion. For example, one segment of the business that strives for long-term profitability in an ill-defined target market can prove as frustrating and counterproductive as another organizational component that seeks a quick killing in a narrow niche in which long-term perseverance is a prerequisite for success. A deliberately considered and focused thrust that is conscientiously adhered to over the long pull lies at the core of many a success story, both organizational and personal—and of our fourteen corporations in particular.

In this chapter, we will first probe the clarity and specificity in each organization's mission statement. Is it concise and clear? Is it understandable and implementable? Does it hang together in a logical and unambiguous way? We will also examine the closely related issue of acquisition and diversification strategies in these several corporations that have elected to pursue that avenue toward growth. Particular attention will be paid to the degree of fit between a firm's primary mission statement and its acquisition-diversification policies.

Clarity of Mission

Far too frequently businesses are established on the spur of the moment with little conscious thought given to the complexity of the undertaking; or they are operated on the basis of the amorphous economic principle—maximize long-run profitability or its more sophisticated modification—optimize the present value of the firm's long-term potential. This latter extension usually has as its outer limit the equally nebulous concept of infinity. As desirable as this motive may be in principle, it provides little substantive direction for running the enterprise. Far more critical is the purpose of the business. What does it seek to accomplish? By what means of production and through which channel of distribution? At the core of the organization is this constantly emerging question: what is the central mission or primary thrust around which activities will focus?

A clear unambiguous statement of what an organization—or for that matter, an individual—seeks to accomplish is probably the most critical building block that can ever be laid in place. Why so little time and attention is devoted to constructing a well fleshed-out statement is one of the continuing mysteries of corporate and human existence. Without some rather precise delineation of organizational purpose, progress commonly becomes sporadic, lethargic, or easily fractionated—if not all three. A concise mission statement emblazoned somewhere in the corporation serves as a touchstone to which executives and associates can refer from time to time as reminders of what it is the firm and they are about. The road made of good intentions is crowded with individuals and organizations who begin a trek with optimism and enthusiasm, only to lose their way once complexity, competitive maneuvers, and hectic activity begin to cloud the way.

All of our fourteen firms have one over-arching similarity—a similarity so apparent and pervasive that even the casual observer quickly perceives its presence. *Each of these organizations has a crystal-clear idea of what it is about—its principal activity and its outstanding expertise.* Each knows full well the focal point toward which most of its energy is directed, and that awareness is well communicated among key executives and to most members of the organization. Little effort is directed to peripheral activities that fall outside the boundaries of its mission statement.

A rather detailed enumeration of each of the fourteen corporate missions is warranted at this juncture, in order to make three points:

To convey how precise, unambiguous, and down-to-earth are most of these focal points that govern the daily lives of so many individuals.

To broaden the summary profile of each company that was presented in chapter 1. Each mission statement will provide a reference point and context within which the rest of the organization's objectives, activities, and behavior can be viewed with sharper perspective.

To illustrate how far removed most of these statements are from the overly simplistic, perhaps almost meaningless, profit maximization motivations noted above.

Here then, are fourteen organizational focal points that for the most part, are neither overly elaborate nor flowery, yet are absolutely germane to the consistent pattern of success achieved by these organizations.

Were our fourteen firms placed on a continuum reflecting the degree of product complexity or number of product lines, Tambrands would occupy the single product line pole position. From its founding in the mid-1930s, the company—Tampax until 1984—has remained a single-product company for all practical purposes. Its expertise is manufacturing and marketing catamenial devices—internal tampons and external pads that absorb the menstrual flow. For only a brief interval in its history did the firm venture beyond that main mission. Hair rinse and rubber baby pants were produced, mainly to avoid any employee layoffs during the Great Depression. Revenues generated from these two lines, however, never exceeded .5 percent of total sales in any year.

Most management experts and top-level business executives agree that the conscious decision to concentrate on a single product line, single market, or single technology is a high-risk decision. That resolution, once firmly implanted, can foreclose entry into other endeavors and commits all organizational resources to focus on a single target. The drawback is loss of mobility and maneuverability to hedge one's bet with other product lines. But the sword is two-edged. The advantage of the single focus is total organizational strength directed toward one point. Andrew Carnegie's method of dealing with the dilemma that arises from placing all of one's eggs in one basket appears in his famous quote: "I watch my one basket *very* carefully"—which is exactly the approach adopted by Tambrand's top management from its inception through the seventeen-year period that the firm has met this study's criteria. The corporation is a superb example of the degree of success that can be achieved when almost all of a firm's energies are directed on a single path—a high-intensity laser beam, if you will.

At the other end of the spectrum lies American Home Products (hereafter AHP) with an assortment of some 1,500 different products. Among its complex mix are ethical drugs (such as the cardiovascular control drug, Inderal—the second largest-selling drug in America, behind SmithKline Beckman's Tagamet), various medical supplies (handled through the Sherwood Medical division), packaged over-the-counter medicines (such as Anacin, Dristan, and Preparation H), and assorted food and household items (among them Brach candies, Chef-Boy-ar-dee foods, and Woolite cold water wash). The first impression and conclusion might be that AHP is a conglomerate, much in the mold of an ITT, Gulf and Western Industries, or Litton Industries. But such comparison is deceptive.

AHP encompasses its complex array of products under a single umbrella of expertise. The organization has, since about 1935, artfully acquired promising companies and products, cultivating and managing them to their full potential, then divesting them (if the need arises) at the propitious moment. In a nutshell, AHP's expertise is the well-orchestrated artistry of timing acquisition, cultivation, and divestment. That orchestration includes a broad range of methods and techniques. Among them are sharp, intensive preacquisition investigation, strong decentralization and divisionalization, tight financial controls, continuous emphasis on profit performance, and shrewd marketing policies—each of which will be touched on in greater detail in subsequent sections of this book. The centerpiece of that orchestration process is, in short, timing.

For example, AHP's Ekco line of metal housewares (pots and pans) was recently divested following a period of considerable success and profit. Although the division's performance was quite respectable at the time of divestment, and several executives were reluctant to part with it, the top echelon believed the division's contribution to the corporation had peaked and was tending downward. Divestment allowed the firm to redeploy resources and concentrate attention on more lucrative opportunities.

Again, AHP's grand strategy of focusing on timing as its central expertise was and continues to be a conscious decision. It is also a high-risk decision. Complexity of product lines often becomes a competitive disadvantage. Covering 1,500 items in different markets, using different channels of distribution, adopting different promotional techniques, and confronting aggressive competitors on several fronts—all pose continuing threats for the corporation. But the decision is made workable—as we will discover in more detail later—by a total commitment of top executives at headquarters and in each division to make the system and process work.

The commonality between single-product Tambrands and multiproduct AHP is that both are superbly honed and tempered machines, each with a precisely defined central thrust that is well understood and attentively adhered to by perceptive managerial teams. Although the profit motive plays a significant role in both organizations, that motivating force does not provide the central thrust nor the focal point around which each firm organizes its energy. Instead, the well-articulated mission statement is the hub around which the organization musters its efforts.

Another of our fourteen that, on the surface, appears to be spread across widely disparate activities with little focus is Dover. Its more than forty product lines include hydraulic elevators, sucker rods for oil-well drilling, circuit profilers, and torque multipliers. The central thrust, however, behind which these seemingly unrelated lines are organized into some semblance of sanity, is well-conceived and purposeful. Dover limits its activities to three industrial sectors: (1) elevators; (2) equipment for *producing* oil wells (not oil exploration, drilling, transport, or refining firms); and (3) narrow niches in aerospace and high-technology electronic products. Each product line is managed as an independent, autonomous division, with New York City headquarters performing the role of a coordinating central banker and financial adviser. Each division's top management is given enormous freedom to pursue its specific niche and expertise—with the stipulation from headquarters that the division maintain a dominant market position in its respective niche while continuing to generate a high return on invested capital. Of the more than forty lines, all but seven hold the number one market position in their selected niche: five are number two, while only two are third-ranked. Briefly put, the focal point of the corporation is clear: maintain a dominant market position in a limited number of industrial sectors in which a high level of expertise has been achieved. Intervention by central top management is kept to a minimum so long as overall objectives are attained.

The expertness with which a complex operation such as Dover is successfully operated and maintained can perhaps be better appreciated with a brief look at another less successful company that is somewhat similarly organized. Charles M. Leighton, one of the founders of CML Group, Incorporated, laid out the principal ingredients of the firm in 1969:[1]

1. Acquire companies in the leisure-time field whose respective presidents wished to be relieved of many of the administrative burdens of being CEO.

2. Retain each president as CEO of his or her respective company and place considerable authority in that individual to manage the business.

3. Provide administrative assistance from central CML headquarters to each subsidiary in the form of long-range planning, marketing, accounting, and strong centralized financial control and support.

One aspect of the third ingredient is that all borrowing and cash flows that occur throughout the entire CML Group would be funneled through headquarters—so that each formerly independent enterprise would be no longer troubled (nor able) to borrow on their own from external sources or to maintain exclusive control over their cash balances.

Until the mid-1970s, CML's "ego-intensive" products encompassed footwear, sports and ski wear, grandfather clock kits, and archery equipment—all sold through mail order catalogs—plus motor boats and boat sails, and like Dover's product mix, not a particularly cohesive nor an excessively dissimilar group of products. The factors that appear to distinguish the CML and Dover organizations (at least until the mid-1970s) fall into two categories: leadership and direction. Each of Dover's divisions or subsidiaries is headed and led by an individual (or group) that retains virtually all administrative responsibilities of managing the business, rather than being free of them, as at CML. Full responsibility for all functional areas of the business continues to reside at the grass roots in each Dover division, with the centralized banking function being the sole exception. It is not so at CML, where considerable responsibility for long-range planning, marketing, accounting, and control in each division resides at central headquarters. With respect to direction, whereas Dover establishes performance criteria in market dominance and high return on invested capital, the CML Group stipulates no such clear mandates. Two characteristics appear to have been absent in CML's organization: (1) committed leaders at the operational level that were eager to manage their respective businesses, and (2) specific mandates with respect to the goals toward which each organizational unit was expected to strive and against which it would be measured.

Betz Laboratories is another organization that, like Tambrands, has adhered very closely to a single product line during its entire history. Betz's focal point is blending an array of chemicals in special mixtures or "prescriptions" to treat water and waste water in complex processing systems at the site of each of its industrial clients. Various ingredients are custom-blended to treat liquids that circulate through boilers, cooling towers, heat exchangers, and other large and complex systems that are associated with the paper-making, petroleum-refining, and steel industries. In essence, Betz keeps open the plumbing and piping in a considerable segment of the industrial plant in the United States.

Betz, at one point, was tempted to enter municipal water and sewage treatment through one of its divisions. But when federal agencies began issuing regulations that would have effectively placed a limitation on the profitability that such ventures might achieve, management arranged to dispose of all municipally dedicated operations by selling them to a group of employees through an employee stock ownership plan (ESOP). In 1977, Betz divested itself of industrial water treatment in Latin America and Asia rather than succumb to cultural norms in those two areas that required payola, bribes, commissions, and other conciliatory payments to secure business.

The almost sole focal point of Commerce Clearing House (CCH) is on particular pieces of federal legislation. Its central thrust is the digestion, translation, and conversion of the *Federal Register* and congressional enactments into intelligible, useful information—in the form of timely loose-leaf reporting services—for accountants, teachers, attorneys, and other professionals. CCH has developed to a high art the translation of the Internal Revenue Code and related regulations, various pieces of federal labor legislation, and federal securities requirements, from the notoriously unreadable bureaucratic idiom into useable prose. Only one other organization—Prentice-Hall—approaches competing with CCH's reputation for reliability, timeliness, and effectiveness in this area. Prentice-Hall, however, is primarily involved in book publishing rather than in providing a loose-leaf service. Basically, CCH has a virtual monopoly franchise on the loose-leaf reporting service for the federal level.

So well does CCH perform its task that two of the firm's perennial clients are the Internal Revenue Service and Congress. The advice and counsel of the Chicago-based cadre of lawyers and accountants are continually sought whenever new or revised income tax and labor law regulations are under consideration in Washington. CCH's well-versed staff provides a degree of continuity, stability, and expertise not otherwise available to those legislative and administrative bodies. Even the organization's few ancillary activities in the selected fields of computer processing of income tax returns and assistance for attorneys and accountants in the complex task of corporate filings with numerous levels of government agencies are directly associated with the legislative and regulatory enactment process.

Both Betz Laboratories and CCH epitomize the trait of "sticking to one's knitting" that Peters and Waterman frequently identified among the sixty-two firms in their *In Search of Excellence* study. The two, who were then consultants, discovered that most of those firms had identified a relatively well-defined niche in which to participate and then had pursued that specialty or expertise and avoided detours into unrelated areas of diversion. Concentrating on a single thrust enables the entire organization—from bottom to top and through each of the functional areas—to focus its entire energy on solving problems, meeting challenges, and devising new opportunities in that one area. Focused attention enables the corporation to become the best in a particular segment—to erect such a standard of superiority in both product and service dimensions that existing competitors or potential entrants, lacking a similar focus, will confront substantial, often insurmountable, difficulties in invading territories carved out by the acknowledged expert.

The strategy of focus is certainly not a recently discovered concept. In fact, it is merely an extension of task specialization in the pin factory that Adam Smith elaborated on in his *Wealth of Nations*. However, it is a strategy the advantages of which are still overlooked by a substantial number of existing businesses. Many a top management succumbs to the temptations of pursuing seemingly lucrative opportunities outside its proven expertise. Blatant greed and ambition for more growth, territory, power, sales, and profit in new areas of unrelated endeavor too often sing their siren songs. A significant measure of organizational discipline is required to maintain a steady pace in sailing a selected course as effectively as possible.

Scripto provides a notable illustration of an enterprise that virtually surrendered an almost insurmountable lead and the major market share in its niche by pursuing a policy of fractionation and excessive diversification. Monie Ferst and Harold Hirsch created Atlanta-based Scripto, Incorporated, in 1923, to manufacture a quality mechanical pencil that would be sold for twenty-five cents or less to a mass market. Disbelief on the part of distributors and retailers that such a feat could be accomplished was initially overcome by the distribution of thousands of free samples. The writing implement won immediate acceptance by the public. When the breakeven point in sales was finally achieved in 1930, Scripto reduced its price to ten cents, thereby becoming one of the first American manufacturers to adopt the "barrier to entry" tactic of reducing price as production costs fell because of progression down the learning curve. The company remained a single product firm into 1947, except during World War II, when it produced ordnance material for the military. Until 1947, Scripto dominated the mechanical pencil market.

In that year, Ferst selected Jimmy Carmichael to succeed Hirsch as president. Carmichael's objectives were to develop Scripto into: (1) a full-line mechanical writing instrument manufacturer and (2) the world's largest manufacturer of mechanical writing instruments. In an industry in which success was tied closely to specific niches, as opposed to a broad product line covering all types of pencils and pens (ballpoint, fountain, and eventually felt-tip), Carmichael's strategy proved overly ambitious and almost diametrically opposed to Scripto's proven expertise. Carmichael's redefined mission preceded by only one year another episode that also "snatched defeat from the jaws of almost certain victory"—Thomas Dewey's ill-fated candidacy for the U.S. presidency in 1948. Scripto introduced the ballpoint pen in 1947 and followed soon afterward with the fountain pen—then raised the price of the mechanical pencil to the level at which it breached the middle- and high-priced market. Cigarette lighters were introduced in 1957; worldwide expansion was aggressively pursued.

During the mid-1960s, under Carl Singer, a large diversification effort was implemented to recover Scripto's deteriorating position. The company entered carpet manufacturing, produced ceramic ashtrays, developed a thermo-fax copier machine and a wide-angle lens camera, and attempted to cover all price lines in the writing instrument field. Although most of these later entries have since been abandoned, Scripto has never fully recovered from Carmichael's grandiose strategy (and its subsequent extensions by Singer) that began in 1947.

Had the company concentrated on the strategy of becoming the world's largest manufacturer of inexpensive quality mechanical pencils it might well have provided sufficient challenge and opportunity to test and satisfy the capabilities of top management, stockholders, and employees alike. Venturing substantially beyond its tested area of expertise, particularly in an industry in which success was closely correlated with niche specialization, proved beyond the capacity of Scripto in the post–World War II era. The company simply pursued too many things in too many diverse and unrelated areas to maintain proficiency in any!

Diametrically opposed to Scripto's fractionated efforts is the particularly well-defined expertise of Deluxe Check Printers—an expertise that has been religiously adhered to since the company's founding in the early 1920s. Very simply, that mission is the printing and distributing of small-lot orders of 200 to 600 personalized checks and deposit slips to individual customers within forty-eight hours of the receipt of the customer's order. The quick turn-around is accomplished through a tightly integrated network of sixty-two printing plants strategically located throughout the United States. Except for retaining a small interest in Mexico, Deluxe has restricted operations to the United States. Few other world cultures are as linked and dedicated to check-writing as is the United States. Although the company has recently probed other preprinted business and personal computer forms, the primary target continues to be the personal check and deposit slip market. So well recognized and respected is Deluxe's expertise and proficiency in its selected niche that its market share exceeds by four times that of its nearest competitor, the John H. Harland Company.

Dow Jones is another organization whose flagship line occupies a near-monopolistic position in a specific market niche. The corporation's mission is to be the leading publisher of business news and information in the United States, if not the world. Its flagship is and always has been *The Wall Street Journal*, supported strongly by *Barron's* and, to a lesser degree, by three recent extensions: a news-retrieval system, a newswire service, and Richard D. Irwin, Incorporated, book publishers. Concentrating its primary attention on the *Journal* has helped make it the "best single newspaper-publishing franchise in the country," according to publishing analyst Richard Howitt of First Manhattan Company.[2]

The primary goal of Dow Jones has never been to be the largest business-news and information-gathering publisher in the country, nor to become a mass media conglomerate. Instead, its aim is to become and remain the best in the field of business news—to excel in the quality and usefulness of the information it provides. The major precept under which the firm has operated since its takeover by Clarence Barron, in 1902, is to strive to make business news understandable and to make the knowledge of how the economy works more widely accessible and intelligible. Warren Phillips, the current CEO, restated the message in 1982: "to take business issues out of the world of the arcane and esoteric, strip them of their mysteries and enable any of us to understand what was going on."[3]

International Flavors and Fragrances has remained sharply focused throughout its history on creating flavor and scent additives for incorporation by other manufacturers into their consumer products. It has resisted the temptation to manufacture and market consumer goods under its own label—preferring instead to defer to others who are more adept and conversant in the complex area of marketing consumer goods in a finished form to the public. Top management is dedicated to the proposition that fractionation of the corporate mission from a particular expertise into a variety of specialities dilutes managerial talent and employee effort. A phenomenon called "creeping managerial overhead" frequently erodes the advantages that might otherwise be gained from a sharpened focus. According to the company's recently retired CEO, Henry G. Walter, Jr., "The pace of technological advance and competitive combativeness are becoming far too rapid and sophisticated to maintain pronounced superiority in more than one or two areas of concentration." Although a new endeavor often appears at first glance to require only a tiny bit more additional effort or extra time, a continuation along the road of fractionation soon usurps more valuable time and effort from other activities—particularly from what was formerly the central thrust—usually to the detriment of both former and new endeavors.

One of our fourteen organizations that at first glance appears to have pursued a conscious policy of fractionation is Philip Morris (PM). Its principal product lines (excluding General Foods, which was not acquired until late 1985) are three inexpensive mass-consumed "tranquilizers"—cigarettes (the mainstay), Miller beer, and 7-Up carbonated beverages. PM's distinctive competence lies in being one of America's premiere consumer marketing organizations. It accomplishes its superior achievements through skillful and imaginative marketing, innovative market segmentation, and aggressive pioneering. Robert H. Miles points out in his *Coffin Nails and Corporate Strategies* that PM's marketing research group and top management identified the emerging environmental pressure of the modern liberated woman—and created Virginia Slims to accommodate that specific market segment.[4] The organization pioneered cigarette advertising on radio, with "Johnnie's" famous "Call for Philip Morris," because the company could not afford high-cost newsprint advertising. PM was the first of the "big six" cigarette companies to venture into overseas markets. It introduced the first low-tar cigarette, the flip-top box, the thin red tear-tape, and the filter-tipped Marlboro brand that is today the world's largest selling cigarette. Nationally distributed light beer also owes its genesis to PM.

In short, the organization is a first-mover, pioneer, creator of change, and an identifier and satisfier of emerging trends—a company that is continuously searching for new market opportunities. We shall see in a subsequent section of this chapter, which deals with acquisitions, how effectively the company has coupled those attributes with its acquisition strategy.

The principal thrust of U.S. Tobacco has two specialities in common with Philip Morris: (1) tobacco, and in the form of (2) an inexpensive mass-consumed "tranquilizer." Its flagship—smokeless tobacco—was originally introduced to accommodate individuals who relish the taste of nicotine and prefer not to shake the habit, but who require their hands free for work, such as lumberjacks, farmers, and athletes. The product has recently attained renewed vigor in the aftermath of society's prolonged concern over the alleged link between smoking and lung cancer, and from the as yet unproven claim of a direct link between chewing tobacco and snuff and oral cancer.

One of the most consistently highly profitable sectors of the American economy since World War II has been the pharmaceutical industry. The *Quarterly Financial Reports* from the Federal Trade Commission and the Bureau of the Census reveal that the rate of return on average stockholders' equity for the drug industry during the twenty-three-year period, 1962 to 1984, exceeded the all-manufacturing average by about 6.5 percentage points (18.7 percent versus 12.3 percent). During that same period, the three predominantly ethical drug corporations in our study, plus American Home Products, exceeded the drug industry average by an additional 6.5 percentage points—in other words, 13 percentage points (or more than double) the all manufacturing average of 12.3 percent, a most impressive statistic.

Eli Lilly regards it as its central mission to remain the industry's premiere marketing machine, distributing its ethical drugs almost exclusively through an elaborate network of 400 wholesalers. Whereas most pharmaceutical manufacturers market their products directly to hospitals and large drug chains (with wholesalers handling smaller and remote-area accounts), Lilly uses some 1,150 technical salespeople (of which about 80 percent are registered pharmacists) to sell its 800 items through this wholesaler network. The organization orients its research development effort toward the acute infectious diseases more than in the direction of chronic long-term maintenance drugs.

On the other hand, Merck focuses more attention on chronic long-term maintenance drugs, such as Timoptic for glaucoma victims. Merck, like Lilly, is a research-driven organization, with a slight difference. Merck is striving to become the world's preeminent drug manufacturer during the 1980s.

SmithKline Beckman (SKB) is also a comprehensive health-care organization, focusing its efforts on pharmaceuticals for humans and animals, as well as on high-technology analytical devices for the detection and treatment of diseases through its Beckman division. SKB's top echelon sees its chief mission as becoming the world's leader in the health-care field. Some observers claim that SKB has become overly dependent, for its outstanding performance in recent years, on the highly successful gastrointestinal drug Tagamet, the world's largest selling prescription drug in history.

Our fourteenth organization is Kellogg, which concentrates the vast majority of its efforts on ready-to-eat breakfast cereals and, to a lesser extent, on convenience foods, as Whitney yogurt and Mrs. Smith's pies.

The message that comes through loud and clear among this group of fourteen is a common motif of concentration, focus, and the targeting of organizational effort toward a very well-defined area of expertise. Drucker refers to this attribute as a "concentration decision."[5] In his book *Leadership in Administration,* P. Selznick calls it a "distinctive competence;"[6] whereas Peters and Waterman label it "sticking to one's knitting."[7] Regardless of the specific term used, all of our fourteen organizations have developed a crystal-clear idea of their particular central mission, expertise, and thrust and they are relentless in perfecting that pursuit. Numerous academicians, consultants, practitioners, and financial analysts steadily maintain that consciously directing organizational energy toward a well-defined expertise is often prerequisite to success. Even those organizations that have pursued some diversification, through internally generated projects or by means of acquisitions, rarely allow themselves to be seriously fractionated or diverted from their central thrust.

Well-Defined Acquisition Strategy

As critical as may be the importance of clarity of mission to organizational success, this attribute cannot stand alone as the sole ingredient. Other elements must be combined with it, much like spokes about a hub. For those among our fourteen that pursue acquisitions and diversification, one of those elements is a well-defined acquisition strategy coupled with a cautious program of diversification activity. Only three of our fourteen companies have pursued acquisitions or diversification activities rather heavily; five others have to a far more limited extent; and the remaining six have evidenced almost no interest in this route. We can quickly deal with these latter six first.

Betz Labs has never evidenced much interest in acquisitions or diversification. Although the company did enter the consulting field at one point and purchased a pumping company plus an electronics firm a number of years ago, these activities were quickly divested as soon as top management realized that these were not their business. Management simply recognized that the organization's mainline operations presented sufficient challenges to keep the entire work force totally occupied.

Commerce Clearing House echoes a similar concern. "We have rarely sought acquisitions, and are extremely cautious in this arena," noted one spokesperson, "having been burned a couple of times in the past." CCH divested an operation in 1983 that provided turnkey microcomputer services to accountants when management finally realized that those activities simply did not fit with the rest of the organization. "From now on," commented the spokesperson interviewed, "if a potential candidate is not in our traditional publishing lines, we're just not interested. Pursuit of peripheral areas would merely end up eroding this organization's time."

Deluxe Check, International Flavors and Fragrances (IFF), and Tambrands also express little interest in seeking candidates for acquisition, although Tambrands has entertained recent thoughts of diversifying beyond its catamenial line. However, any diversification efforts by the Lake Success organization will be restricted primarily to internally generated new consumer nondurables for distribution through its normal retailing channels, as opposed to a search for new products or companies by acquisition. Finally, U.S. Tobacco did acquire a line of smoking accessories that includes pipes, smoking tobacco, and pipe cleaners to complement its smokeless tobacco line and the Ste. Michelle line of Washington state wines. The Ste. Michelle acquisition generated less than 5 percent of total sales volume and a 1.5 percent operating loss in 1984.

Turning to those among the fourteen that have pursued some degree of acquisition or diversification, we can advance a variety of reasons in support of organizations that seek to grow through these routes:

To achieve economies of scale by spreading existent, or slightly higher, fixed costs that are incurred through a merger, over a considerably larger volume of output.

To offset current or likely deterioration in demand or the competitiveness of existing product lines through acquisition of more lucrative products.

To flesh out and complete an existing product line.

To initiate or accomplish the process of integration, either forward or backward, of products or channels of distribution.

To retain in the business profits and excess cash that have been generated by converting them into earning assets, rather than to distribute them to stockholders in the form of taxable cash dividends.

To undertake a challenge to generate renewed organizational vigor or counteract organizational boredom.

One or more of these rationales have been used at one time or another by the eight organizations among our fourteen that have taken the acquisition route. But in almost every case, several added dimensions are present that might account for some of their continuing overall success.

First, for the most part these organizations seek acquisition candidates that will reinforce and complement their existing product and service lines—that bolster and take advantage of their expertise, rather than fractionate or dilute it. Their acquisitions do not violate, nor move the organization quantum leaps beyond, the experience of management and employees that exists at the time of the acquisition. One of the questions most often asked by managers in these several organizations when they are contemplating an acquisition is to what degree is this candidate likely to strengthen or dilute our expertise, key mission, and principal thrust? Second, considerable attention is devoted to thorough and comprehensive preacquisition analysis in order to understand and anticipate the likely pluses and drawbacks of the acquisition before resources are committed to the endeavor, rather than afterward.

Third, most of these managements seemed particularly sensitive and eager to insulate against the proposition that complexity and hugeness often beget competitive disadvantages—that acquisitions are often at the risk of becoming the initial step along the road to excessive, perhaps unmanageable complications. Finally, in the few instances in which some of these organizations have made errors of judgment in making particular acquisitions, crucial lessons were learned about what to avoid in the future.

The move to diversify Dow Jones began when its advertising lineage began to decease significantly, during the 1970 recession. A management consulting group recommended that an attempt be made to offset the organization's heavy concentration in the business-financial area with selected diversification. Shortly after an encounter, on the golf course in 1970, between William Kerby (then the president of Dow Jones) and James Ottaway, Sr. (owner of the Ottaway newspaper group in northeastern United States), Dow Jones acquired the Ottaway chain.

A policy was developed during that process that has continued to govern the firm's acquisition course, according to one of its top executives: "Any candidate must possess a culture that places top priority on high ethical standards, integrity, and quality. The candidate should be in the field of written communications—excluding glossy magazines." Using this acquisition guideline, Richard D. Irwin, which specializes in business and economics textbooks for college, university, and business executive clientele, was acquired, in 1975. Dow Jones' most recent major acquisition was American Demographics, in 1981.

Dow Jones bailed out from short-term excursions with its *Book Digest* (a consumer-oriented magazine) and the *National Observer* (the nationwide Sunday newspaper). The two lessons gleaned from these two exercises were (1) the *Digest* did not fall within Dow's expertise, and (2) the *Observer* lacked a clearly identified readership toward which advertisers could direct their promotional efforts. One Dow Jones spokesman did admit, however, that the organization's continuance of the *Observer* experiment probably lasted too long out of deference to Bernard (Barney) Kilgore's (president of the firm from 1947 to 1966), close association with that publication.

Until the late 1970s, Kellogg adhered to its policy of not diversifying much beyond the existing lines of ready-to-eat (R-T-E) breakfast cereals. But, about 1978, top management began to construct an explicit acquisition policy that would take the firm somewhat beyond that relatively narrow niche in consumer goods. The policy consisted of two primary ingredients: product traits and financial characteristics. First, candidates that produced and distributed top-quality convenience foods, cosmetics, pharmaceuticals, and health-image products would be considered. Second, prospective candidates should generate annual sales of about one-half billion dollars, demonstrate a sales growth (in constant dollars) exceeding 10 percent, and generate a return on owners' investment comparable to Kellogg's existing rate at the time of acquisition. Although recent acquistions have been concentrated in convenience foods, such as Mrs. Smith's pies and Eggo dressings, the almost fanatical single-minded allegiance to R-T-E cereals continues to account for about 97 percent of Kellogg's sales. Some financial analysts criticize the organization for not diversifying sufficiently beyond R-T-E cereals; but top management evidences no anxiety or panic to move a considerable distance beyond its proven expertise. Said one company spokesperson: "The untapped world-wide market for R-T-E cereals is enormous."

Three criteria comprise Lilly's policy with respect to prospective acquisition candidates. The prospect must possess: (1) first-rate R&D capability; (2) high quality of operations; and (3) a culture that is closely compatible with Lilly's. During the past twenty years, a number of medical and scientific instrument products have been acquired and successfully integrated into Lilly's operations. One recent acquisition, however, has created some anxiety within the enterprise.

The 1971 purchase of Elizabeth Arden, a manufacturer and marketer of cosmetics, emerges as Lilly's most controversial acquisition—primarily because it ventured beyond the narrow confines of the medical and scientific community. The acquisition was predicated chiefly on the basis of the compatibility between Arden and Lilly in the area of R&D—particularly Arden's toxicity studies with respect to the short and long-term sensitivity of the human body to externally applied chemical compounds and how the human organism may be subjected to modification through such chemicals. Ancillary compatibilities also existed between the operational climates and cultural attitudes of the two organizations. What emerged as somewhat of a surprise or shock to the Lilly organization was the awareness of its almost total inexperience with the "puffery, hype, and hucksterism" so common in the cosmetic field. Said one Lilly spokesperson, "At the time of the acquisition, we perceived ourselves as a relatively competent marketer of products associated with the medical field; but we soon discovered a void in our understanding of the marketing programs that are demanded in the cosmetic arena. We are still learning the process of integrating the best of both worlds."

A fallacy common with many firms that have acquired products or marketing climates that are foreign to their experience is immediately and aggressively adjusting or forcing the new firm to adopt the orientations of the parent company—often with untimely and disastrous consequences. A basic tenet in Lilly, once an acquisition has been accomplished, is to maintain a hands-off policy with respect to the new organization for about five years. Only after that break-in and acclimatization period are executives "parachuted in" to the acquired enterprise or transferred between it and Lilly. "Extreme patience, tolerance, and understanding are required by both parties to the transaction during this transition period," according to another Lilly spokesperson; "and our philosophy appears to have yielded substantial payoffs."

SmithKline Beckman is another pharmaceutical company that has experienced a problem with a recent acquisition. Most of SKB's pharmaceutical products, including Tagamet, have been internally generated. The outstanding success of that drug provided the company with an enormous cash flow, which altered the firm from what previously could be described as adversity-oriented to opportunity-challenged. One outlet that was considered for the huge cash buildup was diversification through acquisition. The field of promising candidates was narrowed to six finalists in the health-care field—principally diagnostic and analytical instrumentation for use in hospitals and laboratories.

Beckman Instruments emerged as the targeted candidate, and the acquisition was consummated in 1982. The integration of Beckman into the SmithKline organization has, however, been beset with some problems caused by cultural differences between the two entities, a more complete discussion of which is deferred to chapter 5. Suffice to say at this point that the basic differences between the two cultures appear to lie in the style with which conflict resolution occurs. SmithKline traditionally has adopted a "quiet, subdued, genteel approach" to resolving problems that arise—the ultimate objective being to "avoid open combat." Beckman's culture, on the other hand, has fostered fewer behind-the-scenes confrontations and a preference, instead, for "more open combat." As one executive who grew up in the SmithKline environment describes it, "considerable bluff, noise, and a less logical approach to problem-solving seems to permeate Beckman's culture. But we are beginning to accommodate and tolerate each other's conflict resolution styles."

A large number of ethical pharmaceutical companies have either formed or acquired subsidiaries to market their chemical products and proprietary drugs in such a way that the chemicals and proprietaries are not directly nor easily associated in the public's or physician's mind with the ethical drug side of the organization. (*Ethical* drugs are available to the public only by a physician's prescription; whereas *proprietary* drugs are available to the public over the counter, without a physician's prescription). For example, American Home Products formed Ayerst Laboratories and Wyeth Laboratories to concentrate on the manufacture and marketing of ethical drugs; whereas its Whitehall Laboratories generates such over-the-counter drugs as Advil and Anacin (pain relievers) and Preparation H (for treatment of hemorrhoids).

Merck acquired Philadelphia-based Sharp and Dohme as a conduit through which ethical drugs developed in the chemical side of Merck could be marketed. As Walter S. Measday emphasized in "The Pharmaceutical Industry" in 1971, the primary problem in the pharmaceutical industry is not in manufacturing various drugs, but in marketing them. Capital requirements and risk characteristics associated with the marketing side substantially surpass those associated with manufacturing. Although the Sharp and Dohme acquisition has proven extremely satisfactory, Merck became involved in another diversification effort in the late 1950s that turned out to be far less successful.

In deciding to enter the silicon industry during the late 1950s, Merck was determined to be the sole supplier of silicon components to the electronics industry. It intended to make silicon-based products so thoroughly researched and of such high quality that, according to a Merck spokesman, "electronics manufacturers would naturally seek these products from no other source than Merck." Unfortunately, the guiding principle of each electronics manufacturer (a point that had eluded Merck's notice during its analysis prior to entry in this field) was never to allow itself to be at the mercy of only one supplier. The Merck executive recalls: "It was a disaster. We fell victim to building excessive capacity and overconfidence—both in manufacturing facilities and marketing operations—to such an extent that we became unable to compete price-wise with other entrants in the silicon field."

The occasional blunder that a few of our fourteen organizations have experienced in their efforts to diversify or expand into new or related fields can be fortified with numerous examples from other industries and companies. The Intercollegiate Case Clearing House, located at Soldiers Field adjacent to Harvard's Graduate School of Business, contains a library of true case histories replete with examples of firms that entered new business activities without first adequately scanning the environment. A case mentioned previously was Scripto's almost suicidal venture into areas quite foreign to its central expertise in inexpensive mechanical pencils—namely a wide-angle lens camera, household carpeting, ceramic ashtrays, and copying equipment. Exxon discovered, after several years in the office equipment arena, that its preeminence in petroleum failed to provide synergistic skills sufficient to confront IBM and other well-entrenched competitors on their home turf.

In many cases, the disparity between the product expertise of the parent and the acquired firm is more subtle and less obvious. Northeastern Food (the name in this instance has been disguised to protect the guilty in top management), a large supermarket food chain located on the east coast, acquired a family-owned chain of discount stores that sold clothing and household items. The hoped-for complementarity and reinforcement to be gained from operating food, clothing, and household products in adjacent but separate discount retail outlets was overshadowed by two failures on the part of Northeastern's top echelon. First, the styles of management and organization in the two entities were distinctly different. Northeastern was organized along decentralized lines with each store's general manager being the critical focal point in the corporation; whereas the operation and control of all stores in the acquired nonfood organization were almost entirely centralized in its president. In addition, the authority and competence of individual store managers had never been allowed to develop. Northeastern's top management soon discovered the mismatch between the two organizational styles when attempts were made to superimpose Northeastern's control apparatus on the new subsidiary. The nonfood company's infrastructure simply did not exist to accommodate the parent's decentralized operating mode. Second, purchasing and merchandising requirements in food and nonfood discount stores are sufficiently distinctive to require different approaches and competencies. Food customers, for example, are less prone to fads and fashion than are the same individuals when they become shoppers for clothing and household items. In short, the fit between the two organizations has, to this day, never been fully resolved nor adequately reconciled.

But Merck learned from its silicon-entry mistake. Prompted by the experience, Henry W. Gadsen (president of Merck), established a corporate development group, in 1964, to construct a clearly thought through acquisition policy for the organization. The three-point strategy that emerged from that group's efforts was (1) a candidate, and the industrial segment of which it is a part, must offer good growth prospects; (2) the candidate's sector must be closely associated with Merck's experience—preferably science and technology; and (3) Merck must be capable of making a positive contribution to the acquiree. The company has religiously adhered to those guidelines since their inception—the first test case being the Calgon acquisition in 1968. According to one Merck executive commenting during the interview on the relevance and subsequent success of the Calgon purchase, "The step from killing germs and unwanted elements in humans and animals to ridding water of unwanted elements seemed to us a natural."

The three among our fourteen corporations that have heavily pursued the acquisition route are Dover, American Home Products, and Philip Morris, and each of these organizations has developed clearly articulated policies to guide this activity. Dover's top executives keep eyes and ears constantly attuned for rumblings in industrial circles and the investment banking community of potential acquisition candidates that are seeking a buyer. Some of the most productive leads arrive through investment banking contacts that have located companies whose owners wish to sell out because of concerns with estate tax or management succession. Its top manangement in New York City considers about 300 candidates every year.

Dover's policy is clear, unambiguous, and consistently applied. As it is enunciated by a central office executive in New York City, "Only the market leader in its field with top-flight management currently in place need apply. We expect the managerial core in each acquisition candidate to continue in place for the foreseeable future." No expectation exists at headquarters of parachuting individuals in to replace those currently in managerial slots. Candidates must be in one of the following industrial segments: elevators, equipment for producing oil wells, high-tech electronic products, and very select niches in industrial and aerospace products. In addition, each candidate must have demonstrated the capacity to earn a high return on invested capital.

American Home Products is a classic case of an organization that has grown and diversified by acquiring both companies and products. Alvin Brush, president and chairman of AHP for thirty years (beginning in 1935), pioneered the construction of the corporation's current acquisition policy. Simply put it was to acquire existing consumer nondurable specialty items that are easy to make and merchandise, that will be difficult for competitors to match, and that are profitable. If a specific candidate looks appealing, AHP assigns a team of lawyers and accountants to analyze the candidate and to borrow time—while other executives investigate additional aspects of the business to determine how AHP might improve its operations. If top management feels that AHP can make little or no contribution to improving the company or product line, AHP will usually turn thumbs down. These strategies have proven effective and immensely profitable over the years.

AHP's strategy of acquiring ready-made branded product lines that can be improved upon possesses several attractive features. Branded or proprietary products tend to be immune from foreign competition. Customers, once they become convinced of the product's advantages and are won over, tend to remain relatively loyal—and the more successful branded items a company presents to the retailer, the more marketing power and clout it carries with repect to shelf space. Finally, developing and promoting new products from scratch can cost upward to $50 million or $75 million. Obtaining a ready-made and relatively secure brand-name line conserves enormous capital resources that can be directed to other, more productive ventures.

AHP's acquisition policy is supplemented by its often equally profitable divestiture scheme of selling a company or product at the appropriate time. Marietta Dyestuffs was sold to American Cyanamid in 1946, while the Harmon Color Works (also a dye business) was disposed of to B.F. Goodrich in 1950. As baby foods became more of a commodity than a specialty item, AHP sold its Clapp's baby food line to Duffy-Mott in 1953. And the sale of

Ekco Products occurred in 1984. All four divestitures were accomplished at considerable profit to AHP.

From the standpoint of venturing into a relatively new area and then discovering it was a mistake, Philip Morris closely resembles Merck and Betz Labs. Philip Morris side-tracked itself by acquiring American Safety Razor in 1960 and Clark Gum in 1963. At one point in PM's history, a group of top executives had aspirations of becoming another American Home Products, but such visions were quickly squelched. Within a few years of these two acquisitions, PM's top management realized that even if it captured a sizeable segment of those two markets from such well-entrenched competitors as Gillette (razor blades) and Wrigley (chewing gum), the winnings would proably not justify the time and effort expended. Clark Gum was sold in 1973, and American Safety Razor was disposed of in 1977 to ASR employees through a leveraged buyout arrangement. In addition, Philip Morris sold its industrial division in early 1985, asserting that the paper products business no longer fit the company's long-run strategies.

Learning from such strategic experiences, PM has constructed a well fleshed out and rather specific acquisition policy. Some of its central ingredients are

> Seek and make acquisitions in only those sectors where the firm believes it can be a major, if not dominant factor in such areas as pricing, market share, and product leadership. Is the market sufficiently large and profitable to warrant entry and development, and does the reasonable expectation exist for PM to exercise significant clout?

> The acquisition should offer prospects of high profitability, although management is willing to allow a five-year period for that profitability to emerge.

> The candidate must enable PM to capitalize on its distinctive competence in marketing consumer non-durable products.

> An acquisition should satsify a sales growth objective of 20 percent per year; which means that the candidate probably should not already hold the dominant share of its product market.

> The candidate should enable PM to inject something new, different, or better in the market place to avoid competing head-on with existing competitors.

> Potential must exist for worldwide distribution of the candidate's products.

Since the late 1960s, PM has concentrated its diversification effort on turn-around situations that require large injections of capital, strong general management, and marketing expertise. It has sought and acquired companies with highly branded products in large markets, but those that have not yet attained market leadership. Miller Brewing Company was acquired in 1969 under the six-point diversification strategy, and 7-Up was purchased in 1978. Mission Viejo Realty group was acquired in 1970 to serve as a vehicle through which surplus cash that was generated from the tobacco segment could be invested as a hedge against inflation. In administering its acquisitions, PM has developed a noteworthy hallmark of patience, as pointed out in the second guideline above—a willingness to allow each new segment approximately five years from the point of acquisition to develop its earnings potential. However, several industrial and financial analysts openly question whether the Miller and 7-Up acquisitions will pan out over the long run. One PM spokesman observed that the General Foods takeover "appears to offer substantially more positive potential than did the beverage components."

Most, but certainly not all, of the acquisitions and moves toward diversification that were attempted by members of our elite group proved to be as successful as originally anticipated. But even when events do not work out favorably, these acquirers do seem to learn from their infrequent mistakes. For example, these ventures either have been accomplished within relatively clear acquisition-diversification policy guidelines, or errors in judgment have stimulated the development of such guidelines. The dominant acquisition criteria tend to be (1) closeness of fit with existing product lines and expertise of the parent; (2) a good performance record with respect to profitability and market share; (3) an excellent prognosis for future development; and (4) compatibility with the parent's objectives, culture, and organizational environment. These criteria, along with the parent's already well-defined corporate mission and central thrust, often result in fruitful marriages that endure over several years.

A Long-Run Perspective and Patience

Considerable criticism has been directed at the business and industrial sectors during the past ten to fifteen years with respect to the short-term, quick-fix orientation that runs deep and is so prevalent across the United States. Managers of institutional investment (trust and pension) portfolios are accused of excessively churning both equity and debt securities in order to generate lucrative commissions, which, in turn, enhance short-run earnings performance. On the other hand, criticism is leveled at corporate executives who primarily strive for quarterly improvement in profit performance rather than devote attention to long-term commitments that may not reap immediate benefits. Investment in costly and often risky research and development projects, as well as routine repairs and maintenance expenditures on plant and equipment, are often deferred in the short-term to enhance the immediate bottom line—both with respect to profit and cash flow. Many are rightfully accused of short-sightedness in managing the affairs of enterprises for the immediate quarterly "now," as opposed to devoting persistent attention and energy to the long haul. Even U.S. schools of business and MBA programs are not immune from attack. Heard frequently are assertions that budding top executives, middle managers, and staff specialists were and are being trained in the make-it-fast, move-on-and-up, get-out-quick syndromes.

In short, the overemphasis on short-term performance, to the detriment of the long-term pull, is believed by many to lie at the heart of much that is wrong on the current U.S. business scene.

Needless to say, even the most carefully considered and focused strategy may not prove immediately successful. Countless events, ranging from economic downturns and the introduction of new technology to sudden invasions by domestic and offshore competitors can easily delay or frustrate full and profitable return on an investment. But our fourteen seem to have learned the lessons of patience and forebearance well. Traits that are deeply rooted in each of these enterprises include long-term patient persistence, perseverance, and dogged constancy of purpose—as opposed to flash-in-the-pan success or the quick-fix when things go awry. Betz and CCH are not obsessed with achieving the sudden breakthrough or magic formulation. Instead, both see success arising from bulldog perseverance and attention to detail and quality day after week, month in and year out. The Midwestern ethic of steadiness of purpose and consistency of performance are endemic in the Lilly, Kellogg, Deluxe Check Printers, and CCH organizations. Set in the Eastern culture, Philip Morris accomplishes its tasks with somewhat more flair and show biz promotion; but even here, the watchword (according to one high-level executive) is "strive for steady momentum rather than intermittent blips." PM's acquisition policy guideline of allowing new acquisitions five years in which to develop their earnings potential underlines the organization's dedication to a patient gristing process.

The late Liston Pope, a former dean of the Yale Divinity School capsulized, in a sermon at Harvard's Memorial Chapel in the spring of 1950, what appears to be a cultural characteristic that pervades most of our fourteen organizations. "Life," he asserted, "consists of much plodding, dogged determinism, and uneventful persistence."[8] His advice that day to the assembled members of the Harvard community was "Hang tough and look to the long pull. Most of humanity seems to have lost that insight. A bit of faith (blind or otherwise) doesn't hurt either from time to time." Little imagination is required to extend this logic from personal to business-related activities.

The single corporation among these elite that could possibly be accused of adopting a short-run orientation is American Home Products. Its top management targets quarter-by-quarter improvements in earnings, year after year. But this seemingly short-term commitment has been integrated so thoroughly into AHP's culture over a period of three decades, that the so-called short-view has become integral to its continuous record of long-term top performance. As one key executive described it to me, "Quarterly improvement is the engine that drives us. Occasional downturns do occur. But when they do, we are tolerant and allow a reasonable time for turn-arounds to be made."

Likewise, the several divisions and subsidiaries of Dover operate with patient diligence in what some outsiders consider an assemblage of rather mundane manufacturing enterprises. Reporters around the world and editorial copy editors at Dow Jones' *The Wall Street Journal* continually grind out highly credible, impeccably written, and understandable copy concerning the business-financial community. Without a great deal of fanfare or hoopla, IFF quietly and continually—almost anonymously—generates new fragrance "notes" and flavor "enhancers" for integration into industrial and consumer goods. Personnel in research laboratories at Merck, SmithKline Beckman, and Lilly diligently explore new avenues to detect components that may conquer specific diseases or improve current techniques of attacking viruses that invade humans and animals. "Much of the work is tedious, painfully slow, and fraught with failure," recites one spokesman at SmithKline, "but over the long haul, we're convinced that attention to detail and stamina pays off."

To put the matter simply and without great need for additional elaboration, virtually every one of our fourteen elite has a long-run perspective in striving for success in its respective industries or niches. Messages were repeatedly voiced during the several interviews that lead me to believe these organizations cannot be faulted for being myopic or short-sighted in the way operations are usually conducted. Executives in several of these firms stated emphatically that they were reluctant to propose—much less adopt—executive stock option plans in the enterprise if such introduction might encourage top management to focus on monthly or quarterly performance statistics in hopes of enhancing short-term movement in the market price of the firm's stock, to the detriment of the long-term perspective currently in place. And golden parachutes for the top and middle-echelon are generally anathema to these firms—an abomination.

Steadiness of purpose, tenacity, the long pull, perseverance, and consistency. That perspective, combined with a well-defined and focused central thrust, mission, and expertise—and clear acquisition-diversification guidelines in those instances in which that strategic route has been adopted—reflect the prevailing philosophy among these fourteen organizations. "The big breakthrough or windfall profit—if and when it arrives—is merely frosting on the cake," said one Philip Morris executive.

Notes

1. "CML Group, Inc." in C.R. Christensen, N.A. Berg, and M.S. Salter, *Policy Formulation and Administration,* 7th ed. (Homewood, Ill.: R.D. Irwin, 1976), pp. 571–603.
2. In "Dow Jones Joins the Media Conglomerates," *Business Week* (13 Nov. 1978), p. 67.
3. In Lloyd Wendt, *The Wall Street Journal: The Story of Dow Jones and the Nation's Business Newspaper* (Chicago: Rand McNally, 1982), p. 432.
4. Robert H. Miles, *Coffin Nails and Corporate Strategies* (Englewood Cliffs, N.J.: Prentice-Hall, 1982), p. 103.
5. Peter F. Drucker, *Management: Tasks, Responsibilities, Practices* (New York: Harper & Row, 1974).
6. P. Selznick, *Leadership in Administration: A Sociological Interpretation,* (New York: Harper & Row, 1957).
7. Thomas J. Peters and Robert H. Waterman, Jr., *In Search of Excellence: Lessons from America's Best-Run Companies* (New York: Harper & Row, 1982).
8. Unpublished sermon by Liston Pope in The Memorial Chapel at Harvard University, Spring 1950.

3
Internal Operating Procedures: Planning and Monitoring Activities

> The next worst thing to having no objective is to achieve it.
> —Charles Yale Bartholomew, adapted from Oscar Wilde

A quarter century ago, contingents of doctoral candidates in business administration were weaned on the four principle functions of management: Planning, Motivating, Organizing, and Controlling (P.M.O.C.). Those graduate students truncated and parroted these concepts into the familiar P.M.O.C. chant whenever professors sought an answer to the question "What are the most important dimensions of the management process?" In spite of the parody, however, these four functions still continue to serve as valid descriptions of the main elements in the managerial process.

This chapter addresses two of those elements: the planning and controlling (or monitoring) of activities that our fourteen organizations have developed. Also included are a brief look at establishing financial objectives and some highlights of the actual financial results achieved by these enterprises.

Extensive Planning Activity

Planning is the function of management that transforms an organization's mission statement, central thrust, and expertise into implementable focused specifics. Restated, annual (or more frequent) planning and budgeting exercises translate abstract corporate perspectives, philosophies, and policies into specific operating guidelines. Results of these planning efforts are communicated to those in the organization who need to know essential details of goals in order to implement them. Unless constant and serious attention is paid to the various activities connected with the planning function, the enterprise can languish and, at best, grope haphazardly into the future.

It came as no surprise to this observer to detect, early on in the field research, that virtually every one of our fourteen firms engages in extensive and continuous planning and budgeting activities. As one interviewee summarized her firm's planning endeavors: "Many of us in the front office devote almost as much time to planning—in the broadest sense—throughout the year as we do to actually implementing and coordinating those plans. It's a never-ending commitment—and a commitment that continues to serve us well."

In addition to its setting specific financial objectives for forthcoming periods, the overall planning function in these corporations encompasses a broad range of activities, several of which are listed as follows:

Research and development activities and programs.

Product development, including new products and improvements to existing lines.

Capital investment in equipment, plants, and facilities.

Alteration in coverage of territories and regions—domestic and foreign.

Marketing research, merchandising, and promotional campaigns.

Production and scheduling.

Managerial succession and development.

Compensation and fringe benefit packages for all levels of employees.

Acquisitions and their integration into the existing organization.

Although several of these dimensions will be examined in more detail later, a few warrant discussion at this juncture; but, rather than burden the reader with a litany of all the detailed facets in the planning cycle, I will note only some of the more interesting highlights that were discovered among the fourteen.

R&D and new product planning are critical avenues for progress, particularly for the three organizations that are predominantly involved in ethical drugs. One key to Merck's pattern of continued success may lie in its well-structured R&D planning process. "The strategic planning process with respect to R&D activity is critical to our entire operation," notes one Merck vice-president. "It's everywhere. Without it, we would flounder." Detailed plans are laid out five to ten years into the future, with expectant arrivals of new human and animal drugs (and offsetting departures) positioned along a time-line. Adequate slack and flexibility are allowed on the continuum for the unexpected—both good and disadvantageous. "We have a pretty fair picture of what products are expected to enter and exit the stream at any point during the next five to ten years." Though they are less detailed, arrangements for new or augmented facilities are also footnoted, along with unusual aspects of marketing and promotional programs that warrant early attention.

Lilly's planning exercises are extensive and elaborate, beginning with a sophisticated economic forecast for several years that is contructed by a staff of highly trained and experienced "pharmaceutical economists." Said one executive, "Lilly has always been planning-oriented; but with the elevation of Dick Wood to CEO, the organization has become even more deeply dedicated to the planning-cycle regimen. Little is left to surprise or chance."

In highly decentralized Dover, the philosophy of operating autonomy that extends throughout the company forces detailed planning activities deep into each division and subsidiary. Very specific and comprehensive operating budgets and capital equipment plans are developed at the grass roots level—after which, key line and staff officers of each organizational component are invited to present their prospectuses for the next year "plus four" to central office executives in New York City. This review-coordination process is frequently quite grueling and exhausting. But as one headquarters vice-president puts it: "The benefits gained from these annual reviews have proved so useful that I seriously doubt we shall ever cut back on the time we devote to planning activities. It's not the sole item that accounts for whatever success we've enjoyed, but it probably counts for a substantial part."

Others among our fourteen also think five to ten years ahead. Betz Labs continually updates its forecasts and budgets to five years; and Dow Jones (DJ) stresses strategic planning for ten or more years. "We're not just concerned with the numbers for the current years," comments one DJ executive. "We pay close attention to what we wish to accomplish and what new areas of business we plan to probe a considerable distance in the future."

Another organization that nurtures the involvement of line managers at the local level is Deluxe Check Printers. Line executives at each of the sixty-two geographically dispersed plants and regional and divisional offices in the United States prepare the intricate detail that is reflected in the firm's annual budgets. The process is basically bottom-up, with fine-tuning and coordination provided by the planning and general executive staff at the St. Paul central offices. So critical does Deluxe consider the planning dimension that it finally departed from its traditional promotion-from-within philosophy several years ago to obtain a broadened, fresher planning perspective from outside the organization. A top-level executive was brought in as vice-president of planning to supplement and coordinate existent in-house capability. "The 'invader' was accepted within a very short period, and planning exercises proved even more fruitful than several years ago. And those earlier efforts were pretty fair," remarked one key manager.

But not all planning efforts work so well as at Deluxe. Planning for the coming year at International Flavors and Fragrances begins in October-November, with the budget and capital spending plans being firmed up by the end of December. However, what frequently occurs before mid-January in the new year is a "red alert"—the signal that emanates from the front office that the budget for the forthcoming year requires "some redefinition" in the form of significant changes and updates. In a few isolated instances, the original budget is entirely jettisoned and reworked to accommodate changes that emerge during the early part of the new year. While several in the organization have developed some skepticism toward the planning process, derived from the history of what often unfolds, the majority continue to attest to the benefits that accrue from progressing through the annual ritual of examining in detail the numbers, objectives, strategies, and tactics that provide targets for the entire organization.

Where many organizations that are not among our elite fourteen exhibit deficiencies in the planning dimension is in the area of integrating an acquisition into the existing organizational structure. Even though considerable time and effort may be devoted by the courting suitor to analyzing an acquisition candidate's product lines, facilities, and financial performance, often scant attention is paid to the organizational fit and integration. Those crucial items are often left either to chance or hope. Northeastern Food (cited in the previous chapter) gave almost no consideration to how the smaller non-food acquisition would be integrated and accommodated within the parent's existing structure. During the first month of "marriage," executives at both Northeastern's and the recent acquisition's headquarters discovered the almost total incompatability of the two organizational styles of management and operation. Had conscious attention been paid to this aspect during the preacquisition planning stage, points of differences might have been anticipated and strategies developed to deal with expected problems before they became almost insolvable, or, at the other extreme, the acquisition might have been aborted entirely.

Philip Morris has largely avoided this postacquisition trap by anticipating integration problems and planning the coordination of acquired organizations into its existent structure. By and large, new acquisitions remain autonomous units for a predetermined period—usually two to three years—after which time managers flow between PM and the acquired organizations to facilitate coordination of organizational styles. In addition, cross-ties between parents and subsidiary are continually nourished at all levels and in each functional area of the business after acquisition.

The overall planning process has become almost a religion at Philip Morris. Annual forecasts and budgets are revised quarterly, along with an annual update of five-year plans, in a three-tiered framework:

1. Divisonal budgets are constructed from the bottom up.

2. A group vice-president and staff hold special review sessions with each operating division or company.

3. Each operating unit then presents its plan to the chairman and key headquarters executives in New York City, at which time details are fine-tuned and coordinated.

The real planning power resides in this third step—the Corporate Products Committee (CPC), which consists of approximately ten key executives at headquarters. Each member has had extensive line experience, usually in marketing or finance, and hence is completely familiar with most tricks, stratagems, and other devices that are likely to emerge during these review sessions with divisional managers.

Each major product is subject to intense scrutiny by the CPC—including packaging, content, pricing, and promotional strategy. A total marketing plan, including advertising and copy layout is reviewed for each new brand. Test marketing results are used to revise the plan. National sales expectations for existing products are cross-checked, using closely guarded weekly industry sales statistics. Considerable attention is also devoted, during these reviews, to the role that foreign operations are expected to play in the overall corporate strategy. This elaborate process forces subordinates to probe every detail of their business unit prior to recommending new products or major modifications to existing ones. The exercises also keep personnel at headquarters well appraised of marketing and financial plans that are being developed throughout the organization.

Several of the corporations pay particular heed to the managerial succession problems and opportunities that are likely to emerge within the foreseeable future. Here, Lilly, SmithKline Beckman, and Deluxe Check easily come to mind. Each of these organizations attempts to crystal-ball its managerial requirements and shortfalls at least three to five years ahead. They then focus on training and development requirements to ensure that appropriately positioned executives are available and ready when replacements are required. Tangentially related to planning for managerial succession is the regular review of compensation and fringe benefit packages at all levels of the organization. Lilly appears to be near the forefront of our group in this total compensation planning dimension.

Only two companies among the fourteen have not engaged in extensive or detailed planning activities during some period of their appearance among this elite group: Tambrands and American Home Products. Almost no forecasting, budgeting, or planning activity was undertaken during Casey's regime at Tambrands. The focal point with respect to planning during that era was merely to ensure that more cases of catamenial products were shipped from each plant each year. Of little concern was whether its market share increased, remained stable, or eroded. Not until about 1980 was a comprehensive planning and budgeting process installed. Since that point, however, considerable emphasis had been devoted to planning activities.

In light of the thirty-year presence of American Home Products in this elite group (equaled or approached only by Merck and SmithKline Beckman), it was somewhat surprising to discover that little allegiance had been paid to long-range planning during a large segment of its existence. True, annual budgets and capital expenditure plans were and are developed and reviewed in fine detail. In fact, every nonbudgeted expenditure over $250 had to be explained to headquarters and approved by William F. LaPorte, until he retired in 1980. During those years, a voluminous manual spelled out in considerable detail all expenditures that required headquarters' approval.

Any vision beyond the one-year plan was hope, the current year being the most distant horizon of any concern. Long-run planning was almost totally ignored. In spite of this apparent lack of concern with the distant future, however, AHP demonstrated enormous capacity to remain enviably viable and extremely profitable over a period spanning three decades. Perhaps the reason is because they consistently pay such close attention to comprehensive short-term planning year after year.

We will examine some of the financial targets that these enterprises establish and briefly review highlights of their financial performance during the periods they have been members of this most highly and consistently profitable group of large American corporations.

Financial Objectives Established and Performance Results

Aside from personnel decisions, one of the most arduous tasks confronting management is setting specific goals and targets toward which the organization will focus effort in the near future. Not only must specific numbers be pinpointed—such as X earnings per share—but also those areas of the organization that are to receive special attention. For a number of years, General Electric (GE) attacked this setting-objectives dimension by identifying eight areas of concern. Specific objectives were established in each of the following sectors: corporate responsibility, market share, personnel development, productivity, product leadership, profitability, research and development, and balance between short- and long-run objectives.

Management development seminars that were conducted throughout GE consistently emphasized the point that no one of these eight areas was more important than any other. Each stood on an equal footing with respect to organizational criticalness. For instance, failure to achieve product leadership targets in any year could be as devastating to long-term corporate health as not attaining personnel development goals or market share objectives. Despite all this equality rhetoric, however, everyone in the organization knew full well that one dimension seemed to always emerge just ever so slightly above the other seven areas in organizational importance—namely profitability.

Profitability is, has been, and will probably continue to be the prime currency of the realm in U.S. business, just as published research is in academia. Although more dimensions enter today's complex calculus of corporate progress and success, top management's eye still focuses on the bottom line—whether it is defined as total after-tax dollar profit, return on sales, earnings per share, return on stockholders' equity, or return on total assets.

The vast majority of our fourteen organizations has clearly defined its financial objectives, usually stated quite precisely in terms of some measure of profitability. Nebulous phraseology and imprecise targets are generally alien to this elite group. A brief look at the level of precision and detail with which these financial objectives are established by top management in several of our corporations may prove instructive. During this review, frequent reference to appendixes A and B will be useful. (Appendix A reflects the average ROS and ROI of the *Fortune* 500 and the top 20 percent cutoff points for 1954 to 1985; appendix B displays several key financial ratios for each firm.)

Betz Labs has established a three-tiered priority among its financial targets. Of first priority is to increase after-tax profit by about 15 percent annually; second, to generate annual sales growth by the same percentage; and in third place is maintenance of a high gross-margin percentage. Actual results attained during the twelve years it has been in this group reveal that Betz's after-tax profits increased about 18 percent compounded annually, whereas its dollar sales volume grew at about 16 percent annually. The gross margin percentage averaged approximately 59.5 percent during this eleven-year period, with a high of over 63 percent reflected in 1984. In short, Betz achieved each of its three financial aims over this eleven-year period.

Inspection of the financial statement analysis in appendix B indicates that Betz's ROS increased almost steadily, from 8.1 percent in 1974, to around 12 percent in the 1980s, with a significant upward blip in 1978 to 13.6 percent. ROI has hovered around 22.5 percent, again, with a significant climb to 26.4 percent in 1978. The cash cycle decreased markedly and almost steadily during the twelve-year period—from 206 days in 1974 to 96 in 1985. Restated, Betz required 110 fewer days in 1985 to convert its inventory into collected sales than it did in 1974—halving its cash-flow cycle. With respect to leverage, the organization has been a very sparse user of interest-bearing debt to finance operations, averaging less than 2 percent of total assets being financed with interest-bearing debt during this twelve-year period, to virtually zero in 1985.

Like many organizations and individuals, not every entity—even those that are highly successful—attains the financial goals it establishes. Commerce Clearing House strives to achieve an annual before-tax ROS of at least 20 percent, with little concern directed to either ROI or earnings per share. However, its before-tax ROS averaged about 17.5 percent during the most recent eleven years; whereas its after-tax ROS approximated 8.75 percent over the same period, with a low of 6.6 percent in 1983 due to the $15 million pretax writeoff of the turnkey computer systems segment. Its cash cycle centers around four months—quite respectable for a publishing company, but not surprising in view of the fact that demand for its loose-leaf updates is relatively firm (as opposed to the situation of general publishers, who produce for an uncertain demand). Interest-bearing debt is used very sparingly, financing on average less than 1 percent of total assets.

International Flavors and Fragrances (IFF) is another corporation that has fallen just short of attaining its twin financial goals of 15 percent annual increase in after-tax profit and 15 percent ROS during the last seventeen years. Its compound annual growth in after-tax profit is about 12 percent; whereas ROS consistently hovers close to 15 percent. Except for the relatively poor 11 percent in 1975, ROS averaged about 14.5 percent during the seventeen-year period it has been among the elite. Again excluding the below-cutoff point for ROI of 15.2 percent that IFF experienced in 1975, its ROI averaged about 21 percent.

In sharp contrast to many organizations that seek growth for the sake of growth, Deluxe Check has a goal of *controlled* growth—in its words, "to maintain a healthy company, with annual after-tax ROI targets of 20 percent along with a respectable return on total assets." Two additional guidelines are to maintain: (1) sales growth equal to or above the growth rate in its market, and (2) continuity of "respectable" cash dividend payouts. Deluxe has consistently exceeded its primary goal of 20 percent ROI during its seventeen-year membership in this group—rising almost steadily to over 32 percent in 1985. A remarkable record of achievement, despite its meager use of interest-bearing debt to finance operations—averaging around 3 percent during the period. The company's forty-eight-hour production timetable partially accounts for its cash cycle varying within a very narrow range of fifty-seven to sixty-nine days—a notable record of consistency.

One distinguishing characteristic that emerges from a detailed financial analysis of these fourteen organizations is the consistency of their financial ratios. Once a particular financial ratio is established in one of these corporations, the level of that ratio tends to persist for extended periods. Although sudden variation or an occasional blip may occur in a specific ratio in a few of these enterprises, financial performance tends to remain within a fairly narrow spectrum. Some financial analysts refer to this phenomenon as "maintaining the momentum of the inertial mass." Restated, once a large body begins along a particular path at a specific speed, both the direction and velocity tend to perpetuate themselves.

As an example of relative stability, note the experience that American Home Products attained in each of the six ratios reflected in appendix B over the thirty-year period, 1956 to 1985. The largest blips occurred in ROS in its most recent two years—which is about four percentage points above the 11.1 percent average that was earned during the previous twenty-eight years. Another illustration of two noticeable blips is the increase in Kellogg's overall leverage from 33.3 percent, in 1983, to 70.8 percent, in 1984, and its percentage of interest-bearing debt rising from 2.6 percent to 42.3 percent during 1984. Both blips resulted from the 1984 leveraged "buy-up" of over fifteen million shares of its common stock from the W.K. Kellogg Foundation Trust—the largest financial transaction in the company's seventy-eight–year history.

Recall that the planning process in American Home Products deviates somewhat from the long-term perspective found so prevalent among the rest of the group; but that departure has been significantly tempered by consistent application of certain financial objectives quarter by quarter for the last three decades. Several maxims comprise that financial objective framework: Each product must pay its way from the start, or within a few months of introduction. Cultivation of an image (other than profitability) and attainment of high market share are priorities that appear far down AHP's list.

The overriding financial objective is to maximize earnings for stockholders by maximizing corporate income and minimizing expenses.

Almost total emphasis is on current profit—quarter by quarter. Each division and product line is expected to increase dollar sales and profit by 10 percent over the same month the previous year. This goal of immediacy tends to discourage management from assuming risks beyond one year—risks that might penalize short-term profitability and cash flow, but could enhance long-term performance.

These consistently applied guidelines have generated ROS's that range between 10.2 percent and 15.3 percent, and average 11.2 percent during the past thirty years—with the ROS steadily creeping upward from a plateau of about 10.8 percent, prior to 1975, to 21 percent, in 1985. In a like manner, the ROI has been consistently high, averaging 30.3 percent during the last thirty years and never falling below the 26.1 percent of 1968. ROIs in the low 30 percent range have been common since 1976—an extremely notable performance for a large enterprise in the consumer nondurable field. Again, even a short-term financial orientation steadfastly applied over a generation can result in outstanding long-run financial performance—at least in American Home Products.

Another of our fourteen that gives close attention to maximizing earnings for its stockholders is Tambrands. Beginning with its president and later chairman of the board, Thomas F. Casey, and continuing through 1985, Tambrands (previously Tampax) has targeted a high dividend payout as its principal financial objective. During the seventeen year period, 1969–85, the percentage of earnings paid out in dividends averaged 65 percent, reaching a maximum of 79 percent in 1978—a phenomenal payout for a large corporation. Although it dropped to 57.3 percent in 1984, that percentage still remains quite high. The ROS averaged a phenomenal 21 percent during those seventeen years—24 percent during the five years ending in 1974—tapering off to an average or just under 15 percent in the most recent four years. ROI averaged almost 32 percent during those same seventeen years, despite absolutely no interest-bearing debt appearing on the balance sheet at the close of each fiscal year during that period.

Although each of our fourteen organizations establishes rather specific financial performance objectives, no single corporation requires rigid adherence to those targets, should events and developments demand alterations. Recall IFF's "red alerts," cited earlier. In Dover's case, top management fully expects divisional executives to strive for and achieve financial objectives that are established for an upcoming fiscal year. But, should circumstances emerge beyond the control of a particular division's management, those objectives are amended. In short, most of these organizations build in a certain flexibility and reasonableness with respect to the range of acceptable performance.

A Dow Jones policy statement leaves no room for doubt as to its primary priority—that of seeking to be the best business news-gathering and reporting network in the world. It strives to achieve the highest quality in communicating information to the public and fiercely guards the integrity of the free press. The organization believes that, if these goals are achieved, profitability will follow automatically. What financial objectives it does seek are expressed rather unconventionally: "Maintain after-tax net profit ahead of the economy's growth." That seemingly amorphous aim has resulted in remarkably high profitability. During the past sixteen years, its ROS has remained fairly constant—within about one percentage point of 12 percent, rising to about 13.5 percent in 1984 and 1985. The ROI consistently remains within the 25 to 30 percent range.

The three predominantly pharmaceutical enterprises can be viewed as a group. As was pointed out in chapter 2, the ROI for the drug industry during the twenty-three–year period, 1962–84, exceeded the all-manufacturing average by about 6.5 percentage points (18.7 versus 12.3). And our three pharmaceutical organizations (plus AHP) exceeded this industry average an additional 6.5 percentage points during the same period. To repeat, quite an outstanding achievement.

Like Betz Labs, SmithKline Beckman also constructs a three-tiered heirarchy of overall corporate financial objectives. SKB gives top priority to growth in earnings per share and dividend payout, followed closely by ROI, and third by real growth in sales. An additional comment is warranted with respect to its liquidity and use of interest-bearing debt. The organization is a huge generator of cash, despite its lengthened cash cycle, primarily because of the enormous success of the gastrointestinal prescription drug Tagamet. SKB has extremely effective in-house tax-sheltering and tax-planning expertise, evidenced by substantial amounts of cash being held in Puerto Rico under provisions of section 936 of the Internal Revenue Code and awaiting repatriation after the appropriate period. Those off-shore deposits almost entirely offset the interest-bearing debt reflected on the balance sheet, in effect, reducing the interest-bearing percentage to virtually zero.

Two other noteworthy achievements concern U.S. Tobacco and Philip Morris. U.S. Tobacco's ROS has steadily increased during the last seventeen years, more than doubling from about 9 percent in 1969 and 1970 to almost 19.5 percent in 1985. Its ROI has also more than doubled—from 15.3 percent in 1969 to almost 31 percent in both 1984 and 1985. Under pressure from a stringently applied inventory control policy (and after attaining a slightly more "liquid" product mix from Miller beer and 7-Up), Philip Morris' cash cycle has been almost halved, from thirteen months in 1969 to seven months in 1985. In addition, the company systematically uses the highest percentage of interest-bearing debt among our fourteen to finance operations—averaging about 41 percent during the last seventeen years.

In summary, the financial objectives outlined by most members of this group are relatively well defined, providing excellent targets for top executives, division managers, and middle-level supervisors to shoot at with well-directed organizational energy. Precisely configured quantitative guidelines tend to be better understood and more capable of attainment than fuzzy qualitative objectives, such as "improve the corporate responsibility posture of the organization." With the few exceptions noted above, the financial performance of each of the fourteen reveals a remarkable consistency with respect to ROS, ROI, cash cycle, and percentage of total resources obtained through interest-bearing debt arrangements. As indicated, these organizations demonstrate an enormous capacity to maintain their momentum at an extremely high level of profitability. Recall that in only three instances did any of these fourteen fall from grace in that respect—Dover falling .1 and .6 percentage points below our ROI cutoff points in 1983 and 1985, respectively, and IFF dropping .4 percentage points below in 1975. On almost any financial analyst's scorecard, these firms reflect sterling performance in the financial arena.

Intensive Monitoring Activity

The time, money, and effort that are allocated to extensive planning activities and to establishing specific financial goals often prove of little benefit unless appropriate and continuous monitoring activities are functioning throughout the organization. Although monitoring goes by a number of names—controlling, surveillance, cross-checking, verification, intelligence gathering, or periodic review—all functions have one thing in common, which is the detection of signals that indicate how closely plans and targets are being adhered to. A variety of devices and techniques have been devised by which activities are continually monitored, such as daily control charts, monthly volume-mix-price-cost variance analyses, breakeven diagrams, and periodic reviews by top management. Each of the fourteen has integrated effective review and monitoring mechanisms into its organization—mechanisms that have undoubtedly enhanced the ability to remain among the top performers in U.S. industry. Subsequent discussion focuses on seven of these enterprises, which have instituted somewhat interesting schemes or philosophies to facilitate effective control.

Coupled with the planning and goal-setting dimensions in American Home Products is a parallel supportive structure of continuous and intense monitoring activity. Top management and the central staff maintain extremely close tabs on each and every expenditure and income item for each product line and division. Although marketing and promotional programs are decentralized to the divisional level, financial control over all activities is concentrated at headquarters. For example, LaPorte maintained intimate and detailed knowledge of daily operations throughout the company, during his leadership from 1960 to 1980—perhaps as intimate an involvement as undertaken by any CEO of a large U.S. corporation. While AHP is a marketing-driven enterprise, a penchant for financial control and accountability pervades the entire organization. Plans and goals are assured of receiving adequate attention—and of being adhered to, in most cases. Unfortunately, this constant monitoring may have encouraged some of its managers to seek opportunities with competitors offering less stringent working conditions.

In order to facilitate closer control and coordination, Betz Labs has organized itself into several small operating units, coupling that with a rather unique in-house consultative device. Selected top management from several corporate segments are frequently called together to form a mini–board of directors, which provides expert advice to a budding division or one that is experiencing special difficulties. A financial executive from one division, for example, may join with a chemical engineer from another sector, and a marketing manager and an international specialist from a third and fourth segment to address a particular set of expansion problems that confront a product line in another unit. In addition to providing advisory and problem-solving expertise, these mini-boards also monitor activities in the particular unit on a continuous basis. "This mechanism allows us to dispense with external consultants, provides an intimate feel for control activities that are required in new ventures, and enables our managers to broaden their perspective so they can direct their own operations more effectively," states one executive. "The checks and balances provided by this networking prove most valuable."

Overall corporate review in the decentralized Dover organization is concentrated among the central staff and key executives at New York City headquarters. Divisional presidents are evaluated constantly with respect to progress that is being made toward attaining annual budgets. Additional follow-up monitoring is exerted through frequent meetings, and by numerous plant visits throughout the country by top executives. These visitations help front-office managers maintain familiarity with operations, allowing them to see for themselves how specific situations are being handled at the grass roots, and to personally pass out plaudits when circumstances warrant. Applause from headquarters is frequent, according to Gary L. Roubos, president and CEO of Dover. "Bestowing considerable praise for personal achievement is one of my primary tasks. That, plus keeping from getting in the way of their being successful."

At first glance, Dow Jones appears to be run very informally—almost in casual fashion—without any type of monitoring activity in view; but behind this "laid-back" facade is a group of about eleven top officers who are deeply committed and involved in constantly reviewing attainment of annual and long-range plans. "We place heavy emphasis on these activities," noted one member of this group, "and we make use of almost any meeting between us as an opportunity to circulate significant observations." For example, communications with respect to current operations or developing problems are gleaned during morning coffee clatches at which top executives routinely gather. Bits of information dropped during relaxed, but pointed, verbal exchanges are scribbled on note pads for further follow-up. "We're forever seeking better ways to accomplish the task of control. Few stones are left unturned. And one of the most effective devices we've found so far is this coffee-communication linkage."

S.J. Spitz, president and chief operating officer of International Flavors and Fragrances until 1986, installed effective cost control, economic measures, and streamlined monitoring activities upon his arrival at IFF from Tenneco in 1970. Probably the most critical control device in the organization, however, is the Odor Evaluation Board (OEB), which is composed of eight individuals. It has little to do directly with the financial dimension, but, indirectly, its impact on financial performance is enormous. The OEB is the vital control hub of IFF, composed of expert "sniffers, tasters, and analysts" who have been with the firm a considerable number of years. These persons are responsible for maintaining the absolutely critical quality control of each product in the organization's "orchestra of flavor and fragrance notes. . . . Should one note in that ensemble go sour during our client's manufacturing process because of quality control failure on our part," remarked one top IFF executive, "our financial picture could be in serious difficulty."

A driving force that underlies Lilly's review and monitoring process is a pervasive introspective, self-motivated, and self-critiquing attitude. Each manager in Lilly has risen through a culture that emphasizes self-motivated self-analysis—not only of his or her individual relationship with the company, but of the division's or section's progress toward goals over which he or she has responsibility and control. Review committees and coordinating boards do operate at various levels in the corporation, but the impetus to meet budgets, forecasts, and objectives is derived from a built-in corporate consciousness that has been instilled in each manager to achieve or exceed goals. As one executive expresses it, "It's an article of faith in Lilly not to rely on others to provide the goad or prod."

Top management at Philip Morris, like Dover's, believes that control of detailed operations is better left to managers at the local level. Heavy-handed monitoring at New York City headquarters is not the norm by which corrections are made, but everyone throughout PM knows that those in "the City" maintain an eagle eye on interim financial statements that are prepared for each operating segment. Patterns of the company's daily cigarette, soft drink, and beer sales—along with each competitor's volume—in every domestic region and country in the world are under constant surveillance. A phone call between the right persons can address and begin to correct a tactical error or resolve an issue that requires immediate attention within minutes of the deficiency's detection.

The major negative aspect of control activities in many organizations is the feeling that "Big Brother" is watching each movement and that the sword of severance or demotion is ready to drop on the guilty where infractions or unmet objectives are detected. This syndrome emerges among our fourteen to a very limited extent. What is far more pervasive in the vast majority of this elite group is the sense on the part of most managers and employees that "Yes, we are being monitored; but we view this process as culminating in helpful suggestions and constructive advice rather than inflictions of punishment." What seems apparent in these organizations is a continuing reinforcement process that helps supervisors and managers meet previously approved budgets, goals, and targets, and that others exist elsewhere in the corporation who stand ready, willing, and able to provide helpful assistance when things go awry. As one individual at Deluxe Check describes its atmosphere: "Most of us do not feel at all denigrated or intimidated by the monitoring process. It's more a feeling of mutual support and cooperation—not confrontation, threat, or heavy-handedness."

This discussion would be remiss if I failed to point out that not every one of our organizations closely monitors each operating unit in the corporation. Most of these entities allow a certain degree of freedom from constant control in such areas as pure research, such as frequently occurs in the pharmaceutical companies. For example, it is not uncommon for a director of research in such firms to allocate or be allocated a certain amount of discretionary funds—often sizeable—to investigate and probe new "off-the-wall" ideas that may (or may not) yield marketable products years down the road. The hope, of course, is that such unconstrained research will ultimately find some of that effort resulting in profitable ventures. Peters and Waterman refer to such activity in their *In Search of Excellence* as "skunkworks" or "off-the-books activity"—activities that often serve to keep morale high and an unfettered entrepreneurial spirit alive in the organization.

In summary, planning activities that encompass detailed budgeting and forecasting are in place in each of our fourteen organizations. Financial objectives are usually well defined and clearly understood at various managerial levels. Because targets are pinpointed, the probabilities of achieving them increase.

The financial results achieved by these companies as a group—with respect to measures of profitability, liquidity, and leverage—generally reflect level and steadiness of achievement. With respect to profitability, there is a level of attainment that is probably unexcelled elsewhere in U.S. business. Results are monitored and carefully evaluated in most organizations, sometimes as frequently as daily. The several staffs at central headquarters play a central role in directing planning and monitoring activities in most of these enterprises.

At this juncture, we can draw together several key points made thus far in this report. A well-integrated framework of focused mission, well-defined acquisition strategy, relatively long-run perspective, extensive planning activity, clear financial objectives, and intensive monitoring activity are dominant characteristics among these fourteen.

Next up for investigation are several aspects of organizational structure, development, and continuity that exist in this elite group.

4

The Top Echelon and the Front Office

> A man to carry on a successful business must have imagination. He must see things as in a vision, a dream of the whole thing.
> —Charles M. Schwab
> *How to Succeed*

Drawing for a moment on the previous chapter, the reader may raise the point that numerous other U.S. corporations also institute rigorous planning activities, establish specific financial goals, and install extensive monitoring control systems. Yet those same organizations fail to appear among this group of the most highly and consistently successful companies. It might be inferred that planning, setting goals, and monitoring progress should be—but may not be—sufficient to ensure long-run extraordinary success. Recall the precaution that appears in the last paragraph of chapter 1 that continued success in any business is probably the result of a complex interaction of several factors rather than the simple accumulation of single attributes until some magic number of items have been implemented. Although sound planning, well defined objectives, and effective controls are common attributes among the fourteen, other factors in combination with these undoubtedly play significant roles in any pattern of enduring success. Among these other factors are matters that fall within the area of top management and its organization structure.

Concisely put, management is the direction of others toward a goal—"others" being monetary, physical, and most important, human resources. And top management, or the top echelon, includes those individuals at corporate and divisonal headquarters that are responsible for the overall conduct of corporate and divisional activity—the chairman of the board, president, members of the president's office—such as various executive and senior vice-presidents—and division heads.

We focus, in this chapter, on three features of the top echelon that are generally common among the fourteen:

Presence of a visionary founder and notably influential chief executive officers.

Planned managerial succession into top management.

Promotion from within the organization.

A few peripheral points surrounding the role of top management in several of these companies will also be touched on:

The type of individuals most likely to rise into the top ranks.

The use of budding divisions as training grounds for entry into top management.

Cross-fertilization of managerial talent.

The principal feature that is discussed under the umbrella of *organizational structure* is the existence in most of these enterprises of a very lean headquarters and central staff. Also addressed are the degrees of centralization and decentralization present among these fourteen, and two tangential points—(1) transition from the entrepreneurial mode in a particular company to a "professionally managed" organization, and (2) recent developments in the overall control of selected firms that stem largely from the hostile takeover environment.

Visionary Founder and Influential CEO's

A select few visionaries can be identified in each of our fourteen companies who have exerted significant influence on the evolution of their organizations. These individuals are usually either founders or subsequent chief executive officers, such as the board chairman or president.

Two principal architects that set the tone and pattern of development in American Home Products were Alvin Brush and William F. Laporte. Brush became president of AHP in 1935 at age 38, and subsequently rose to the position of chairman of the board, where he remained until his death in 1964. Several policies that he designed and introduced into the company are outlined here. All of them continue substantially unchanged as integral parts of the company:

> He transformed the company from a loosely organized holding company into a well-disciplined, tightly knit operating entity composed of various divisions and groups, such as household products, packaged drugs and cosmetics, food, and ethical pharmaceuticals.
>
> Although various operating plants and divisions were geographically dispersed throughout the United States, the head of each subsidiary or

division (with one or two exceptions) was and is expected to work out of corporate headquarters in New York City.

He selected excellent individuals to head the divisions and gave each manager full latitude in such activities as production and marketing—but with budgetary control and capital expenditure approval residing at headquarters. In selecting executive talent, Brush searched for and hired outstanding individuals even when no immediate opening was available for the person. In effect, he stockpiled executive talent pending openings as they developed in the organization.

He strived to avoid acquiring products or companies that do everything well. Sufficient opportunity must exist for AHP to make significant improvements and contributions to the acquired line.

Brush dismissed as misguided the myth of achieving a balanced, full line of competing products in order to build volume and market share. Instead, his guideline was "Acquire an existing specialty item that is easy to make, package, and merchandise—but which competition will find difficult to match—and which is profitable."

Brush recognized in the 1960s that AHP could no longer continue its traditional formula of expanding its basic drug business by licensing ethical drugs from other pharmaceutical manufacturers. He saw the need to build up internal pharmaceutical research capability, and he began to direct considerable financial resources toward that endeavor.

He felt advertising and promoting the corporate name was a waste of money. "Spend enormous amounts advertising each product—but *never* push the corporate name or a corporate image."

In regards to this last point, several financial analysts, corporate strategists, and academicians have recently criticized Beatrice Company for taking the opposite tack. During the 1984 Olympics, for example, Beatrice spent huge sums advertising on television the virtues of its numerous individual products, such as Samsonite luggage, as well as buying additional time to tie those items to "the family of Beatrice products." Brush's philosophy was that it is sufficiently difficult and expensive to convey positive attributes about a single brand-name product (for example, Anacin) in one well-aimed message amid the noise of the mass media, let alone attempt to simultaneously push the company name with which the product is associated—particularly if the brand and company names are clearly different.

Laporte became president in 1960 and continued after 1964 as chairman of the board until 1980. He supervised the in-house R&D buildup in ethical drugs begun under Brush and also continued the policy of allowing each division to be relatively autonomous, except for finances, which continued to be controlled through the central office. His vision was risk averse—cultivating and maintaining a strong sense of financial discipline in the company. During his two-decade tenure as AHP's chief steward, interest-bearing debt as a percentage of total assets steadily fell from a not-exorbitant 4.7 percent, in 1960, to about .6 percent in 1980. Many accused him of being too penny-pinching—allowing no executive frills or perquisites. He commonly probed into the most intimate corporate operating details. One executive reported that an order had once come from Laporte's office to decrease expenditures for toilet tissue. The corporate response was to purchase a tissue that was 9 millimeters narrower than the standard sheet.

He disclaimed participative management when (and long after) it became a stylish concept, and his view of long-range strategic planning fell just short of his calling it utter nonesense. "Any vision beyond this year's budget is hope," he often declared. He shunned the press to such an extent that it soon became corporate practice to rarely grant interviews or to talk with security analysts and other media representatives; he insisted instead that "our earnings per share tells our story quite adequately." In opposition to philosophies that existed among his competitors, Laporte required that all products pay their way from the point of introduction. And as did Brush, he much preferred a smaller market share and larger profit to a bigger share that generated a smaller profit.

During the three decades that AHP has maintained membership in our elite group, both Brush's and Laporte's vision appear to have been instrumental in instilling in the corporation the following characteristics: shrewd acquisitions and divestitures; financial discipline with tight control over all expenditures; constant pressure for profits; and anonymity for the corporate name. The AHP experience helps illustrate that continuity and complementarity of vision among successors in or near the top helps contribute to long-term success. Adherence by those at the top to a common set of key organizational strategies and values over an extended period of time provides a sense of coherence, stability, and confidence.

A number of outstanding individuals have left Dow Jones with enduring legacies that reinforce and at least partially account for a great deal of the company's success since its founding, in 1882, by Charles H. Dow, Edward D. Jones, and Charles M. Bergstresser. (Bergstresser wisely agreed early on to omit his trisyllabic name from the company's title). The three created, on July 8, 1889, what was to become the firm's most durable and profitable product line, *The Wall Street Journal*. The first single-sheet issue sold for two cents, carried a news bulletin of the Sullivan-Kilrain fight, and mentioned a remote spot on the midwestern plains—Kansas and its capital, Topeka—no fewer than five times.

Clarence Walker Barron bought Dow Jones and Company, including the *Journal,* in 1902, for about $130,000. Shortly thereafter, he constructed a journalistic maxim for the paper: "Never write from the standpoint of yourself, but always from the standpoint of the reader. Economize the reader's time." That clearly stated creed remains a cornerstone of the newspaper to this day.

Bernard "Barney" Kilgore, president and CEO from 1945 to 1966, and chairman from 1966 until his death one year later, was largely responsible for transforming the *Journal* into a sophisticated national business publication. According to Vermont Royster, *The Wall Street Journal's* two-time Pulitzer prize-winner:

> The chief architect of the transformation was Bernard Kilgore, the one who was my bureau chief so long ago. While many others contributed to this growth—able editors, executives and pioneers in the printing trade—his was the vision of a newspaper that could span this huge country delivering the same news on the same day to readers in Portland, Maine, and Portland, Ore. Doubters said it could not be done but the newspaper you hold today, better edited and more complete, is his monument. Other publishers of national newspapers came thereafter. Kilgore had the dream first and saw it fulfilled.[1]

The emphasis on business news was expanded during Kilgore's tenure to include involvement in political and international affairs. He also invented many substantive and stylistic aspects that are currently reflected in the *Journal,* such as comprehensive fact-filled leader articles in both outside columns of page 1; the "What's News Digest" column also on page 1; and clustering related stories inside the paper. Above all, he persisted in continuing Barron's clear-writing edict—absolutely refusing to allow technical jargon to creep into articles without a clarifying explanation and insisting on defining all terms in the simplest language possible.

William F. Kerby served as chairman from 1967 to 1978, and continued to build on his predecessors' principles. He is referred to by many in the company as the father of the organization's diversification efforts into related news areas. In addition, he probed new uses of advanced technology, particularly satellitery, computerization, and data retrieval systems. Warren H. Phillips became president in 1972, CEO in 1975, and chairman in 1978—further extending Kerby's focused diversification efforts. In 1984, Phillips commented on Dow Jones's enormous success since its founding: "We set high standards of performance in terms of content and quality. Financial excellence follows from that. Sounds kind of cornball, but we find that it works."[2]

A striking example of how disjointed and discontinuous visions among occupants of the front office can affect the progress and success of an organization can be drawn from Scripto, previously cited. From its founding in 1923 until at least well into the 1970s, Scripto was led by a series of individuals who appear to have ignored linking their individual visions for the organization into a coherent pattern. Harold Hirsch, from 1923 to 1939 forged Scripto's expertise into a highly successful well-oiled machine, concentrating solely on manufacturing and marketing an inexpensive, high quality, mass-produced mechanical pencil. From necessity, Eugene Stern and E.P. Rogers dedicated the bulk of the firm's capacity during 1940 to 1945 toward manufacturing ordnance items for the war effort, but immediately at the war's conclusion, Scripto redirected it total effort back to its strength in mechanical pencils.

As soon as James Carmichael came aboard to head the company in 1947, however, he departed from a well-proven corporate track record and initiated the dual strategy of (1) making Scripto into a full-line mechanical writing instrument manufacturer and (2) striving to become the largest manufacturer of writing instruments in the world. Grandiose ambitions, particularly in light of the industry's experience that narrow-niche specialization in one, at most two, product lines was a critical key to success. Departure from its well-defined niche and hard-earned success, coupled with over-extended ambitions saw the beginning of Scripto's demise.

Following Carmichael's death in 1964, Carl Singer was named president-CEO, and he immediately instituted a multi-pronged attack. He reversed his predecessor's decision to modernize manufacturing operations with highly automated equipment that would have enabled high-volume, low-cost production; phased out the less expensive ball point and fountain pens (at a time when consumer demand was for less expensive writing instruments); drastically reduced advertising support; and proceeded with a large-scale diversification program into unrelated products—copying machines, wide-angle lens cameras, cigarette lighters, carpet manufacturing, and ceramic ashtrays.

In successive disarray, Robert H. Ferst (1967 to 1968), Arthur Harris (1968 to 1971), and Herbert "Bo" Sams (1971 to well into the 1970s) instituted their own separate and uncoordinated visions for Scripto that left the organization floundering and financially weakened. Each believed that his particular vision contained the appropriate ingredients for a turn-around, and each exerted his best efforts to embark on a more successful course. But the revolutionary departures from the organization's prime underpinnings (ignoring the ingredients for success in this particular industry), the uncoordinated strategies and pursuit of an excessive number of unrelated produuct lines eventually proved unworkable and unmanageable.

Startlingly different from Scripto's experience has been Deluxe Check Printer's development. In 1915, W.R. Hotchkiss foresaw an opportunity and developed a manfacturing system, coupled with a philosophy that still enables the company to provide its clientele with forty-eight-hour service. Remarked a Deluxe vice-president: "Our two-day turnaround is the bedrock on which this company has built its reputation. That plus the founder's obsession with flawless quality have stood us in good stead since the company's creation." Similarly, at Dover, Thomas C. Sutton and Gary L. Roubos (chairman and president, respectively) have developed and continuously implement the two-pronged policy under which the enterprise operates: First, a highly selective acquisition policy—an acquisition must be a recognized leader in its market, possess excellent growth prospects, and reflect a higher-than-average ROI; second, a clear statement on control—give the head of each division or subsidiary complete control over all operations, with the single exception being that New York City headquarters functions as the corporate central banker, providing long-term capital and financing direction.

Although not among our fourteen, John F. Connelly's very successful Crown Cork and Seal provides another example of continuous adherence to the clear vision of its leadership. Connelly took control of the ailing corporation in 1959 and quickly implemented what he perceived to be a turnaround strategy. Instead of adopting the can-manufacturing industry's norm of product diversification and covering all bases, Connelly saw greater opportunity and wisdom in specializing in aerosol, beer, and other difficult-to-manufacture metal containers. He decided to leave the conventional easy-to-make food and beverage can market to the diversified giants such as American Can and Continental Can. He coupled specialization with strong dedicated customer service, assisting clients in solving their in-house canning problems, and pursued overseas expansion in developing markets. He was convinced that the specialization-strong service-overseas expansion triad would allow Crown Cork to sidestep the perennial problems of price competition and low value-added that plagued the can manufacturing industry. And the past three decades have proven the still active octogenarian head of Crown Cork correct.

Although the company was founded by his father in 1925, probably the most influential individual in the early development (well into the 1970s) of Betz Labs was John Drew (hereafter J.D.) Betz. He served as president and CEO until he became a busy chairman emeritus in 1975. A brief overview of his philosophies and significant contributions—which persist in the company to the present—includes:

Stay out of peripheral business and tangential activities that divert managerial time and effort from the main thrust of the organization—keeping open the industrial plumbing systems of our clients.

Ensure that each operating unit and division in the company remains small, manageable, and entrepreneurial in orientation. Subdivide operations into separate divisions when they exceed a certain size in terms of sales volume or number of employees. This allegiance to entrepreneurship reflects J.D.'s personal penchant and love for maneuverability and flexibility—and his profound hatred of stultifying bureauracracy.

Develop and maintain a team concept throughout the organization. Tolerate mistakes and errors—in fact, encourage them for growth and development of the individual and the business. "But," in his own words, "the individual who attempts a coverup is out!"

Adhere to high ethical standards in dealing with both customers and competitors—as exemplified by his terminating several foreign operations when it became apparent that payola and other undercover activities were necessary to compete in those cultures—but do anything within legal constraints to retain customers. Treat each potential loss as a crisis to be avoided.

During his term of leadership, J.D. generated two ideas that became significant in Betz's subsequent success as a corporate entity: First, the use of budding divisions in the company as training grounds to develop individuals who appear to possess the talent and initiative to become future Betz executives; second, developing a process to cross-fertilize managerial talent.

With respect to the first point, individuals who J.D. and other top executives felt were potential stars were placed in responsible positions in operations that were in the initial stages of development. These individuals were given full exposure to all the complexities likely to befall a full-fledged corporate unit. By giving them a sufficiently small unit around which they could completely get their hands—in order to experience how "it all fitted together"—J.D. believed superior managerial talent could be developed in a shorter time than pigeon-holing individuals in an overly narrow specialty allows. "Managers exposed to this challenge have performed admirably in the company," he emphasized. He also remarked that persons whose skills and talents are tested in this way seem to function with a higher degree of confidence and greater breadth of perspective as they move through the organization, compared to their counterparts with whom he had become acquainted in competitors' operations.

His cross-fertilization innovation provides another example of creative vision at the top. The corporation is divided into some eight or nine divisions, subsidiaries, and groups, each of which specializes in a particular industrial segment or geographical area of the world. For example, Betz Paperchem concentrates on providing water and liquid treatment services for customers in the paper industry. Liquids that constantly circulate through paper manfacturing plants must be kept free of slime, corrosion, and biological foulings. This particular subsidiary (as others), is fully staffed with engineering specialists and managerial talent in the several functional areas. In addition, however, Betz Paperchem (like each of the other Betz subsidiaries) has its own mini–board of directors that is composed of representatives from other subsidiaries in the corporation. The board may be composed of a marketing specialist, controller, financial analyst, president, and R&D director from other Betz divisions. This internal board is summoned to assist and furnish counsel whenever unique or particularly troublesome challenges confront the subsidiary's management. This vehicle provides a number of benefits to the entire organization:

> The services of outside consultants are rarely required—at considerable savings to the corporation—and the expertise that is obtained from within Betz is fully familiar with organizational goals, style, and philosophies. No break-in familiarization with the company is required.
>
> Managers who participate on these mini-boards get a chance to broaden their horizons and expertise and to apply their knowledge to nonroutine challenges. New opportunities provide a welcome change of pace.
>
> In gaining additional exposure to other than their own unit of primary responsibility, members of these mini-boards become more productive and effective. In commenting on this facet of the boards, J.D. indicated that "the chief contribution is a sharper, better informed, and more useful group of managers. The boards provide opportunities to get acquainted with the parts that comprise this outfit—and how they all fit together. The concepts of teamwork and smallness are continuously being reinforced."

These two relatively novel managerial devices are particularly intriguing in light of—perhaps even because of—J.D.'s inability to complete his undergraduate degree in chemical engineering, due to illness, and his decision not to pursue an MBA degree as so many of his contemporaries had been inclined to do. His intense curiosity, entrepreneurial drive, and risk-taking proclivities are traits that some educational programs and institutions tend to stifle rather than nourish. "Relatively novel" is, however, used advisedly at the beginning of this paragraph, since Dow Jones recently introduced the practice of using its budding operations as training grounds for individuals whom the top echelon identifies as potential high-level executives. For example, the two small and germinal overseas editions of the *Journal* (European and Asian) provide opportunities for young talented managers to gain a thorough and wide exposure to a complete business unit prior to taking over larger, more complex operations in the Dow Jones organization.

Strong family affiliations have also played a significant role among several other of our fourteen organizations. Eli Lilly continues to reflect numerous ideals and practices instilled in that company by its founder, Colonel Eli Lilly. During his leadership of the firm, from 1867 to 1898, he was determined to make medicines of the highest quality for only physicians to dispense, rather than for snake-oil merchants and itinerant quacks. Although his son Josiah ruled Lilly from 1898 to 1932 with an iron-hand, he disciplined with compassion. He pioneered the installation of several personnel relations policies, such as a wholly-funded company pension plan, a company cafeteria, and employee health insurance. And he instilled in the organization the still current and widespread notion that each employee, with the assistance of the company, outline a career path for himself or herself. Josiah, Jr., the corporate head from 1948 to 1953, expanded that idea to what has since become known within the Lilly organization as "reciprocal bonds of loyalty between company and employee"—a concept that continues to form the cornerstone of corporate personnel policy. "Reciprocal bonds" is an extension of his brother Eli's philosophy, developed during the latter's presidency, from 1932 to 1948, that no employee should ever be laid off due to eonomic hardship.

George W. Merck, son of the founder of that company, began heading the organization in 1926. The following statement, attributed to him, has served as a corporate creed through most of its eighty-five-year history of making chemicals and pharmaceuticals:

> Medicine is for patients. It is not for the profits. The profits follow, and if we remembered that, they have never failed to appear. The better we have remembered it, the larger they have been.[3]

Henry W. Gadsen, CEO from 1965 to 1976, extended that philosophy of service and transformed the company into an aggressive competitor that was also concerned with costs and the bottom line. In fact, some old-timers still with the company suggest that Gadsen might have become too obsessed with "the bottom line."

Another key element in George Merck's strategy to remake the company from a relatively insignificant pharmaceutical house to a predominant role in U.S. industry was, according to Peter Drucker, recruiting outstanding visionaries for its board of directors. One such individual that Merck brought onto the board as its parttime chairman at the close of World War II was Vannevar Bush, a distinguished scientist at the Massachusetts Institute of Technology and a person who had played a principal role as science adviser and administrator during that war effort. As Drucker puts it in his *Management*, Bush's chief assignment was

> to think through what the top management of the company should be and should do. One of his conclusions was the need for an effective board which

could review and guide top management, and could create access for it to major publics such as the scientific community. . . . This, in turn, led to a long-run strategy for Merck which, within a decade, gave a company that had started far behind the old pros in its industry, worldwide leadership in an extremely competitive industry.[4]

Merck well understood that the key to success in the pharmaceutical industry was basic scientific knowledge and organized research.

John J. Horan undertook renewed dedication to the research side of R&D during his tenure as chief executive (from 1976 to 1985) by pumping enormous sums of money into that aspect of the business in an effort to generate more funds for even more research. P. Roy Vagelos implemented Horan's strategy as head of Merck's research laboratories from 1975 until his selection as CEO in 1985. As CEO, Vagelos intends to stress throughout the corporation an orientation to research that many competitors are just beginning to pay serious heed to—namely, learn first how a specific disease works; then start to design, develop, and manipulate the structure of compounds to fight it. (As opposed to the shotgun approach of testing an almost infinite array of chemical compounds by trial and error in the hope that a possible treatment for a specific ailment might eventually emerge.)

Two other visionaries easily come to mind as being instrumental in the continuing success of their respective organizations. Oakleigh Thorne bought into Commerce Clearing House in 1907, fifteen years after its founding. Six years later he expanded the company's product line of a legal reporting service to include what he then thought might hold some profitable potential—a tax reporting service to clarify and interpret legislation that he felt sure would follow passage of the sixteenth amendment to the Constitution. That premonition, along with his insistence on unyielding devotion to quality and reliability of information, has generated enormous dividends for CCH and its stockholders.

On the foods side of the list, William Keith Kellogg founded Kellogg Company twelve years following the accidental discovery by his brother, John Harvey, in 1894 that wheat flakes could be made from boiled and dried wheat. He quickly became interested in selling these wheat (and subsequently corn) flakes by carload lots nationally—rather than simply in mere hundreds of $5 mail orders to sanitarium patients and the health-conscious in nearby regions. The vehicle he envisioned to accomplish the task was a blind, abiding faith in massive advertising—a tradition still at the heart of Kellogg's current corporate philosophy. The founder coupled overwhelming doses of mass media promotion with the display of his signature in bright red script on each package of the company's ready-to-eat cereals, where it remains today openly displayed in each supermarket across the country.

A.L. van Ameringen created International Flavors and Fragrances in 1958, instilling throughout the organization a close-knit, very personalized, almost paternalistic style of management. But it was Henry G. Walter, Jr. who began to transform the firm into a worldwide operation upon his assumption of the presidency in 1963, three years before van Ameringen's death. Walter was the corporate visionary. Until his retirement as chairman in 1985 (in his mid-seventies), he continued to probe uncharted areas in the flavor and fragrance field. For example, he nudged and prodded the research arm of the firm to seek out possible relationships between fragrances and physical reactions, and the subliminal effects of flavors on humans—as opposed to concentrating solely on the typical pyschological reactions induced by aromas and taste enhancers.

Perhaps the most enduring contribution made by Joseph F. Cullman III to Philip Morris during his almost two-decade tenure as CEO (from 1959 to 1977) was his uncanny ability to identify and cultivate seasoned groups of young, energetic managers to operate and carry the enterprise forward. He was able to develop an unusually cohesive and intensely loyal group of individuals to direct the company—by no means a simple task, considering the level of drive, competitiveness, and ambition among the contestants. Cullman demanded that his managers spend 100 percent of their working hours on company business; and he expected a steady flow of results. He loaded each person to the hilt with responsibilities and clout, allowing each individual considerable latitude to succeed and fail. Two other qualities that enabled him to successfully execute his CEO responsibilities were (1) an ability to cut quickly to the essence of a problem and (2) the ability to maintain the spirit of a small company by instilling in the organization a participative nonbureaucratic approach to management.

Some enterprises must struggle through a period in which two conflicting visions compete for organizational predominance. Vail Associates, for example, was founded by Peter W. Seibert, who found his ski-Shangri-la in Eagle County, Colorado. Seibert placed top priority on concern for the environment, the people aspect of the business, and the fun and pure joy encompassed by the physical setting in which Vail was situated. As the company's success mounted, however, the complexity of the organization grew to the point at which Seibert finally succumbed to bringing in a cadre of professional managers. This group, under the direction of Richard L. Peterson, shifted from Seibert's behavioral-environmental inclination toward an economics-efficiency-bottom line orientation. The clash and cleavage between the two segments became so intense that Seibert finally extricated himself from the organization, migrating to Snow Basin, Utah, to pioneer another recreational facility.

Such cleavage and conflict did not emerge in Tambrands (renamed from Tampax in 1984) under the stewardship of Thomas F. Casey until very near to his retirement as CEO in 1978. One of the company's three founders (the other two being Ellery Mann and Earle Griswold), Casey ran the organization with iron-fisted control. He commandeered with a quiet steady leadership, remarking at one point, in response to an inquiry on whether or not he would alter any company policy in the future: "We plan to go on doing what we've always done." A four-pronged company policy, which remained in place almost unchanged until Casey's retirement, included:

1. Concentrate solely on menstrual tampons.
2. Make no radical changes in the product (such as competitors do every few years).
3. Attempt no diversification.
4. Use no massive promotional campaigns.

Not until 1977 did he respond to an eroding market share by increasing his advertising budget 50 percent over the previous year—to $19 million, or 11.6 percent of sales.

Edwin H. Shutt, Jr. joined the organization in 1981, having previously served with Procter and Gamble as president of its Clorox division. His main initiatives at Tambrands have centered on heavy promotional activity and related expenditures, the realignment of the sales and marketing forces, and an eye toward diversification into selected consumer nondurables such as monoclonal antibodies under the "First Response" brand name.

What appears most striking among the majority of visionary leaderships in our fourteen organizations is a focus on long-term strategies and on fundamental building blocks—as opposed to sole concentration on resolving short-run problems and challenges. Most seemed to grasp organizational problems with a broad perspective and to possess an ability to draw and encompass others within their field of vision.

Planning Managerial Succession into Top Management

Developing continuity of leadership in an organization and nurturing individuals to assume those positions may be obligations of the corporate top echelon as critical as clearly identifying the central mission and focus of the enterprise. Although the creative engineering geniuses of Bill Lear and Howard Head are reflected in their respective innovations—the Lear jet and the Head ski—neither was able to successfully manage the enterprises they founded. What is even sadder is that neither individual was able to identify and nourish managers to carry on the organizations their pioneering achievements created. Bill Ruger, although a superb creator of small firearms and the dynamic head of Sturm, Ruger, and Company, may be confronting a similar problem of managerial succession. The task of planning succession into the top echelon demands subtle insight that is critical to the continued success of any organization.

Except for three relatively recent instances, considerable attention appears to have been devoted in each of our organizations to the process of developing managerial talent to occupy its top positions. Although some concern was voiced by several lower level executives in American Home Products, little deliberate effort appears to have been exerted by those officials near the top, during the late 1970s, to nurture a cadre of individuals to replace Laporte as CEO. At International Flavors and Fragrances, conscious thought as to who would eventually replace Henry Walter and S.J. Spitz (aged 75 and 64, respectively, in 1985) seemed to be continuously absent from the corporation's list of issues to resolve until well into 1985,— when successors were finally appointed. And very little effort was exerted toward identifying Casey's successor at Tambrands until his retirement in 1978.

At the other extreme, five or six examples can be drawn from among the remaining eleven entreprises to provide some evidence that deliberate, conscious attention toward resolving progression into the top echelon is an astute investment by top policymakers. Betz Labs has a long-standing commitment to rotating among senior positions in its various divisions and functional areas those whom top management has identified as prospective candidates for vice-presidencies and above. The company believes this practice, plus the previously mentioned mini-board device, exposes these individuals to a variety of experiences and responsibilities that no amount of outside seminars or in-house training sessions could accomplish. Reflecting on this practice, J.D. Betz remarked: "A two to three year stint as head of a division's marketing or sales function, followed by directing an international activity, and finally leading a full-scale domestic division provides us with a bevy of executive talent I cannot easily visualize another scheme accomplishing so superbly for us."

Deluxe Check Printers pursues a different course. It developed an extremely successful in-house training scheme in the late 1970s that is the envy of, and a model for, many *Fortune* 500 corporations. Each manager—whether plant, functional, divisional, or president-CEO—is expected to develop and maintain a stable of trainees for each supervisory position in his or her organizational unit, including his or her own position. The program consists of three parts: (1) upper level managers discuss the goals and job objectives of candidates for managerial positions with the candidates; (2) senior corporate officials participate as counselors and advisers at critical decision points in each candidate's career; and (3) candidates construct an action plan to implement the statement of management philosophy that he or she is constantly in the process of creating. Whenever a person moves up within managerial ranks, the internal promotion sequence—"the snake dance"—begins. According to one top-level executive, "expectations are fulfilled, and the management development process is transmitted in an immediately visible and concrete way to another generation of Deluxe managers."

Dover does not engage to any large extent in actively rotating executives between its various divisions and subsidiaries. Instead, top management in each organizational unit is expected to develop its own executive talent. It is a process that is constantly being encouraged and monitored from New York City headquarters. Occasionally an individual from a subsidiary will migrate to the central office, as did Gary Roubos, who became executive vice-president of the corporation in the mid-1970s, after serving as president of the Dietrich Standard subsidiary.

Lilly is deeply concerned about selecting and cultivating its executive talent for eventual movement into top corporate slots. Although no specific road map is constructed for individuals who become candidates for vice-presidential and higher responsibilities, the company makes every effort to provide those individuals with a variety of experiences and exposures that will prepare them to assume enlarged responsibilities. Putting into practice the concepts of career planning that were introduced by Josiah, the firm is committed to giving every employee a long-term productive career with Lilly, especially those destined to move into its top positions.

As mentioned previously, Philip Morris is constantly nurturing executives for the top echelon. Cullman initiated the process of loading aspirants to the hilt with responsibilities and decision-making opportunities—a framework that appears in no danger of being aborted. The company does, however, have a deep-seated aversion to individuals, especially young MBAs from prestigous graduate schools, who have a detailed, preprogrammed flight path worked out for themselves as to how they are going to progress through the company to their predetermined objectives. One corporate spokesperson emphatically pointed out, "we simply will not hire the aspiring MBA who has laid out a pre-planned route and destiny to top positions in this company. The organization is too fluid and dynamic to accommodate such tactics. No way!"

SmithKline Beckman spends considerable time identifying and recruiting very intelligent individuals for entry into its managerial ranks, particularly those who have been exposed to rigorous liberal arts and science backgrounds. They must evidence "generalist" potential, as opposed to becoming merely an outstanding specialist in a particular field. A reservoir of executive material is continually being replenished to provide a pool of managerial talent. Contrary to the procedures of many other companies in this study, SKB does develop a specific plan for each candidate who is identified as a "comer," a promotion path that will enable the individual's strengths and special energies to be detected early and be utilized. Until recently, the

"2 + 2 + 2" formula appeared to be the well-proven pathway to top echelon positions: two line positions in different divisions or groups; plus two exposures to different functional areas of the business; plus exposure in two countries—in some combination. Such seasoning is no longer the sure-fire route to a top position because, according to a highly placed personnel officer, "sufficient opportunities now exist in any one of several divisions to satisfy the necessary exposure and developmental needs of most aspirants."

Promotion from Within

It would seem, from the foregoing, that promotion from within would be the normal pattern among our fourteen organizations, and such is the case. In almost every instance, promotion of those currently in the enterprise is standard operating procedure—whether it is to supervisory, staff specialist, middle management, or top echelon slots. Continuity and perpetuation of an organization's culture seems to be of paramount importance in virtually all of these organizations. As one top executive at Philip Morris put it: "The time, effort, and attention we pay to developing our people is enormous and painstaking. Why shouldn't we avail ourselves at every opportunity of reaping the best of what we sow?" The same individual commented that, during his thirty-five years with the company, he could recall top management regretting the loss of only one potential candidate for a top slot in PM. "We make every effort to keep the best we've got."

All of the CEOs and almost every vice-president at Deluxe and most managers at all levels in Betz Labs, have been homegrown. It is almost a fetish at Kellogg to promote from within. Elaborate in-house training and a variety of management development programs are continuously in process at Merck, SmithKline Beckman, and Lilly.

Only on rare occasion is a high-level executive brought in from the outside. Betty A. Duval was lured from General Foods, in 1980, to assume the vice-presidency for staff development at Dow Jones. As mentioned previously, the vice-president for planning at Deluxe was hired from the outside—primarily because of the special expertise he had developed elsewhere. Commerce Clearing House rarely seeks outside talent. In fact, their on-campus recruiting activity for even entry-level positions is an extremely small operation. "Most of our so-called recruiting entails interviewing those who seek us out and come knocking on our door," according to one CCH executive. He did remark, however, that two executives were recently hired to handle the cash management area within the enterprise.

In only one instance did I discover that the occupant of the top job had been recruited from outside directly for that position. Ed Shutt was recruited from Clorox, in 1981, to head Tambrands following his dismissal from that Procter and Gamble division because of a policy disagreement.

A potential morale problem at Dow Jones, however, may be in the making because of its recent efforts to recruit and hire "superstars" from the outside to occupy positions of prestige and influence on the staff of *The Wall Street Journal*. With the exception of Duval, hiring senior staff people was unheard of in the past at Dow Jones, and some older staff members at the *Journal* are concerned about the negative impact that this superstar-hiring practice may have on organizational morale. "We'll just have to wait and see how these new individuals assimilate into the organization," said one long-time member of the editorial staff. "If the celebrity arrivals maintain a relatively low profile and go about their tasks methodically, quietly, and professionally—I think we can weather the transition. But it's going to be a bit touchy and uncomfortable for some oldsters—unquestionably."

Routes to the Top

The vast majority of those who rise into top positions in our fourteen organizations are a widely assorted group, with highly diverse backgrounds being represented. However, a few organizations evidence a bias for certain types of individuals to assume top echelon positions. Betz Labs candidly asserts that chemical engineers are its "chosen ones"—as, incidentally, also does Minnesota, Mining and Manufacturing. Remarked a Betz spokesman, "Not all chemical engineers make good top executives, but we've got lots of good Chem E's to select from. And our expertise is chemical engineering." Dow Jones has a well-established and well-understood policy that only individuals with news reporting and editorial backgrounds are potential candidates for the very top slots. According to one senior vice-president, however, this convention causes little distress in the organization because a sufficient number of other high-level positions exist in other sectors of the company that provide ample opportunities for responsibility, challenge, and compensation for aspiring executives.

Virtually all top executives at Kellogg rise through the sales ranks, and most managers at Lilly were in charge of a sales territory during their career with the organization. Even Lilly's chief economist had responsibility for a sales territory during his early career in the enterprise. However, two tracks are now being groomed in Lilly by which aspiring executives may rise through the enterprise without prejudice—the research side and the management side.

Most top executives in Philip Morris have spent a significant portion of their careers in the marketing area. The company makes no excuses for having marketers occupy top positions in this heavily consumer-oriented company. Reflected one spokeman, "For marketing people to head this marketing company makes tremendous sense, and is a natural. I can't visualize PM ever being operated another way."

Lean Headquarters and Central Staff

The most pervasive component of organizational structure among the fourteen enterprises is a lean, spare headquarters and central staff. The empire building and excessive executive-suite fluff that are so commonplace in many U.S. enterprises appear relatively alien to most of our corporations. C. Northcote Parkinson would probably have uncovered insufficient material among our fourteen firms on which to construct his infamous law of 1957. These firms may spend vast sums on R&D activities (the pharmaceutical houses and IFF), for promotional and marketing endeavors (AHP, Kellogg, Philip Morris, and U.S. Tobacco), and to implement production floor innovations (Betz, CCH, and Deluxe)—but relatively little resources are allocated to front-office overhead. These enterprises are convinced that the bulk of profits are generated in the field and from lower level operations rather than in the executive suite.

Dover maintains a central office staff of fewer than twenty-five persons, including secretaries, to monitor and control a geographically dispersed network that generates about $1.4 billion sales and $100 million after-tax profit. During a recent visit to the United States, a European competitor asked a Dover executive at headquarters how such a feat could be accomplished with so small a pool of talent, since he used more than seventy in his West German headquarters. The Dover spokesman replied, "We just do it. It's that simple." Even the accoutrements in its fifth floor Park Avenue headquarters are sparse and not elaborate. "It's the people at the grassroots that need the funds to make it happen," stressed the executive, "not those of us here in the Big Apple."

International Flavors and Fragrances, Deluxe Check, and Commerce Clearing House, each, run a trim, streamlined central office in New York City, St. Paul, and Chicago, respectively. CCH's top management is no-nonsense, work-oriented, with a great deal of hands-on activity. On its first floor, almost every top executive, secretary, and nonproduction floor manager is easily visible. The physical furnishings at IFF are very conservative and bare-bones, reflecting a quiet simplicity. Kellogg prides itself on maintaining a tight, lean, and efficient front office—a standard that permeates the entire organization.

Considering the $16 billion total revenues that Philip Morris generated in 1985, its headquarters staff is quite small. The organization tries to keep communication lines short to facilitate quick decision making. The company is convinced that a streamlined central staff aids this objective. SmithKline Beckman presents another example of an enterprise that maintains its headquarters staff at the bare minimum—a simplifying process that began during Thomas Rauch's tenure as CEO from 1966 to 1972.

Betz Labs insists on keeping each of its several operating units small and manned by only a few divisional executives. The use of interlocking miniboards throughout the company enables each division to function without duplicate trappings, excess costly administrative personnel, or, for that matter, outside consultants. Approximately 100 people are now housed in Tambrands's headquarters—the remaining 2,500 employees being scattered among its several plant locations in its northeastern United States and five offshore facilities. Of those 100 at Lake Success, the large majority are marketing personnel.

Quick decision making, short lines of communication, little bureaucracy, and informality (recall the morning coffee clatches) are facilitated through Dow Jones's extremely thin top management structure. Its dozen top executives are split about eight to four between its Liberty Street headquarters, near Wall Street, and the South Brunswick, New Jersey, facility, respectively. A helicopter can put all of the dozen executives in the same location within the hour.

Perhaps American Home Products best epitomizes the tightness with which these firms run their front offices. The number of individuals in its New York City headquarters is minimal—some say almost too few. Even divisional top management are, according to one manager, "very small shops." The company shuns opulence. Green metal desks are still found atop linoleum floors, and the most elaborately furnished small conference rooms are, at best, stark. It is not uncommon for an outsider to come away from AHP with the sense of having witnessed the epitome of parsimonious frugality. Top executives enjoy few, if any, perquisites, and expense accounts that cover above the bare minimum are anathema. More than a few AHP former managers have remarked that the company is a great place to invest one's dollars, but a harsh and frugal environment in which to make a living.

Degree of Centralization and Decentralization

There has been considerable controversy during the last two decades concerning whether decentralization or centralization is the better organizational strategy. Depending on one's inclinations, an ample number of experts—business executives such as Alfred Sloan and Ralph Cordiner, consultants, and academicians—are available to support either viewpoint. Although a majority of our fourteen companies may be classified as decentralized, several have functioned very effectively and profitably for a considerable period of time within a centralized organizational framework. In other words, it is not patently clear whether the optimum form of organization is decentralized divisonalization or decision making that is concentrated in one or a very few at the top.

Many allege that, for almost twenty years, Laporte treated American Home Products as his personal fiefdom—probing the most minute details in operating divisions, auditing every capital expenditure that exceeded $250, taping numerous conversations, firing endless pointed questions at subordinates during luncheon meetings, and topping it all with an autocratic demeanor. Oddly enough, however, and despite the tight financial control that is exercised by headquarters, considerable responsibility has always been delegated to each division's top management.

However, no organization among our fourteen appears to have been more autocratically run during a large portion of its existence than Tambrands. Thomas Casey made virtually all the important (and many less critical) decisions during his reign from 1955 through 1978. He instilled fear and allegiance in many of his subordinates, hiring only those who he felt would likely agree with him and acquiesce to his way of operating the firm. Those who slipped through his initial screening devices and were subsequently discovered to disagree or be of a different mind than Casey, were shortly thereafter given the opportunity to seek employment elsewhere. Many veteran employees recall that he had an almost complete lack of trust in his underlings—that he considered them less than competent unless they carried out his directives to the letter. One executive, recalling those years, remarked that the firm would probably have been successful during that period regardless of how it was run, primarily because of its superior, almost monopoly-like product. Only one top executive seems to have been able to consistently insulate himself from Casey. "Somehow Earle Griswold (one of the three founders and an engineer), erected, up in the Palmer, Massachusetts plant, a Chinese wall between himself and Casey's front office. He survived as a loner." Since E. Russell Sprague's interim tenure as CEO, Tambrands has become far more decentralized, democratic, and participatory. Ed Shutt has further decentralized and democratized the company since his appointment as CEO. Remarked one top manager: "He's like a sea of fresh air."

International Flavors and Fragrances reflects a contrast in organizational style. Until their simultaneous retirement in 1985, Walter and Spitz made most of the critical decisions. Yet, each of the overseas divisions was operated as a personal fiefdom of its managing head. "Several managers of those overseas units posted 'Keep off and out' signs at the front door," a former IFF top executive recalled. Until the late 1960s, J.D. Betz organized Betz Labs with himself at the hub of most decisions. There was little delegation of responsibility. But as the corporation grew, more delegation and decentralized decision making occurred. "It had to," according to J.D.—until today, the firm is run as a collection of small units, each with considerable autonomy and delegation of powers. Several additional facets of what occurred in Betz Labs during this transition are summarized in the next segment of this chapter.

Commerce Clearing House, Philip Morris, and SmithKline Beckman are essentially decentralized operations, with the chief task of the headquarters personnel being to draw the total picture together. Line management is given great latitude, with headquaters simply requiring that it be kept informed of what is going on at each divisional level. Robert Dee has pushed decentralization even further during his term as SKB's CEO; and Henry Wendt (its current president) would like to further eliminate red-tape, bureaucratic controls, and numerous other "evils associated with bigness." Deluxe Check Printers is decentralized down to the plant level—throughout the United States—with the St. Paul facility also pulling the total corporate picture together.

Dow Jones delegates considerable responsibility to its groups and divisions, among which are Ottaway newspapers, Richard D. Irwin (publisher), the information and operating services (including news retrieval activities), and *The Wall Street Journal*. Dover probably reflects the highest degree of decentralization among the fourteen, giving almost total discretionary powers to its divisions and subsidiaries.

Whether these companies are operated as centralized or decentralized entities—or headed by autocratic or participatory-type CEOs—may be far less critical than that each entity has a clear idea of its central task, that the decisions that are made at the very top are respected (even if not loved), that managerial succession occurs in a relatively methodical manner, and that the vast majority of promotions occur primarily from within the organization. In short, that the "snake dance" be perpetuated among long-time participants that are well acquainted with the prevailing system.

Transition from Entrepreneurial to Professional Management

Quite accidently, I uncovered a somewhat intriguing facet of corporate evolution during my investigation of Betz Laboratories. Seldom is the transition from a small entreprenuerial family business into a large, very profitable, professionally managed, and publicly-owned corporation executed so successfully. Howard Head was unable to accomplish it at Head Ski Company, and William Lear experienced serious managerial difficulties in attempting to convert Lear Jet Industries into a durable entity. But John Drew (J.D.) Betz—a born maverick entrepreneur—steered Betz Labs through similar straits with skill and perception. Although not unique among U.S. corporations, the Betz experience warrants a brief recount.

Betz Labs was founded by J.D.'s father, in 1925, to treat water that flowed through industrial boilers. J.D. entered Lehigh University, in 1937, as a chemical engineering major, but he developed a serious illness between his junior and senior years that prevented him from graduating with his class in 1941. In fact, so serious was the ailment that he never returned to complete the degree requirements. However, as pointed out previously, he undertook a self-study program that equipped him with the chemical engineering essentials required to run the budding Betz operation. In addition, he gleaned sufficient business administration skills from several of his fraternity brothers who did complete their degree requirements and from frequent attendance at seminars sponsored by various management associations.

The corporation was operated as a closely held entrepreneurial family partnership from 1941 to 1955. During that period, each of four functional areas—R&D, production, marketing-sales, and finance-legal—reported directly to J.D. He handled all central policy and high level decision making, delegating only the daily operating details to the head of each functional area. Only J.D. and his treasurer were familiar with the intimate financial details of the company. During this fifteen-year period, sales increased from $300,000, in 1941, to about $1 million, in 1955.

By 1961 sales had reached $10 million, and the corporation began to become more complex, due, in part, to geographically dispersed plants and diversification into aspects of water treatment other than boilers. During the period 1961 to 1965, J.D. perceived that it would not be in the too distant future that some type of nonfamily, professionally managed type of operation would be required. In 1965, with sales at $17 million, the company went public, and its stock was traded over the counter.

At that point, wheels were set in motion to shift from the single-handed entrepreneurial stage toward a professional management team concept. Long-range planning, extensive budgeting, formalized lines of communication, and a considerably larger, more complicated organization were almost forcing themselves to be installed. In an interview, J.D. recalled:

> I sensed that team decision-making would have to be the way to operate the company, even though that was not my personal preference or style. I had to learn to accept the mistakes of others; and that others would have to make more of the important decisions from that point onward. It almost broke my heart to yield the decision-making function to which I had grown accustomed at the hub of the organization. But it was essential—absolutely crucial—that it be done!"[5]

What is most remarkable about this transformation from family-run to professionally managed enterprise was that the former entrepreneur, John

Drew Betz, perceived that a fundamental change in managerial style had become essential. Furthermore, he then proceeded to initiate and facilitate that complex evolutionary (if not revolutionary) process of transition—a process that countless numbers of other entrepreneurs have either failed to understand, to respond to, or to implement. He decided that when sales hit $25 million he would resign as president and CEO—which he did. He remained as chairman of the board until sales reached $50 million in 1971—at which point he elevated himself to chairman emeritus, a position he still occupied in 1986.

Although inactive in daily corporate affairs, he continued to maintain an avid interest in its progress, problems, challenges, and opportunities. In reflecting on his active years of tenure with the company, he said his greatest accomplishments were those that helped:

Keep operating units in the company small, with an entrepreneurial orientation;

Set in motion a concern to maintain and nurture a common culture of teamwork in the firm—long before it became the in thing to do;

Create the mini–board of directors device (referred to earlier in this chapter); and

Encourage at least two former president-CEOs of the corporation to remain aboard as directors after their retirement from active involvement in the firm.

J.D. felt this last accomplishment was particularly valuable to the corporation, in that those who have devoted a significant portion of their active executive lives to the firm could and should continue to monitor the current leadership "to insure it doesn't mess up too badly." He believed that "the perspective and collective wisdom accumulated by those who served in high places" could prove valuable to those actively engaged in meeting the daily challenges of the business.

What makes this particular transition especially satisfying is its epilogue. Although J.D. handcrafted the mechansims that facilitated the transformation of Betz Labs from a small family to large professionally managed enterprise, he never surrendered his first love—involvement in entrepreneurial, high-risk, capital ventures. At the time this information was gathered, he had both hands deeply immersed in some ten to fifteen budding capital venture arrangements. When he discovered that Betz Labs had moved beyond the capital venture-entrepreneurial stage, J.D. redirected his frustration at losing that outlet for his abilities to new ventures outside the corporation. That is his personal salvation, a point that many others in similar straits seem to overlook or ignore as a viable alternative to enduring "the growing pains of an overly successful family enterprise."

Control of the Corporation

Considering the current maelstrom of leveraged buy outs, buy backs, hostile takeovers, and "greenmail" payoffs (*greenmail* is the practice whereby a company repurchases its stock from an unwanted suitor at above-market prices), a few words may be warranted with respect to how several of our fourteen organizations are attempting to protect their corporate identity and control. Although the majority of raiders concentrate on identifying firms that deploy their resources in a less-than-optimum manner, or are heavily leveraged with debt, superbly run organizations are not immune from being identified as takeover targets.

Recall that in 1978, Commerce Clearing House, repurchased 2.5 million shares of its common stock from the Thorne estate, plus an additional one million on the open market in 1978–79. These buybacks were accomplished to achieve three objectives: (1) enable the Thorne estate to meet various estate tax assessments; (2) make effective use of some surplus cash; and (3) forestall any attempt by outsiders to gain a significant equity influence in the affairs of this relatively small, but highly successful enterprise. In addition to accomplishing these objectives, the repurchasing produced a residual benefit for CCH of almost doubling its ROI from an already quite respectable 32 percent in 1978, to 63 percent in 1980.

Likewise, Dover bought back about 627,000 shares of its common stock in 1982 and 1984 to achieve objectives (2) and (3) outlined in the CCH case, and provide the corporation with shares in its treasury with which to grant executive stock options. Subsequently at its April 1985, annual stockholders' meeting, shareholders approved an "antigreenmail" device, whereby shareholder approval is required for any company repurchase of its outstanding shares from a hostile investor, at a premium of 5 percent or more. Lilly's stockholders also approved two antitakeover measures in April 1985: (1) the requirement of staggered terms for its directors; and (2) the necessity for the approval by holders of 80 percent of the corporation's common shares outstanding to consummate a merger or sale of assets. In addition, shareholders authorized the corporation to repurchase up to 750,000 (about 1 percent) of its common shares for use in stock option plans. In 1985, Merck also asked its stockholders to approve several measures designed to block certain types of takeover bids and curtail the payment of greenmail.

Kellogg accomplished the massive repurchase of 15.15 million of its common shares in late 1984, primarily in response to a federal law that stipulates that a foundation (the W.K. Kellogg Foundation, in this case) cannot hold more than 35 percent of its assets in any single company's stock after 1993. Although Kellogg was not threatened by an immediate takeover, several financial analysts believe this leveraged buyback was motivated in part by the recent pandemic of hostile takeovers. The transaction also enabled Kellogg to almost double its ROI—from 26 percent in 1983, to 48 percent in 1985.

The most dramatic recent effort to retain control among present stockholders in our fourteen corporations, however, emerged in Dow Jones. First, we need a brief recap of history to put the 1985 transaction in context. Clarence Barron bought 90 percent control of Dow Jones in 1902 and immediately transferred the stock to his wife, Jessie Waldron Barron. The stock subsequently passed to Barron's adopted daughter, Jane Bancroft, one of Jessie's two daughters. That side of the Bancroft family currently controls about 54.7 percent of Dow Jones's common stock, and their shares are currently held in a maze of complex interlocking trusts, which provide an almost impenetrable barrier against any takeover attempt (hostile or friendly) that might conceivably arise.

To ensure continuity of family control of the corporation and to eliminate any possibility of a takeover, the corporation sought approval from its stockholders in April 1985, to create a new Class B common stock. Each new share would have ten times the voting power of an existing share, but could be sold only to members of a current shareholder's family or to trusts in which they are beneficiaries. Class B stock would never be publicly traded. Approved and upheld in the courts in 1986, the provision enables members of the Bancroft family to sell shares of existing common stock on the open market, when necessary to pay estate taxes or meet current living expenses, but the Class B shares would continue to be held by current stockholders or their families—especially the 55 percent held by members of the Bancroft family in the intricate maze of interlocking trusts.

One Dow Jones spokesman explained that the prime objective of Dow Jones throughout its entire history has been to maintain a fiercely independent business newspaper. The Bancroft family continues to wholeheartedly subscribe to that purpose, agreeing to place total trust and confidence in the management of the firm by adopting a hands-off policy. This arrangement provides the corporation with the best of both worlds—general freedom from intervention by owners that allows management an independence to pursue the principal objectives of the firm, and the simultaneous removal of the possibility of a radical alteration in owner-manager philosophy. Managerial leadership undertakes its stewardship role very seriously. This arrangement is further reinforced by the organizational policy cited earlier, which enables only those who progress through the editorial-journalistic side of Dow Jones to rise to top positions of leadership in the company.

Summary

Several of the commonalities outlined with respect to top management and organizational characteristics in these fourteen enterprises may *in part* account for their outstanding success over the recent past:

> Strong, influential, and visionary founders or chief executive officers;
>
> Planned succession to positions of leadership in the organization;
>
> The running of a tight ship—as reflected in a lean headquarters and central staff.

Of doubtful importance as a contributor to success, however, is whether the company's form of organization is decentralized or centralized. Though the majority of these fourteen during the recent past have operated within what might be termed a decentralized mode, a few have been run quite successfully—at least profitably—under a rather centralized, even autocratic, philosophy of management.

The next chapter will examine in some detail several behavioral aspects that are associated with the internal organization of these firms.

Notes

1. Vermont Royster, "End of a Chapter," *The Wall Street Journal* (March 5, 1986), p. 32. Reprinted by permission.
2. In Nancy J. Perry, "America's Most Admired Corporations," *Fortune* (9 January, 1984), pp. 54–55.
3. M. Moskowwitz, M. Katz, and R. Levering, eds., *Everybody's Business: An Almanac* (New York: Harper & Row, 1980), p. 231.
4. Peter F. Drucker, *Management: Tasks, Responsbilities, Practices* (New York: Harper & Row, 1974), p. 634–35. Reprinted by permission.
5. Interview with John Drew Betz on February 14, 1984.

5
Cultural Characteristics of the Organization

> Culture is one thing and varnish is another.
> —Ralph Waldo Emerson
>
> [People] have to believe that it really makes a difference whether they do well or badly. They have to care.
> —John W. Gardner

Executives, consultants, and acadamecians have focused considerable attention on the phenomenon of culture in business and industrial organizations during the past decade. The level of interest in this topic runs the gamut from serious investigation and analysis to blatant chicanery—the latter tack pursued by those seeking to capitalize on the latest managerial fad and organizational gimmick. More level-headed investigators readily assert that "culture" is probably present in some form or other in any social grouping—village, religious, or otherwise—and that the presence of the concept in a commercial setting should by no means be considered new or novel. In fact, it is doubtful that any business enterprise has endured very long without some common bond among its members.

Briefly stated, culture is the total pattern of human behavior—composed of customs, beliefs, social norms, and material traits that form the tradition of a group of individuals—that is transmitted to succeeding generations through language, symbols, thought, and action. Ruth Benedict phrased it succinctly in her *Patterns of Culture* in 1934: "What really binds men together is their cultures—the ideas and standards they have in common."[1] *In Search of Excellence* highlighted several examples of corporate culture that were observed in their study of U.S. companies, including "skunk works" (informal enclaves of people and money that function outside the confines of the corporate bureaucracy), "entrepreneurial champions" who become heroes to be emulated by other creative members of the organizations, "management by walking about," and group events the primary purpose of which is to honor individual achievement with monetary awards, prizes, and assorted celebration.[2]

In this chapter, we venture into this "soft" behavioral side (as opposed to its "hard" quantifiable, numbers-oriented, and production aspects) of corporate life. Specifically, we will examine several dimensions of corporate culture that exist among our fourteen organizations, including: (1)) the degree to which a corporate culture is nourished and preserved; (2) attributes that may account for the high esprit de corps that is present in most of these companies; (3) the presence of a "give-a-damn" attitude that permeates each firm; (4) the mutual concern that is evidenced in these organizations for its members; and (5) the impact that the presence or absence of unionization appears to exert on the corporate success of these fourteen.

Cultivation of a Culture

Perhaps it is not surprising that each of these fourteen organizations embodies and reflects—in fact is—a unique culture. Within minutes of walking into the executive suites on the twenty-second floor of Philip Morris's headquarters, in the heart of New York City, and the first floor central offices of Commerce Clearing House, on the outskirts of Chicago, one senses that a different style, pace, and ethos permeate each organization. Whereas PM evidences a decidedly more cosmopolitan, big city, ebullient, gregarious, and outgoing personality, CCH appears more suburban, open, low key, quiet, and down-to-earth.

A particular attribute that caught my attention early in this investigation was the difference in degree to which each company devotes conscious attention to nurturing its culture. The spectrum depicted below ranges from seven companies that devote considerable effort to developing a corporate mystique or bond among its members, to the remaining half that vary from moderate concern to benign neglect.

Considerable Attention	Moderate to Low-Key Attention	Benign Neglect
Betz Labs	American Home Products	Dover
Deluxe Check Printers	Commerce Clearing House	International Flavors
Kellogg	Dow-Jones	& Fragrances
Lilly	Tambrands	
Merck	U.S. Tobacco	
Philip Morris		
SmithKline Beckman		

A few selected vignettes will add some perspective to this array; however, the reader should bear in mind one prime limitation. The written word scarcely begins to touch the intricate attributes, patterns, relationships, and nuances that form the gestalt of a group's culture. Nonetheless, a cursory glance may shed some light on the nature and content of corporate culture in several of these organizations.

The vast majority of managers and a large number of employees in Betz Labs are very much concerned about maintaining and nourishing a common culture. The fundamental ingredients are surviving legacies that were instilled in the organization during the almost thirty-year leadership of John Drew Betz: Keep operating units small in terms of physical size and number of employees; and develop close teamwork among all employees in each division and among the executives in all divisions. Close rapport is developed and maintained among sales technicians-engineers, staff personnel, and managers in each operating unit. In addition, numerous policies are instituted to facilitate an entrepreneurial spirit in these units, one of the key ones of which is "Encourage mistakes—It's an excellent way to learn and improve."

Problems commonly associated with large-scale depersonalized bureaucracies are notably absent within Betz. In fact, two important common bonds that exist between middle- and upper-level managers are an overwhelming number of individuals with chemical engineering degrees and a distaste, if not hatred, of corporate bureaucracy. The mini-boards, discussed in the previous chapter, help provide cross-fertilization of managerial talent and serve to maintain close working relationships among divisions at a relatively high executive level.

Deluxe Check copes with what could become its bigness problem by subdividing the organization into about sixty plants that are strategically located throughout the continental United States. All printing-production plants are almost clones of each other—much like the common physical layout that exists in most K-Mart discount stores from coast to coast. Each plant is operated at top efficiency with almost no slack personnel. Pervasive in the organization is an allegiance, at all levels, to a Midwestern work ethic. As one executive explained it: "A great number of us thoroughly enjoy our work; we like to work, and work hard. In fact, it can be tremendously enjoyable in an outfit like this. We don't often talk about it. We just do it." Along with these elements are the extensive training programs and the intensity with which each individual, from top to bottom, participates in its operation. The "snake dance," referred to earlier, provides a tangible bond among all employees as it unfolds each week somewhere in the corporation. "That process alone furnishes tangible proof that our system and culture are alive, working, and well," reflected one plant manager.

Each of our three predominantly pharmaceutical corporations is seriously concerned with maintaining a corporate culture. As in Deluxe, the work ethic is also highly valued in Lilly. Although some outsiders accuse the Lilly corporate family of being a bit stodgy, rigid, and self-righteous, a propensity does exist in the corporation to approach problems pragmatically and with down-to-earth style. As one staff member put it; "We try to get at the nub of a problem—in terms of the old saw—where the rubber meets the road." Part of the stodginess image that some perceive may be explained by the extremely sensitive approach that the corporation has developed in dealing with the external world. The surrounding community (Lilly is an extremely philanthropic and community service–oriented company) and the pharmaceutical world pay close heed to public pronouncements that emanate from its front office. Hence, extreme caution has become standard operating procedure when presenting the firm's public face, more so now than in the past.

In fact, a somewhat cautious, if not almost adversarial, atmosphere is beginning to creep into Lilly's dealings with internal relationships. The litigation consciousness that has arisen in the American culture is starting to infiltrate this most stalwart of corporate environments. Part of this phenomenon arises as an aftermath of the Oraflex controversy. The impact of that issue permeated deep into the organization, and, as one top-level executive recalled: "Some members of the Lilly complex are beginning to deal very cautiously with persons in other divisions and departments of the company—let alone the public." More elaborate clearance procedures and compartmentalization of activities are starting to create a protective maze through which managers must navigate. "It's something we must be more watchful of and make every effort to alleviate," remarked the same executive. Still, the organization relies very heavily on running operations substantially on eye-to-eye contact, in-person communication, an open door policy, and a bare minimum of in-house memoranda.

Some organizations enjoy the luxury—but more likely contend with the pitfalls—of two cultures. Recall that Vail Associates endured dual cultures during the final three to four years of Peter Seibert's leadership of the company. He and those loyal to him nourished a behavioral and environmental perspective, whereas the cadre of executives that joined the firm to restore its financial health stressed the quantitative analysis and economic efficiency dimensions. Compromise and accommodation between the two competing views was the initial response of both sides. Then tensions began to develop. Considerable conflict and confrontation arose, until the issue was finally resolved when Seibert (and several others of his persuasion) removed themselves from daily operations and ultimately severed all connections with the enterprise.

Twin cultures have also recently emerged, although far less contentiously, in SmithKline Beckman since the merger with Beckman Instruments in March, 1982. The corporate culture that was consciously nourished in SKB when it was still Smith Kline and French (and subsequently SmithKline) can be summarized as follows:

> Deep concern for the human community and human relationships stemming from its Quaker heritage;

A very participative style of management;

Conservative and genteel, with few pretentious, ostentatious, or flaunting displays;

The upper levels of management well-populated with pragmatically oriented, liberal arts and science–trained, generalist-type managers;

An intuitive approach to problem solving (as opposed to exhaustive quantitative dissection of all the evidence), with considerable informal communication, handshakes to seal agreements, and little need for CYA (cover your ass) memoranda.

Quiet teamwork lay at the heart of the organization; and any disagreements were handled obliquely and with style—avoiding show-down confrontations at almost any cost.

Extensive use of its Management Executive Development Institute device began in the mid-1970s to strengthen cultural bonds in the corporation. In fact, its principal purpose was quite openly stated: "To communicate an integrated corporate style." Originally designed to bring top and upper-to-middle management executives together to discuss a specific theme or topic for about one week twice each year, the program was so well-received and proved so beneficial that it was soon extended into lower levels of managers. Separate, but closely coordinated, training seminars for entering and first-level managerial levels coexist with these executive-level programs. In short, a very concerted conscious effort has long been devoted toward the creation of a common culture throughout the SmithKline side—using well-conceived devices to implement that process.

What has caused some concern among several long-time SmithKline executives since the Beckman merger, however, is the degree of difference between the SmithKline mode of operations and the Beckman way. (This concern is aside from Beckman's failure to perform up to expectations since its acquisition in 1982). As described by a SmithKline-bred executive, the Beckman culture stresses more out-in-the-open confrontations when disagreements arise. "Whereas battles in the SmithKline side are negotiated quietly behind the scenes, Beckman execs are more prone to have at it with all their excess degrees of freedom showing. In addition, the Beckman organization relies more on loudness, bravado, and a somewhat less logical approach to reconciliation."

Although things are evolving to the point at which the two styles are becoming more commingled, consternation still arises on occasion. Even though the two organizations may never completely evolve into a common culture, cross-fertilization is expected to help move individuals toward a more common modus operandi. But little fear exists in either stem of the organization that an irreconcilable rift—the magnitude of which caused problems at Vail—will emerge.

Much of the cultural underpinnings that bind Philip Morris together originate in the organization's intense and aggressive marketing orientation. Practically all members of management—from first level supervisor to front office—have "earned their spurs" in the rough-and-tumble world of brand-name promotion activity. One top executive remarked: "Even our financial and production people are well-bathed in a marketing/promotion perspective." Considerable effort is exerted to stay close to the marketplace, especially in the major distributorship area. Eyeball contact between members of the organization and peripheral agencies is commonplace. The personal call, rather than an impersonal bureaucracy and written memos, is the standard of behavior throughout the organization whether in tobacco, beverage, or food.

It is probably no coincidence that the conscious effort that these five firms, along with Kellogg and Merck, devote to nourishing a common corporate culture is instrumental in the success of each enterprise. The common bond that helps unite a large organization is just one additional aspect in the arsenal of attributes that assist these companies in sustaining outstanding records of performance.

Even the five organizations that evidence a moderate to low-key conscious concern toward developing an organizational culture extend the relevance of this insight. Commerce Clearing House is a very democratically run organization. For example, its top echelon receives no bonuses and stock option plans that are not available to rank-and-file employees. The culture is low key, pragmatic, productively busy, one in which hard work is deeply appreciated and rewarded, and employees at all levels project a very conservative, down-to-earth, evenly paced quality that the visitor senses almost immediately. As one of its top financial executives proclaims: "What's the big deal? Few of us feel married to the company, and most of us can leave our workplace at 5 p.m. Yet we're all willing to pitch in with extra effort when unusual problems arise. We don't go out of our way to puff a culture. It's just a fact of life here."

A similar attitude pervades Dow-Jones, especially with those associated with the firm's flagship, *The Wall Street Journal*. As one front office executive noted: "It's almost a love we here have for our product—it runs extremely high. Even our news distribution organization senses the importance of getting the paper to our readership on time five days a week." Great concern is shared throughout the organization—from news-gathering reporters, editorial staff, and press operators—in perfecting the product. Constant attention is devoted to quality surveillance, and (as in Lilly) on-going concerns with organizational and individual self-criticism to maintain high standards of excellence are of paramount importance. But again, no great conscious concern is directed at nourishing these attitudes in the enterprise. They tend to develop from the very character of the place, seemingly without much explicit attention or fanfare.

Nonetheless, two somewhat different cultures seem to be emerging in a headquarters that is split between the heart of New York City's financial district and South Brunswick, New Jersey. A bit of a friendly "them-us" attitude has arisen between the two groups, which serves to stimulate good-natured rivalry, rather than animosity as it might in some organizations. The South Brunswick operation tends to function in a slightly more relaxed atmosphere than does the Liberty Street segment, but cross-fertilization between individuals at the two locations is frequent, widespread, and deep. Of particular interest were the eight to nine celebrations that were held in plush surroundings around the country during Dow Jones's one hundreth anniversary a few years ago. Recalled one manager: "We all had great fun. All the top execs attended. Levity, games, and good spirits abounded in great profusion. It really made those of us who attended these functions feel pretty fortunate to belong to such a playful yet devoted and dedicated group of individuals. Yet in my long career here, I can recall few other exercises that were developed exclusively, or even tangentially, to consciously cultivate 'our culture'."

American Home Products and Tambrands occupy somewhat ambiguous positions with respect to culture development—somewhere between low-key conscious attention and benign neglect. Distinctive cultural traits have emerged in American Home Products almost in spite of the lack of a consciously nurtured organizational culture. In fact, several top AHP executives regard concern for culture as "corporate-family nonsense." No annual get-togethers or corporatewide picnics are held. The corporation historically has striven for anonymity, secrecy, and aloofness with respect to external constituencies, as financial analysts and the mass media. Until quite recently, the corporation took very little interest in initiating contact with outside interests other than advertising entities and customers. It did not maintain a public relations department, and, for a substantial portion of its existence, corporate executives were urged not to talk with the press. The standard response given to those who seek to interview members of management is "We simply never talk outside our organization." Outsiders are distrusted.

Another AHP cultural trait that has arisen is a shunning of opulence. "It's a parsimonious, sequestered place in which to work," remarked one executive who requested that his identity not be disclosed. "Those qualities seem to be our character. We don't advertise it, but neither do we begrudge the reality of our situation. It's just AHP." In short, what seems to prevail in the organization is a paradox—the emergence of a culture because middle and top management pay such little attention to it. That in itself can become a cultural trait.

John Connelly's Crown Cork and Seal Company, although not one of our fourteen, bears a close resemblance to AHP's corporate stance. Mr. Connelly still answers his own phone in an almost austere, bare-bones office. Accoutrements are sparse throughout that corporation. Instead of attention being directed to massaging some corporate culture facade, it is directed to servicing its customers and generating high return on capital and total investment. In spite of the lack of conscious attention, however, a culture does emerge. Such was the case, also, at Tambrands during Thomas Casey's leadership when a culture arose despite the very low level of interest directed toward its cultivation. There was extreme secrecy on all production operations at its various plants. It was a cloistered community that restricted itself to talking only with itself. Only Casey conversed with the press and financial community, and it remained so until Casey resigned as CEO on December 31, 1978.

Dover and International Flavors and Fragrances are placed in the category of cultural development that might be termed benign neglect. Very little of what might be called a common culture binds Dover's several divisions and subsidiaries together. Part of this arises from historical circumstances. The vast majority of its approximately forty units were once independent companies, each having developed its own separate character when it operated as an independent entity. About the only identifiable traits that are common among this loose federation of organizations arise at the upper executive levels—a competitive environment is fostered among individual enterprises that must seek funds annually from the "central banker" in New York City for capital investment projects; tensions develop before, during, and after the tough and strenuous periodic review sessions that are conducted with each division's top personnel at central headquarters—the results of which usually filter quite rapidly through the corporate grapevine; and relatively sparse accoutrements and furnishings are evident at headquarters—a style that is frequently duplicated in divisional offices. But geographic isolation and technological specialization among the divisions, plus rare rotation of managers among these entities, help reinforce a relative lack of common culture in the Dover organization.

Whatever culture has arisen at International Flavors and Fragrances during the last twenty years can be characterized as artistic, emotional, and "non-rational"—traits not totally foreign or out of synchronization with an organization that specializes in creating sensory enhancers. In many respects, these attitudes may reflect characteristics of its recently retired CEO, Henry Walter, who was characterized by one former senior executive as "extremely sharp of mind, irascible, frequently brilliant, unpredictable, temperamental, and idiosyncratic." Perhaps the independence with which IFF's overseas executives carry on their operations is founded in the irascible, temperamental behavior they saw at headquarters.

On a broader scale, many severely criticize the recent emphasis on the corporate cultural phenomenon, asserting that too much is being made about nothing, or—at the other extreme—the obvious. Other analysts and practitioners detect much that is significant in the various dimensions of a corporation's culture. Attitudes are built up over a long stretch of its history, myths arise, and legends are transmitted by word and deed among the old and new members of the organization, along with the sharing of numerous trials and tribulations that each enterprise experiences during its existence. All of this transforms the organization into something more than a mere manufacturer or merchandiser of goods and services for profit. Culture is what gives life, spirit, and, in some cases, a joie de vivre to an assemblage of people, but, although an organization's culture is important, its impact need not be overplayed.

Esprit de Corps

One notable cultural trait that is easily detectable among these fourteen organizations is an extremely high degree of esprit de corps. Closely allied is a relative freedom from internecine warfare and debilitating political struggle. A sense of camaraderie and a common bond unite a large number of each organization's officers and rank-and-file employees. A portion of this presence undoubtedly stems from the well-understood and clear definition of the organization's central thrust and mission; but an even larger segment seems to arise from a shared belief that the employees are indeed embarked on a common and meaningful endeavor. In many respects, the phenomenon closely resembles what Fritz Roethlisberger, William Dickson, and Elton Mayo discovered among Western Electric employees in Chicago during the Hawthorne experiments of the early 1930s and what can today be observed in quality circles in Japan and America.[3]

A large segment of those associated with Commerce Clearing House feel they are engaged in the highly useful common endeavor of clarifying for practitioners, teachers, and students of tax regulations, labor law, and other federal legislation the almost impenetrable language and jargon with which these enactments are customarily written. Said one executive: "If our staff can clearly communicate what Congress and various federal agencies had in mind when they wrote what they did, we have indeed performed a valuable—and what we believe will be a never ending—service. The task of translating governmental gobbledegook and legalese into useable information is our mission and our raison d'être. And without boasting, we as a group feel we do that job pretty damn well."

Another organization whose primary task is communicating with the public, Dow Jones, also takes great pride in what it does and how it does it. One vice-president remarked: "Putting together a story—such as a major merger or corporate takeover—often requires a number of people ferreting out information and facts in various areas of the country and world, then piecing them together into a coherent pattern. This process takes enormous coordination and sequencing—an undertaking which is becoming one of our primary expertises. Without the goodwill and shared common purpose among our backbone news-reporting and editorial staffs, we would be unable to execute the job."

Of course, some internecine warfare and internal politics do occasionally arise in these corporations; but these elements appear to exist far less frequently than they do in most business enterprises. Bernard Kilgore, during his tenure as Dow Jones's CEO, quashed very quickly what he saw as cleavages arising among some departments in the organization. At one point, when interdepartmental tension approached heated exchange, Kilgore pointed out during a joint meeting: "You people in circulation needn't be concerned about your colleagues in advertising doing their job. You in circulation know you're the best in the business. Likewise, so are those in advertising." Emphasizing that both teams were "Number One" in their respective areas almost immediately converted the flare-up into a sense of common purpose and intense departmental and corporate pride. More important, the spirit that arose during that confrontation soon trickled down into the rest of the organization. To this day, when any individual or group in the *Journal* wins a Pulitzer prize, (eleven of which have been won by *Journal* staff members since 1947), the entire organization basks in the glory of that award. Those occasions generate a feeling that the entire enterprise has again risen another notch above whatever competition is out there.

At *CCH*, too, there is little back-biting and few turf squabbles. If anything, good-natured ribbing is the usual order of the day. At Deluxe Check, each of the 62 plants takes enormous pride in maintaining and beating the forty-eight–hour turnaround clock on customer orders that serves as a key objective of the company. Said one executive: "It's become a good-natured interdivisional rivalry in the company to 'beat that clock'." And this attitude of interdivisional rivalry also arises in Betz Labs, where great personal pride in a division's growth is the stuff from which overall corporate growth and progress derives much of its strength and thrust.

In Philip Morris, a high level of mutual respect exists among personnel in each of the various divisions. Concurrently, a sense of "competitive contentiousness" has arisen in PM. Fearing that the concept could be easily misunderstood, one manager quickly clarified its central message. "Here what is meant by competitive contentiousness is not an adversarial relationship between organizational segments—but rather constant challenges and suggestions for improvements that arise in one sector for other divisions to consider for adoption and implementation. It's a mutual sharing and challenge orientation that permeates and fits well in what is a relatively gregarious and aggressive organization."

Another facet of high organizational morale is reflected in U.S. Tobacco's response to attacks toward its various product lines. Mused one manager: "Our response to government agencies and consumer groups that snipe at any of our main products is that we immediately 'circle the wagons,' draw together to muster our collective strength, and strive to move beyond the immediate conflict as rapidly as possible. To what extent our efforts prove successful requires time to assess. But the main point of these external challenges is they draw us together and make us a better, more united team in the long run."

In only one company among the fourteen has notable internecine warfare arisen in its recent past. Shortly after the profitability downturn in 1975, a character change emerged in International Flavors and Fragrances. One former executive recalled: "The organizational response to that unexpected and marked downturn was finger-pointing, some back-stabbing, potboiling disturbances, and CYA memoranda. The '75 financial performance disturbed the entire organization; and what resulted was an attempt to internalize its root causes by inflicting pins in ourselves and each other." The company has made an impressive sustained recovery from that financial trough, but vestiges of the squabbles that arose during its aftermath have not entirely disappeared.

One characteristic that is frequently seen among employees in these enterprises is their seemingly genuine pleasure in working in the organizations and with their colleagues. Such comments as "pleasurable experiences," "look forward to arriving at work," "it's great fun," punctuated several conversations with employees and managers. The impression obtained during these interviews was not one of a utopian dream, or of unreal rose-colored glasses being worn, but rather the simple fact that these people liked working with their colleagues and doing what they all did quite well in these particular organizations—certainly not a unique experience among the millions who undertake their tasks each day, but certainly unusually prevalent among our fourteen enterprises.

A Give-a-Damn Attitude

Americans are constantly being bombarded with news that Japanese, West German, and other overseas manufacturers are beating us at quality, service, and dependability of products. It is alleged that U.S.-produced automobiles, steel, and small appliances (among other items) no longer measure up to our previous standards of durability and quality. Our reputation for service has also fallen on difficult times, but such is not the case with the goods and services that are provided by these fourteen companies.

Employees, executives, and middle managers, alike, in every single one of these organizations care deeply about what is produced, how long the product lasts, the quality that goes into the product and service, the reputation that is earned, and the receptivity that output garners in the marketplace. In short, employees from top to bottom seriously are concerned about what the organization stands for, what is produced, and the continuity of a lasting commitment to high standards.

One top executive at Deluxe Check, who was familiar with most of the firms among our fourteen, made the following remark: "One thing that immediately comes to my mind with respect to these fourteen is that most often give constant attention to this matter of caring for the customer, their product, and the organization's integrity." At Deluxe Check, excuses are not made for (nor is any customer complaint ignored regarding) an order that fails to reach its destination accurately or in timely fashion. "Not only do we immediately notify the customer of our concern, but usually an extra supply of personalized checks are furnished to help assuage any fault on our part," remarked one production supervisor.

Indeed, the vast majority of these organizations respond immediately to the smallest customer complaint. Betz personnel react to the slightest customer disgruntlement as the beginning of the possible loss of that customer. "Loss of a customer—potential or actual—due to our negligence or misfeasance is a matter of crisis in this outfit. We try to assure that complaints never arise. But when they do, we react—and promptly," stressed one executive. For example, sales technicians go out of their way to correct the slightest glitch caused by a chemical mixture that the company has prescribed. CCH personnel feel similarly inclined. "For us to allow gobbledegook, misinformation, and error to creep into our publications is an almost 'unforgiveable sin' so far as we're concerned. We're very careful about our output, and take painstaking care to hold to high standards of accuracy. But when we make errors, we act quickly to correct, amend, and update."

Coupled with this approach to customer and internal relations is the existence of a high sense of ethics in these enterprises. Of particular note in this regard is the action that Betz Labs took in response to requests that the company offer bribes and under-the-table payola to secure business in several foreign countries in which it had operated formerly. It simply closed down those operations and never returned. Similarly, Deluxe Check extends no mercy or condolences to any employee who besmirches the Deluxe name. The guilty are not "outplaced," "retired early for personal reasons," nor are "connections severed by mutual consent." They are simply fired. And despite its post-1975 internal problems, IFF continued to operate using absolute above-board ethics with respect to customers and competitors. SmithKline

Beckman and Tambrands also share a high sense of corporate ethics and morals.

Example after example could be cited to document the caring attitude that is engrained in these organizations. Suffice it to say, however, that this dedication to top-flight service and product quality is of paramount importance to the individuals connected with these enterprises. Restated, what impressed this observer in each of our fourteen organizations is an allegiance to a moral precept that is reflected in Matthew 5:41—"And whosoever shall compel thee to go a mile, go with him twain."

What clearly distinguishes these fourteen is that each enthusiastically and willingly goes three or more miles in many cases. Unfortunately, equally high marks cannot be awarded to a considerable number of firms in this country that have allowed service, quality, and reliability to be suboptimized and given a priority somewhere substantially beneath the objective of short-term profitability.

Concern for Employees and Degree of Unionization

The degree of an organization's concern for its employees often becomes apparent with an examination of various working conditions that exist in the corporation, along with fringe benefit packages that are provided. Some business enterprises offer their executives and rank-and-file employees excessively lucrative fringe packages, salaries, and working conditions compared to the effort expended and work performance, while others are extremely tightfisted compared to competitors in their industry. One general objective that is sought by personnel directors and others who are charged with setting salary-benefits-working condition guidelines is to achieve an optimum balance between work performance, work environment, and the financial reward structure.

The vast majority of our fourteen organizations seem to have accomplished this often tenuous task of "balanced optimization" of these several elements, while concurrently moving toward another dimension—a genuine caring attitude toward its organizational members. It is in respect to this added dimension that these elite corporations distinguish themselves.

Few among our fourteen waste time reciting the old cliche that "our employees are our most important resource." Their actions speak far louder than words. Philip Morris explicitly strives to provide the finest working conditions, highest salary structure, and best fringe benefit package of any company in its industry. That includes physical surroundings, flex-time, top compensation schemes, health and disability insurance benefits, retirement programs, and stock purchase, stock sharing, and stock option plans. One outcome that this entire package of benefits has generated is an intense loyalty to the organization by all employees at all levels.

Along with their own very lucrative compensation schemes, Deluxe Check, Lilly, and Tambrands support what they term a "full employment" policy. This translates into steady employment for all full-time employees in these organizations. Deluxe utilizes part-time employees only for unusual peak periods of activity, relying on its very productive full-time labor force to maintain production levels through the normal course of each year. Lilly adheres closely to its stated policy of "eliminating jobs but not people," stressing its commitment to enable each employee to develop a career within the organization from first day of employment to retirement. As it has with Philip Morris, this organizational attitude has nurtured very close bonds of loyalty between employees and Lilly.

Merck also seeks to offer its entire staff an outstanding compensation package that is the envy of the pharmaceutical industry. One mid-level employee exclaimed: "Why any of us would want to seek out another employer is quite baffling. This is a great place to work." Apparently a substantial majority feel similarly inclined, as reflected in the extremely low turnover rate. In addition to well implemented training programs for various levels in the company, Merck also has initiated an in-house television program through which employees are interviewed "on the street" at their work locations. They express their opinions concerning numerous aspects of their specific job, research activity that is under development, their progress in the company, and problems that warrant correction in the company.

Although Dow Jones restricts stock options to relatively high executive levels, CCH enables all levels of employees and executives to participate to the same degree in all of its stock purchase and bonus programs. Remarked a top financial executive at CCH: "We've believed in uniform incentives for a number of years. They support our desire to create a very democratic organization." Lilly also strives to ensure equity among its fringe packages at all levels throughout the organization.

As to union activity, mixed degrees of unionization were in evidence among the fourteen. No unions exist at Betz Labs (although two attempts were made in the recent past to establish a union), Deluxe Check, Tambrands, or IFF, in its domestic operations. (Unions do exist in some of IFF's overseas operations due to local custom, but interest is strong on the domestic scene to discourage unionization efforts). Similarly, SmithKline Beckman actively seeks to discourage unionization in its domestic operations, and Lilly is almost completely devoid of unions.

CCH works well with a printer's union; while Dow Jones has relations with several union organizations—the majority of which are located outside New York City. Fortunately, most unions connected with DJ respect technological innovations and advancements that are recommended by management; and agreements between company and union do not place stumbling blocks in implementing these improvements. Merck, AHP, and many Dover divisions have negotiated very workable agreements with several national unions.

On balance, the presence or absence of unions seems not to have adversely affected the outstanding performance of these fourteen companies. Where unions exist, considerable effort is expended to assure excellent continuing relations—and no union has created insurmountable problems in any of our fourteen. As one executive in a nonunionized company described the situation: "Our benefit, compensation, working conditions, and total employee performance package are probably far superior to whatever programs any union would be likely to bargain for and win if they were to enter our organization."

With respect to the total spectrum of cultural characteristics discovered among these elite companies, each company fosters, either explicitly or unconsciously, a corporate culture that nurtures and reinforces outstanding successful performance in several dimensions. Esprit de corps runs high; the vast majority of employees and executives deeply care about what they do and how they do it; and compensation packages make organizational members feel good about themselves.

A long-time Lilly employee echoed a general feeling with which this investigator came away from these companies: "One facet of this culture builds on another sector—which ties to another. They somehow all reinforce each other. How and why all these factors interrelate is something I've never been able to pin down or wholly understand. Perhaps if I'd try to analyze the mystery in greater detail I would destroy the miracle. I'll leave well enough alone."

Notes

1. Ruth Benedict, *Patterns of Culture* (Boston: Houghton Mifflin, 1934), p. 16.
2. Thomas J. Peters and Robert H. Waterman, *In Search of Excellence: Lessons from America's Best-Run Companies* (New York: Harper & Row, 1982).
3. F.J. Roethlisberger and William J. Dickson, *Management and the Worker: An Account of a Research Program Conducted by the Western Electric Company, Hawthorne Works, Chicago* (Cambridge: Harvard University Press, 1947).

6
The External Community: Customers and Competitors

> Keep close to the customer.
> —Peters and Waterman
> *In Search of Excellence*

> I was lucky. When God rained manna from heaven, I had a spoon.
> —Peter Drucker
> *Drucker: The Man Who Invented Corporate Society*

"Once the idea for a product is generated and proven feasible, the largest problem confronting us is *not* the manufacturing component," said a vice-president of SmithKline Beckman. "It's the marketing dimension that most severely tests our capabilities." This observation was echoed by spokespersons in virtually every organization in this study. To be sure, solving manufacturing and production problems requires skilled expertise. But making external constituencies aware of products and services, then distributing them through appropriate channels, and providing after-sale services present most business enterprises with their toughest challenges and highest risks, both psychic and economic. Will the product or service be accepted? What is the potential volume? How sure are we? What if it bombs? Is it really worth the hassles involved? And how do we finance it? Queries such as these constantly perplex and gnaw at most executives—and probably account for the hefty levels of gastric juices produced that products such as Tagamet are designed to alleviate and control.

We will explore several postproduction aspects, in this chapter, and attempt to convey a sense of how our fourteen elite organizations deal with the accompanying challenges and evaluate the associated risks. The specific topics that will be examined include:

An obsession with providing top quality, superior performance, and outstanding service;

The critical role of ongoing innovations and R&D activity;

Involvement on the international scene;

Selected marketing, promotional, and advertising strategies and programs;

Attitudes toward the competition; and

The forcing of a competitive advantage.

Elements surrounding these six dimensions of dealing with the external environment are carefully orchestrated by most of our select corporations into well-coordinated, superbly fine-tuned approaches.

One final topic that we must address in this chapter concerns a dimension of business life that is too frequently overlooked by most analysts of commercial enterprises—namely, being in the right place at the right time, plus luck. Both of these entail, at least in our enterprises, the astuteness to recognize opportunity when it appears, the willingness to take hold of the "brass ring" and assume the risks in pursuing the challenge, and the intelligence and ability to assemble appropriate resources.

Obsession with Top Quality, Superior Performance, and Outstanding Service

Our fourteen organizations represent slightly less than .0001 percent of the almost fifteen million business enterprises that exist in this country, thereby comprising the absolute pinnacle of consistently outstanding performance among large publicly held American commercial ventures. And it came as no sudden shock to this investigator to note that one of the common attributes that probably accounts for their enormously successful performances is their dedication to—indeed, obsession with—rendering superb quality, performance, and service to their clientele. Commerce Clearing House puts most reliance on maintaining impeccable accuracy in its almost real-time on-line reporting services. Similarly, Kellogg, can ill afford to allow the quality in any of its ready-to-eat cereals and other convenience foods to be compromised. Witness its voluntary call-back and subsequent destruction of an entire production lot of its Just Right cereal, during the spring of 1986, when some metal filings were discovered in a few boxes of the product. "It takes guts to do what Kellogg did," said the local manager of a large interstate food distributor in eastern Pennsylvania. "But action like this convinces the public and supermarket chains that Kellogg is seriously concerned with maintaining product integrity."

Tambrands also gives close attention to pursuing the highest quality and ready availability of its main product line. According to one top executive: "Our product is an intensely personal product. And although we're quite aware that most women keep a reserve supply of tampons on their bathroom shelf for the irregular and unexpected occurrence, our sensitivity to their plight motivates us to go the extra mile in making sure that our product is always at the ready—throughout the world." And one aspect that encourages the entire Tambrands organization to pay close heed to product quality is their social conscience. "As self-serving as it may sound," remarked one of its marketing managers, "our product name is almost generic in this catamenial industry—like Kleenex with facial tissue. Ours is an enormous franchise, with all the rights, privileges, and *responsibilities* attached thereto, and we fully intend to protect that name." This point becomes increasingly important when one realizes the degree of concern that women harbor for quality in feminine hygienic products. Women tend to allow price to enter the purchase decision when considering externally applied devices, but, quality and excellence becomes paramount—at almost any price—when the product is to be applied internally. "The essence of our endeavor and survival is continuous trust and confidence," reminded a Tambrands vice-president.

Concern for quality in prescription drugs forces its own unique discipline on our four pharmaceutical firms. Merck, SmithKline Beckman, Lilly, and AHP rank continuity of product quality at the top of corporate concerns with respect to their clientele. The Lilly organization believes that its adherence to product quality has become the standard of excellence for the industry worldwide. That belief stems from the legacy of its founder, Eli Lilly, who committed the firm from the start to producing pharmaceuticals of the highest quality solely for physicians. The company's concern for availability of its medications where and when needed has been continuous ever since the great San Francisco fire-earthquake disaster in April 1906. Said one Lilly executive: "We've always striven to do better on this 'availability' dimension than any of our competitors. And any acquisition candidate we're considering must likewise measure up to our standards in this respect."

As indicated previously, outstanding service and timely availability of product is of paramount concern at Deluxe Check. To facilitate this endeavor, the organization has almost entirely taken over the process of distributing its checks and deposit slips to individual customers. Completed packets are addressed at each of its plants; presorted by three, five, or nine digit ZIP code, bagged; and hand-delivered to postal authorities in readily identifiable zone-designated batches and bags. "The sole thing we've not yet undertaken is hand delivery to the check-user's home," said one plant manager. "We have attempted to remove delays and glitches in the postal system by taking upon ourselves many of the distribution problems associated with mailing. Whatever additional cost this process has placed on Deluxe has paid off handsomely in expedited delivery—and satisfied customers."

A large part of the success of International Flavors and Fragrances is dependent on the client's absolute confidence in the company's ability to deliver the exact product to specifications, at the right time, and at the agreed-on price. Considering that some flavor and fragrance blends entail upward to 200 separate ingredients, the task of achieving continuous reliability is by no means easily executed. Nonetheless, IFF's range of products and services is unmatched in the world; and its reputation for quality and service sets the standard for the industry, both domestic and foreign.

Both artistry and reliability are closely associated with Dow Jones's product lines, especially its flagship *The Wall Street Journal*. The *Journal* is a "paper of record" with respect to such items as stock and bond market quotations, call notices for bond issues, and other legal announcements made by business enterprises to the public. Therefore, those statistics and notifications must be accurate, timely, and complete—each day throughout the year. "All too often our readership takes such items for granted—and we don't begrudge them that perspective," mused one DJ executive, "but the process does entail an enormous amount of electronic equipment, intricate attention to detail, and supervisory wizardry."

On the other hand, the product shelf life of the *Journal* and *Barron's* is extremely short—a mere twenty-four hours in many cases. This in itself demands a constant cycle of search for newness, extensive research, and almost immediate production response. Closely combined with these requisites are scrupulous accuracy, extensive in-house rewriting, and intensive self-criticism. Added to those dimensions is the current practice of same-day delivery to 99 percent of its subscribers, which is made possible by state-of-the-art satellite telemetry and a magnificent in-house circulation system. Said one top DJ executive: "We're engaged in a constant effort to make what we belive to be a high-quality product even better. Not necessarily the biggest. Just the best. It's quite a hubub of a life, yet most of us truly love the complex, frantic pace."

The Critical Role of Innovation and R&D Activity

Robert Miles identifies Philip Morris in his *Coffin Nails and Corporate Strategies* (pp. 102–103) as the quintessential "prospector" organization in the tobacco industry—perhaps in the even broader category of consumer nondurables.[1] According to Miles, the product marketing strategy of a prospector is one of continually searching for market opportunities. Such companies are constantly on the lookout for emerging environmental trends, either to pioneer or to capitalize on. They regularly experiment with new products and modifications of existing ones to test consumer response to those trends. Consequently, according to Miles, they frequently become the "creators of market change to which the competition must react and adapt." The prospector capitalizes on the advantages of being the industry's "first mover," but it also assumes the several risks associated with such undertakings.

PM is probably the most innovative member of the tobacco industry. The organization has developed an acute ability to sense customer needs and appetites early, then to move swiftly to solidify its position when findings proved positive. It was the first to pursue the female market in cigarettes, develop the flip-top box, initiate the red tear-strip, and cultivate the vast overseas markets. (Appendix D reflects the extent to which the fourteen organizations are involved in international operations.) PM, long the small "odd boy out" in the industry, transformed the image of cigarettes in the 1950s from a product that was associated with the aristocratic elite and celebrities in posh nightclubs, into items that tapped the rugged, independent, pioneer-type instincts that lay dormant in the American psyche. Even when it was not the first to initiate a product change, PM has been able to borrow innovative ideas from others, and then do them one better. Although they were one of the last to adopt filter tips and 100s, when these features were finally incorporated into PM's products, the company bested the industry by perfecting the recessed filter and promoting 100s as the chic line in smoking.

This prospector role is not solely limited to the tobacco side of its operation. Under PM's direction, Miller was the first to successfully develop and market "light beer" and create the new seven-ounce bottle for the 7-UP division.

The organization often aligns itself squarely opposite from the conventional wisdom. For example, when competitors were cutting back expansion plans during the early 1970s, in response to the increased health warnings associated with smoking, PM aggressively moved forward by building a quarter-billion dollar cigarette manufacturing plant in Richmond, Virginia. The rationale at the time was that PM was convinced that its volume and market share would undoubtedly increase, irrespective of whether or not total industry demand increased or remained stable; and that it must be ready to take advantage of the upsurge in its demand. In addition, $25 million began to be poured annually into R&D work at the Richmond facility.

The pharmaceutical industry is probably regarded as the most R&D-oriented of any of those represented among our fourteen select companies. A constant stream of research activity must be undertaken in order for these firms to remain on top and in the forefront of new developments. Both Lilly and Merck pursue an extremely aggressive R&D policy—Merck expending about 17 to 18 percent of its sales revenue on such activity, thereby placing it in or near the number one position in the industry worldwide. Merck asserts that its total corporate activity follows from this commitment to extraordinary effort in the R&D dimension, and this commitment is very likely to be accelerated under the leadership of its new CEO (as of 1985), Roy Vagelos, the former director of research.

Scientists meet monthly in review groups to establish criteria and goals and to separate likely winners from apparent losers. Rather than spending large blocks of time and effort modifying existing products, the company focuses its energies on generating genuinely new and different drugs that will represent major improvements in the treatment of specific diseases. Simultaneously, support is gradually withdrawn from older drugs that have passed the point of maximum returns. Consequently, its sales force usually has a portfolio containing items that are really new and different to discuss with the physician and hospital. This systematic plan for drug research, adopted in the late 1940s, has been largely instrumental in transforming Merck from a marginal distributor of patent medicines into the largest and one of the most successful of American drug manufacturers and marketers.

Patents contain both good and bad aspects for pharmaceutical firms. The upside is that a patent grants the inventor the right to exclude others from making, using, or selling the invention or discovery, usually for seventeen years. Unfortunately, however, the normal *effective* life of a patent on a prescription drug varies from five to eight years, as reflected in the time-line in figure 6–1. Filing with the Federal Drug Administration (FDA) usually occurs about two years after the patent has been granted. Testing, application procedures, and awaiting FDA approval can entail from seven to ten years. Since a patented drug cannot be sold in the United States prior to that approval, the effective life of the patent may be truncated to eight, or as little as five, years. In short, the payout and recovery of R&D expenditures from even the most successful drug must be generated during less than ten years—far short of the entire seventeen-year exclusive period granted by the patent right. At the end of the seventeenth year, any manufacturer is entitled to reap rewards from the specific drug. The risks are extremely high for all pharmaceutical manufacturers that are engaged in creating new products, and engaging in R&D activity is an absolute must for organizations that seek to excel.

The trend in this industry during the past fifteen years has been for each major drug manufacturer to concentrate on a relatively narrow band of human ailments, as opposed to covering the entire spectrum of maladies. Hardly any pharmaceutical company today attempts to be expert in all classes of drugs and treat all kinds of human ailments. Thomas M. Rauch, during his tenure as SmithKline Beckman's CEO from 1966 to 1972 (the Smith

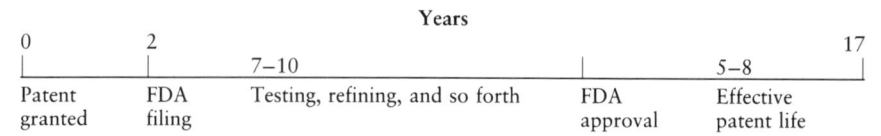

```
                                    Years
0               2                                                                    17
|               |       7–10                         |           5–8                 |
Patent          FDA     Testing, refining, and so forth   FDA         Effective
granted         filing                                    approval    patent life
```

Figure 6–1. Effective Patent Life of a Pharmaceutical Product

Kline and French Laboratories then), directed researchers to concentrate on six ailments, including gastrointestinal disorders, cardiovascular and renal (kidney) diseases, and arthritis. He urged scientists to search for improvements in existing drugs, rather than concentrate only on finding the big blockbusters. Ironically, the biggest blockbuster ever to hit the ethical pharmaceutical industry—Tagamet—was born in the early 1970s from Rauch's redirected development program, reaching the market place in November 1976. SKB has recently revitalized its R&D efforts because of a deep concern that the company might have become overly dependent on the success of this single drug, the patent on which will expire in the very near future.

Just as SKB is narrowing its focus, Lilly is beginning to concentrate its R&D on shorter-run infectious diseases—those that present acute problems over a period of one to two weeks—despite its often avowed claim that the "company goes wherever research leads." On the other hand, Merck relies on the long-run maintenance, chronic-disorder field, in which refill prescriptions provide the bulk of revenue. These maintenance drugs include Timoptic, for the treatment of glaucoma; Aldomet, for cardiovascular problems; Indocin and Clinoril, for arthritis; and a variety of diuretic drugs.

The general perception in the industry is that specialization by field will become more of a necessity in the future, as the task of probing the frontiers of science becomes more costly, time-consuming, and risky. Of 8,000 candidate drugs in the laboratory, generally only one makes it to market; and of this group, only about 25 percent eventually become successful in terms of return on investment. The two problems that account for the largest number of drug failures are discovery of adverse side effects and toxicity.

Each of the four ethical drug companies in our group is, as briefly sketched out in previous chapters, undergoing a revolution in the way pharmaceutical research is executed. The traditional approach was to devise and amass new chemical compounds—then to test them on animals and in other experiments to determine their effect with respect to general well-being or on specific ailments. It was very much a hit-or-miss proposition—similar to a shotgun blast at the side of a barn with the hope that one pellet would hit a specific nailhead. During the last ten years, however, the new wave of research has been dedicated to exploring and understanding, first, a particular disease and what makes it function, then a breakdown of its characteristics to determine points of vulnerability. Subsequently, various compounds and their derivatives, whose properties are relatively well understood, are identified and manipulated, molecule by molecule, to ascertain the degree to which they might attack the particular element in the disease or organ that could ultimately lead to the desired physiological effect. As one research director explained: "It's now like aiming a rifle, loaded with a custom-made cartridge, at a designated target we want to hit. Chances of success are far greater in less time than under the previous approach. But it is costly."

Lilly has been criticized for developing relatively few truly new drugs (given the level of effort and dollars directed toward its R&D activity). In 1985, its total R&D effort represented about 9 percent of sales revenue. The company got its first real boost in pharmaceuticals with its development—in a joint venture with a Canadian organization—of insulin in October 1923. That "blockbuster" was followed, during the 1950s, with the development of the Salk vaccine. Since then, however a significant impetus behind the firm's success has been derived from its ability to translate some small improvement or an edge on product superiority into market dominance. For a considerable period of its history, it has developed a unique ability to "cut itself in" on new developments, whether originated in-house or by competitors. Currently, it is redirecting its R&D efforts toward the internal creation of specialty, trademarked, products.

American Home Product's in-house research program in prescription drugs has, until very recently, suffered (1) underfunding, and (2) extensive licensing agreements. Although an outstanding marketing organization, AHP has traditionally underfunded its R&D programs in ethical drugs. Several financial analysts observe that this underfunding stems from the organization's traditional dedication to frugality, to establishing excessively stringent risk-reward policies, and to extremely tight monitoring of all funds (including R&D) to ensure their effective use. Laporte's attitude, during the early years of his leadership of AHP, was to let the competition do the basic research, then move in later and try to do better. The end result, over a period of years, according to one analyst, has been a stifling, nonadventurous atmosphere with respect to ethical drug R&D. Remarked a SmithKline Beckman research chemist on this point: "We in SKB found that pharmaceutical research is fraught with constant uncertainty and enormous risk. So what else is new with the price of discovery? But we've also discovered that accountants are usually not the best watchdogs over the research dimension."

The second aspect that discouraged an aggressively adventurous R&D spirit within the organization was its emphasis on licensing drug products, particularly from overseas manufacturers. A foreign firm, having discovered a particular drug, would be contacted by AHP to license the drug—such as Inderal—for distribution in the United States under one of AHP's subsidiary ethical drug houses. Under such arrangements, AHP's primary efforts were directed to the development aspect of R&D—instead of basic research—and to marketing. Under LaPorte's later-period leadership, the internal research capability in ethical drugs was built up, and those efforts are continuing today. In 1986, approximately 35 to 40 percent of AHP ethical drugs were generated from in-house R&D—and that percentage is being forced upward through redirected attention to specific human applications. Current research activity is concentrated on cardiovascular agents, analgesics, antiarthritics, and psychotropics.

Deluxe Check is very secretive about the inner workings of its production layout and design—and of its continuous introduction of new ideas that place it at the forefront of the industry's state of the art. When an innovation proves successful at one of its sixty-two plant sites, it is, within a short time, introduced in most of the other locations. The company constantly challenges every employee to use imagination, skill, and the latest technology to improve the production and distribution process. Said one vice-president: "We've been encouraging even miniscule improvements in our operations—and appropriately rewarding the discoverers—long before we got word that the Japanese were doing the same thing. We've always done it this way." One of the key innovations pioneered by Deluxe was the magnetic coding system that appears at the bottom of each personal and business check. That, and the special paper to accept the MICR (Magnetic Ink Character Recognition system) imprint, were developed in St. Paul to automate the bank-clearing network. "It put us and the American banking system quantum jumps ahead of whatever else was out there," remarked a Deluxe sales executive.

Although Dow Jones has retained the same front-page format in the *Journal* for a number of years, it is not averse to reorganizing other sections of the paper, making incremental improvements that often escape the reader's eye. But it is in the area of satellite technology that the paper has left other newsprint media in the shadows. The *Journal* moved into satellite-telemetry feeds from the New York editorial offices to its 17 U.S. printing plants. It is called point-to-points broadcast communication, and it uses geostationary satellites positioned 23,000 miles above the earth. Eventually, DJ expects to introduce points-to-point and points-to-points communication—in other words, to feed information from scattered locations on the globe to a central place, and from a certain number of locations to a selected number of other points, simultaneously.

Another dimension in which the organization is constantly innovating involves devising ways to recycle basic financial and news data in different ways for different constituencies—such as repackaging similar business information with slight adaptation for the Asian or European editions of the *Journal* or for use in its new retrieval systems. The promotional side of the business is certainly not immune to innovations: DJ recently inaugurated arrangements with radio and television stations to receive free advertising for its several product lines, in return for providing daily financial and business data "feeds" for local and regional broadcasts. The arrangement is called "reciprocal commerical time." Another introduction is the "per inquiry commercial," whereby DJ pays a local broadcast station a commission for individuals who subscribe to *Barron's* or the *Journal* as a result of hearing or seeing the commerical over that station. One final example of DJ's dedication to constant innovation lies in its delivery system. Rather than rely entirely on the postal system for delivery of its product, the organization maintains its own privately contracted delivery system in most metropolitan sections of the country. According to a vice-president, "This is a critical part of the system that enables us to place today's *Journal* in the hands of 99 percent of our subscribers Today!"

Betz Labs devotes considerable financial and human resources to developing more effective chemical mixtures to combat the build-up of algaes, slimes, scales, and other incrustations that invade industrial piping and conduits. Quite frequently, these innovations are discovered by sales engineers who work at a particular client's plant. Even those in the front office, far from the research laboratory and customer plants, often play a role in discovering major process or production improvements. John Drew Betz, early in his CEO assignment, devised a system whereby bulky, dirty container tanks at a client's plant could be economically removed and replaced with clean tanks containing fresh batches of chemical mixtures. With this system, called "cherry picking," the freshly filled tanks are transported to the customer's location on flat-bed trucks on which a winch and crane system is installed. At the plant site, empty dirty containers are removed from their foundation and replaced with freshly filled ones. The old are then transported to a central facility for cleaning, overhauling, and recharging—instead of having these time-consuming tasks performed at the client's plant site. "A small innovation perhaps," remarked Betz, "but a huge success in saving us considerable sums over these decades."

So, also, does Commerce Clearing House keep eyes peeled for market niches to cultivate and new ways to maintain its production facilities in state-of-the-art condition. Likewise, each of Dover's divisions and subsidiaries is directed to keep its respective product pipelines filled with devices that represent the latest technology. Although innovations in the smokeless tobacco field appear less frequently, U.S. Tobacco revolutionized the industry by being the first to put small parcels of snuff or a pinch of tobacco in teabag-like pouches. "The image of the product changed almost overnight, and opened up entirely new segments of the population to the pleasures of smokeless tobacco—including many in the so-called professions," asserted one of its key marketing executives.

Not only is Kellogg creating new plants to expand production but it is also directing renewed research activity in such biotechnology areas as:

Developing new strains of grain that will provide the full complement of the eight essential amino acid groups.

Reducing from years to perhaps days the ability to detect the results of cross-breeding experiments.

Locating and developing new nitrogen-fixing plants and agents.

Devising new strains of grain that have a higher tolerance for salty water.

All of these should eventually provide a new generation of revitalized products to augment its R-T-E cereal and convenience food lines.

Patents are of little value in helping protect a specific combination of ingredients in a particular aroma or taste compound that is manufactured by International Flavors and Fragrances. In fact, were a patent secured, the exact formula of the mixture would then be revealed to all competitors. A far more secure guarantee of secrecy is to place each formula in the company vaults and safe deposit boxes scattered throughout New York City.

But the methodology that leads IFF to concoct some of its most saleable mixtures may represent an even more secure form of confidentiality. Harry Walter, during his reign as CEO, inculcated into the organization an ability to cut through corporate nonsense, "hype," and "noise" to get at the core of a problem, and he transferred that practice into the international arena. For example, he personally travelled throughout the world seeking those who actually used or might use IFF's products. He and his staff refused to rely on hearsay obtained from surrogates or from leaders of a country who advised what products, odors, or tastes they believed their citizens might use or be impressed with. "To find out what precise flavor ingredients comprise an Indonesian mother's milk that is eagerly consumed by her infant (when trying to develop a taste additive to a milk substitute for use in that area), you don't talk to male embassy officials in Washington, nor to the bureaucracy in Djakarta. You go directly to nursing mothers in the villages on Borneo, Java, and Sumatra," said an IFF research chemist. "The best bet is to obtain samples of the mother's milk, then perform exhaustive analysis on it." Such tactics continue to survive beyond Walter's 1985 retirement; and they help account for IFF's astounding success in the field of taste and scent additives.

Because product life cycles of various blends and ingredients have been shortened from eight to the current three or four years, IFF scientists, sniffers, and tasters are probing hitherto untouched areas of microorganisms, microbiological genetic engineering, and fallouts from the neurosciences to locate new taste and aroma enhancers. One particularly fruitful area lies in developing new blends to augment and "revitalize" tastebuds and odor-sensitive sensory spots in the aged. Improved mixtures with more "bite and penetration" are being developed in the labs for senior citizens who are prone to lose significant portions of both taste and smell sensitivities.

Selected Marketing, Promotional, and Advertising Strategies

The few examples cited previously of an ever-abiding dedication to quality, reliability, and service among our fourteen elite also require ensuring that the marketing function reinforces those efforts. One thing that these organizations are not guilty of is hiding their talents and wares under a bushel. Each enterprise constantly reaches out to the marketplace in an attempt to convince potential clientele of the value of its product or service through timely promotional strategies and programs. A few highlights may serve to convey the nature, content, and scope of some of the activities undertaken by these corporations.

As alluded to earlier, an almost blind faith in massive advertising is the cornerstone of Kellogg's promotional strategy. Implemented by its founder, William Keith Kellogg in 1906, it has been an essential ingredient from which the corporation has never departed. The corporation's signature is displayed in brilliant red on each R-T-E cereal box on supermarket shelves throughout the world. A specific cartoon character, once identified with a particular cereal, remains inseparably linked with that product—and none other—for life. Tony the Tiger *is* Frosted Flakes to millions of youngsters. That product-animal image linkage incessantly bombards television's children-and-mom audience from sunup to bed-down. Recently, under the creative hand of the Leo Burnett advertising agency, the company has adopted Tony as its corporate mascot.

As an aside, the Burnett agency and Kellogg have developed an extremely unusual relationship over the past thirty-seven years. They have stuck with each other through both good and bad times, especially during the 1980–82 period when Kellogg focused undue attention on battling the suit brought against the company by the Federal Trade Commission alleging restraint of trade and price-fixing with its two prime competitors, General Foods and General Mills. Because of inattention to market developments during that period, Kellogg saw its market share slip from over 40 percent to under 35 percent. But neither Kellogg nor Burnett blamed each other. Somehow both entities created environments that encouraged people to overcome adversity and perform above their heads—"better than anyone had a right to expect them to perform," according to Leo Burnett and a top Kellogg executive.

One of Kellogg's competitors recently asserted that the organization was past its prime in so far as aggressive marketing is concerned. Recent evidence, however, suggests otherwise. The company remains one of the dominant advertising concerns in the United States in terms of advertising outlays as a percentage of sales—never relinquishing its objective to "reach everyone who eats." One current tactic is to identify and segment the market into a wide spectrum of discrete niches, such as health-conscious young adults, children of various ethnic groups, active women whose body systems require iron enhancement, and senior citizens who have begun to lose tastebud sensitivity.

The "Big K" will gladly enter a market or country and lose money to gain a foothold—then cultivate that inroad to eventual dominance. For example, the company used the vehicle of refried beans in Mexico to introduce the corporate name to the population. After the name had become accepted on an indigenous product, other non-Mexican cereal products were introduced—with considerable success. "Our bean entry generated some losses," remarked a marketing manager, "but it paved the way for acceptance of our traditional products. Very profitable returns began to be generated shortly thereafter." Because R-T-E cereals have remarkable longevity once they are accepted, Kellogg is willing to sacrifice immediate profitability to gain volume and market share increases in the longer run. Currently the company has eighteen manufacturing facilities outside the United States and distributes its products in about 130 countries.

One of the prime problems that Kellogg has encountered in many overseas markets is that specific cultures frequently have no word for "breakfast," let alone ready-to-eat cereals. The morning meal is not distinguished in any way from other meals. Also, the firm believes that a strong and substantial middle-class segment must exist before convenience foods can be profitably marketed. Lower socioeconomic classes tend to regard R-T-E cereals and convenience foods as luxury items, rather than necessities. Another frequently encountered problem is the presence of overseas consumer organizations that attack United States–style convenience products as symbols of "Yankee, American imperialism." Remarked a company officer: "We have our work cut out for us in these foreign districts. We'll do all right—but it'll take time."

Another huge marketing machine is American Home Products—an organization that has developed several idiosyncratic promotional perspectives since the mid-1930s. In contrast to Kellogg, AHP never puffs the corporate name on its products. The specific brand name gets the big play—not the division or subisidary, which, at best, will appear only in small print. Only brand name items are sold—never commodities or generics—even though some of its products are essentially commodities. For example, Anacin's active ingredient is aspirin, with a small amount of caffeine. One Anacin tablet contains 400 milligrams of aspirin (acetylsalicylic acid) compared to the ordinary 325 milligrams in a pure aspirin tablet. Yet Anacin sells at three to eight times the price per milligram of ordinary low-cost aspirin. It is one of the most heavily promoted products in the over-the-counter market and the consumer appears to have expressed a willingness to pay a substantial premium for that extra 75 milligram of aspirin per tablet, plus the amount of caffeine in a quarter cup of coffee. AHP strongly believes that brand name items are less vulnerable to price-cutting and competition. Again, AHP's experience is like Kellogg's experience: once the customer becomes loyal to products such as Anacin, Preparation H, and Woolite, that loyalty endures. However, the company pays close attention to ensure that the public never overrates an AHP product, for example, harboring the unfounded belief that Anacin can cure pneumonia.

LaPorte's strategy—which still holds in the company although he left his position as AHP's CEO in 1980—is to pump advertising dollars into established products that possess significant volume or market share. From that point on, the tactic is to gain incremental sales and profit, rather than to advertise new products that merely proliferate the product line. This tactic enables the firm to focus its energies and keep current products highly successful. Furthermore, it avoids wasting large sums on promotional activity to expand a market that is dominated by others. In addition, the products selected are those whose sales can be strengthened by use of AHP's huge distribution clout to get them positioned on the retailer's shelf, rather than those requiring heavy expenditures for development that may fail in the end.

Another of AHP's promotional hallmarks is that each of its products (unlike Kellogg or Procter and Gamble) must pay its way from the start. It does not wish to wait two to three years to reap the benefits after spending substantial sums on a new product. AHP intensively and carefully tests each market, evaluating consumer response before probing further and committing additional resources. Said one AHP product manager: "The consumer must demonstrate a willingness to buy before we commit heavy promotional expenditures. In my tenure here, we departed from that principle only once that I can recall—with Youth Garde."

In the advertising trade, the company is notorious for getting every penny's worth that can be squeezed from ad agencies. "We operate with almost no fat," said one top AHP executive, "and we expect the agencies we hire to do likewise." In fact, the John F. Murray advertising agency—an AHP subsidiary that does about 25 percent of AHP's advertising—serves primarily as a hedge and a constant threat to external ad agencies that evidence reluctance to work within AHP guidelines. AHP's approach to advertising is aggressive hard sell with such sledge-hammer, shock techniques as the throbbing head, pulsating stomachs, or "nine out of ten doctors recommend." Despite the criticism continually leveled at these "unsophisticated" tactics, the bottom-line performance of AHP has far exceeded that of most of its competitors.

The ethical drug side of AHP, however, projects quite a different image and approach to marketing and promotional activity. In this respect, AHP resembles other ethical drug manufacturers, most of whom form separate divisions or acquire subsidiaries to insulate the marketing of ethical pharmaceuticals from their over-the-counter remedies. The practice shields their ethical drugs and contact with physicians from the typical mass media hype and heavy commercialism that is characteristic of over-the-counter products.

It is interesting, however, that few products are as intensely promoted by their manufacturers as are prescription drugs. The pharmaceutical industry annually spends the equivalent of between $5,000 and $9,000 per physician advertising and promoting prescription drugs. For example, Wyeth Labs (a division of AHP), known as an extremely aggressive merchandiser of ethical drugs, uses both a very effective force of detail men to personally contact physicians, dentists, and hospitals and modern media technology. In one instance, the division urged 9,000 physicians, by means of engraved invitations, to watch the closed-circuit television promotion of its severe-blood pressure-control prescription drug, Ansolysen.

Merck acquired Sharp and Dohme in 1953 to market and distribute many of the pharmaceutical drugs that were being derived in Merck's chemical research laboratories. The primary purpose in acquiring Sharp and Dohme, however, was not so much to insulate the ethical drug aspect of Merck from its chemical side, as to purchase and integrate as a subsidiary a well recognized organization that contained a strong sales force to market pharmaceuticals. The division currently employs about 1,400 professional representatives who systematically call on physicians and hospitals to promote the various drugs in the company's arsenal.

It is Lilly that is frequently identified as the ethical drug industry's premiere marketing machine. The company distributes its wares almost exclusively through some 400 wholesalers—an uncommon channel in this particular industry—using about 1,500 detail men, 80 percent of whom are registered pharmacists. Lilly has consciously steered clear of the area of heavily advertised over-the-counter drugs. As one executive stated: "It's just not our image. We do almost no advertising direct to the public." The company is reluctant to over-promote its products, having become sensitive to some concern that it might have been overly aggressive in selling such products as its anti-inflammatory drug, Oraflex, which was withdrawn from the market several years ago.

One strategy that Lilly uses in promoting its array of products is to establish clearly identifiable and separate channels of distribution for each of its four major categories: human prescription drugs, animal medications, technological instruments, and Elizabeth Arden cosmetics. The biggest difference in promotional style probably exists between Arden and the other three branches. "Cosmetics entail considerable fluff and puff—which is something new to us," remarked a marketing executive. "And we have taken care to carefully isolate promotional activities and images that are associated with that aspect of our company from our other three medical-related segments."

A rather unusual characteristic that the pharmaceutical companies have in common with three other of our fourteen organizations concerns their respective targeted customer bases. Although the patient ultimately purchases, then consumes or applies the prescribed medication, that patient is not the primary decision maker in the health care sequence, nor is the patient the targeted group for promotional efforts by manufacturers. Instead, it is the physician (and to some extent the hospital) audience to which almost all advertising and merchandising activity is directed. And our three pharmaceuticals—Lilly, Merck, and SmithKline Beckman—plus AHP's medical side do it very well.

The targeted groups for three other companies are even less readily apparent. True, the holder of a checking account is the recipient and end-user of the checks and deposit slips that are manufactured and distributed by Deluxe Check, but the principal clientele that Deluxe cultivates is the financial institution (bank, savings and loan, brokerage firm, or money market management group) on which individual checks are drawn. In many cases, the depositor at a particular institution has only one source company for checks, the company that enters into agreement with that institution to furnish checks for all depositors. Deluxe goes well beyond even this targeting step in the marketing process. It strives to be a partner with each of its client financial institutions and the entire banking industry, rather than to operate merely in the role of a printing company. The firm tries to make each financial institution and the total banking system function better by offering continuing service. Witness, for example, its pioneering role in developing the MICR system, which is currently used throughout much of the U.S. banking community. In short, Deluxe's real clientele base consists of three disparate, yet related, groups, each of which has different needs that must be satisfied: the individual depositer, the financial institution, and the banking system.

Richard D. Irwin Company, a subsidiary of Dow Jones, is a major publisher, particularly in the area of business and economics textbooks. But although students are the ultimate buyers of these books, it is not they who really decide whether or not the books should be purchased for a particular course or curriculum. Instead, the course instructor or group of professors makes that decision for the student. Hence, although textbooks are written to assist students in learning a subject, they are directly marketed and promoted to the professors—who sometimes may never have read the books they assigned. (On the other hand, the instructor may well have written the book for Irwin.) Rarely, if ever, is promotional literature or the army of textbook sales persons directed toward students in the Halls of Ivy—only the professors. From my own personal experience, I can say that Irwin accomplishes that professorial contact more adroitly and aggressively than do many of its competitors.

Although all of the taste and scent enhancements made by International

Flavors and Fragrances are incorporated into products that the individual consumer picks off the market shelf, none of IFF's separate compounds is sold directly to those end-users. Again, its clientele is the manufacturer of products into which are blended IFF ingredients and mixtures.

What these seven firms possess in common is expertise in satisfying at least two, perhaps three, distinct groups of clientele—each group having different needs and decision making ability in the marketing sequence. Each group must be fully serviced and satisfied simultaneously, without disaffecting any other group in the chain—not an insignificant balancing act.

Regarding sales personnel, each of our fourteen organizations recruits, develops, and then successfully retains a superb sales staff. Commerce Clearing House maintains a 500 to 700 person sales force, which is in constant contact with current and prospective customers. This group not only sells the firm's various product lines but also gleans suggestions from the field for improvements in or additions to the existing lines of reference services. In essence, the sales staff serves the dual role of clientele contact point and listening post. Likewise, Philip Morris's approximately 900 person sales force—composed of sales people, product managers, and marketing specialists—also functions in this dual capacity.

Betz Labs, on the other hand, devotes considerable and continuous energy recruiting a large sales-engineer staff. The main source of those recruits is the specific industries that Betz serves. Said one of its former CEOs: "We let what eventually becomes our sales force receive their training in our clients' industries—then we select the cream of the crop from appropriate sources and under amiable circumstances." Rarely are sales engineers hired directly from competitors. When that rare event does occur, however, something quite interesting also happens. In this business, unseating a customer from a competitor is extremely difficult to accomplish, basically because of the strong almost personal relationships that develop between the sales engineer and the client. When a competitor's sales engineer is persuaded to switch employment (to Betz Labs, for example), that individual usually brings along the client account that the long-term relationship has nurtured. "A couple of our best sales engineers and most lucrative accounts arose through this mechanism," recalls one manager. "That's why we make every effort to regard the slightest innuendo of a complaint from one of *our* customers as an impending crisis."

Another interesting facet of the Betz organization is the way it perceives and promotes the service dimension of its operation. According to one headquarters executive, "Any of our competitors could probably arrive at a similar blend of chemicals that we would prescribe for each of our individual clients. Where we believe we are unique, however, is in the emphasis we place on service—and the continuity of that service." Essentially, Betz stresses to its clients that service is free—charging only for the chemical mixtures that are prescribed. Of course, included in the charge for the chemical additives is sufficient "load" to cover sales engineering, overhead, and other service costs. But the goodwill derived from this piece of customer relations seems to have benefited Betz enormously.

International Flavors and Fragrances maintains a special type of highly motivated and experienced salesperson whose task is to cultivate, secure, and nurture customers, but who also must be equally adept at "sniffing out" trends, needs, and new potentials and—above all—be able to sell ethereal ideas. Working with laboratory scientists and artistically inclined technicians, they first translate scent and taste sensations into communicable vocabularies, then into specific products. "It's high-tech art," indicates one product manager, "which takes at least three years of hard work and exposure before an individual begins to approach productive usefulness." And the process by which the essence of a taste sensation or waft of odor is finally captured in the form of a specific chemical formula involves a long chain of individuals that may well include the idea-generator, expert perfumer or taster, PhDs in the laboratory, an alert commodity buyer in worldwide spot and futures markets, and finally, expert export clerks who are familiar with the local logistical routines required to get exotic ingredients from such places as the tropical rain forests of Brazil to a laboratory in the United States.

Another of our fourteen organizations has developed an ability to understand and take advantage of a quite different chain of events. Tambrands begins its promotional efforts by making contact with premenstrual girls through educational programs in public and private schools, in the belief that, once a woman becomes familiar with a personal hygiene product, uses it, and becomes comfortable with it, she will remain a sold customer for the next forty or more years. Another productive avenue that the company has found to promote and market its flagship line is the hospital maternity ward. Every effort is made to make available free samples of Tampax and Maxithins to new mothers, who may have previously been unaware that the company's products help relieve postdelivery trauma and discomfort. Otherwise, the large sales force normally works almost exclusively through its main distribution channel of food brokers.

Tambrands believes the untapped overseas demand is enormous. Although Tampax is currently sold in about one hundred countries, many areas of the world have still not felt the impact of modern-day hygienic products that deal with the menstrual cycle. Also, a revolutionary change in overseas advertising has occurred since Thomas Casey's departure as CEO. During his tenure, the same advertising message appeared in all markets in the world, regardless of cultural differences in attitudes toward menses. Since his retirement, however, separate promotional materials have been designated for each country or major cultural region of the world—each piece being oriented to speak directly to a specific culture's perspective on the monthly cycle of women.

One benefactor of a considerable amount of free advertising is *The Wall Street Journal*. The newspaper is, in most areas of the country—indeed, the world—a symbol of wealth, power, prestige, and influence. A copy of the *Journal* casually, but obviously, tucked under an executive's arm or lying in an open briefcase conveys the appropriate image that the particular line of business suits or luggage being advertised is proper attire for the aspiring manager. In fact, the *Journal* may well be the most widely used device to advertise products and services of other business enterprises. It has become the emblem of corporate United States and the financial districts of the world—a rather unusual symbiotic relationship.

U.S. Tobacco benefits from an entirely different promotional syndrome, one that permeates all of its marketing efforts for smokeless tobacco. The company has capitalized on the close bonding relationship that develops among users of snuff and chewing tobacco. The novice user seeks guidance on how to handle this particular form of tobacco, invariably looking to a veteran for suggestions and advice on appropriate techniques. This personalized instruction by the experienced veteran is conveyed in the firm's promotional material, whether on television, billboards, or in newsprint. The image created is that the product is spread among friends through a one-on-one relationship by word of mouth and the chain reaction of close comradeship. Said one corporate spokesman: "We've a superb in-house national distribution system. But our most effective channel is the millions of adopters of our product who assist their associates in becoming acquainted and comfortable with our primary product line. You couldn't ask for a more effective sales force." The vehicle that is used to convey that concept is exuberant, vigorous sporting events, such as car racing, rodeos, football, and other outdoor activities.

This segment on marketing and promotional activity would be incomplete without a mention of a few facets associated with one of America's premiere consumer marketing companies, Philip Morris. As mentioned previously, an aggressive promotional philosophy permeates all planning and operating activity throughout the organization. A cluster of reinforcing activities comprise the nucleus of that orientation, running the spectrum of image-creation, quality control, massive advertising, market segmentation, modern plant facilities, price-cutting promotions, and innovative packaging. Remarked an executive at one of PM's competitors: "That outfit brings to the marketplace an incredible array of weaponry that is adroitly manipulated, usually in a manner that is much the envy of the entire industry."

PM has artfully developed the ability to create and build a specific image for any particular segment of the market. The principal ingredient in this process is the construction of a product reputation for the item that enables the consumer to link that product and its "reputation" with what he or she wants to be or become. Two classic cases illustrate the process.

In 1954, PM (with the help of the Leo Burnett advertising agency) took Marlboro and transformed it from a sophisticated, upper-class, women's cigarette into the kind of product adopted by the fiercely independent, stalwart, range-riding Western hero. The "Marlboro man" was expanded to embrace "Marlboro country" in the early 1960s, to provide an overall cohesive setting for the cigarette's image. Apparently the new image appeals to a vast crosssection of humanity, since that brand is now the number one seller in the world. This broad acceptance, incidentally, helped make the filter cigarette more acceptable.

Another cigarette, Virginia Slims, was created to appeal to today's lithe, youthful, liberated woman, and its tie to the sports world is secured by sponsorship of the annual Virginia Slims tennis tournament. In short, a particular personality is created for each PM product—whether cigarette or beverage—that then becomes the power and continuity behind the promotional activity for that item.

Since the 1970 ban on cigarette advertising on television, PM has become an even more flexible advertiser. It has expertly adapted to other mass media, such as newspapers, magazines, billboards, trade-oriented devices, point-of-sale displays, sponsorship of sporting events, premium offers, and shelf-position purchase in supermarket and drug chains.

Each brand manager in PM operates with the power of a marketing vice-president in a small company, having control over a large promotional budget and manpower resources. The most resourceful and creative ad agencies in the country are sought out to handle PM's advertising schedule. The Roper organization has for some time carried out most of PM's tracking studies. The in-house marketing staff constantly reviews the effectiveness of all marketing programs—to the point of monitoring daily sales statistics by region and metropolitan area—for every brand sold in the country. To complete this impressive mix of talent and progress, its top marketing managers maintain intimate awareness of the market through close personal contact with clients and distributors.

Without exception, the marketing and promotional endeavors in each of our fourteen represents an impressive spectrum of activity, dedication, and astuteness. Those items, along with attention to quality, service, and reliability help support their well-earned places in a very small and elite class.

Attitudes toward the Competition

One common attribute among this elite group—and one that may in large measure account for their standing head and shoulders above the competition—is their reaction to that competition. In a nutshell, each of these enterprises is concerned with competitors and does keep a watchful eye peeled for their activities and progress. But in the main, it is not "the competition" that drives our select group. Instead, each of these fourteen organizations is driven by some internal instinct to excell, exceed, outdo, and surpass its own—not the competition's—previous or current performance. Each has developed a powerful inherent drive to do it better, simply because almost unlimited opportunities exist to do so. They seem to be so far in front of their colleagues that they seldom look back to see who is gaining. It is not a cocky superiority complex, nor a lack of concern when a competitor introduces a significant improvement, but rather a healthy, confident self-awareness in each of our organizations that it represents the standard of excellence in its respective industrial niche.

Dow Jones constantly strives to make its flagship *Journal* better—with or without competition. New entrants to the field of financial and business news cause DJ little concern because of high entry costs, heavy capital investment, and the elaborate infrastructure and established reputation that are needed to enter and survive in this arena. Except for some selected aspects of the business and financial section of *The New York Times*, no other daily newspaper in the United States approaches touching the depth and breadth of coverage and competence that *The Wall Street Journal* does. The sole nationally circulated written medium that could be considered competitive is the weekly and semi-monthly (not daily) periodical, such as *Business Week, Forbes,* and *Fortune*. DJ has no intention of losing its place at the forefront of national and world financial and business reporting and commentary. But it is far more concerned with improving its present products, as evidenced by its dedication to keep production technology, satellitery competence, and editorial policy guidelines at the cutting edge of the art.

The first-order priority of each of Dover's forty divisions is to improve its own performance and achieve the objectives it has agreed to accomplish each year during the budget-review process. Next in priority is to exceed the rate of return on investment that is being achieved by other Dover divisions, and, finally, to surpass in performance and achievements other companies in the same industrial niche. Even when (for example, because slack demand exists in the petroleum industry for various items that some Dover divisions manufacture) performance objectives are barely met, and shortfalls develop, the attitude within the entire organization still is to excel and exceed.

Commerce Clearning House sees its sole competitor in the tax reporting service field as Prentice-Hall, but the challenge is not regarded as great, since Prentice-Hall's expertise is in textbooks (including its annually updated *Federal Tax Course*) not the loose-leaf folio field. According to one CCH executive: "We've got more than enough challenges and opportunities ahead of us than to be unduly concerned with competitive threats." U.S. Tobacco feels similarly inclined, partially because it also far surpasses any competitive threat on the horizon. It is currently targeting Western Europe (the United Kingdom, France, and Italy), the Far East (Taiwan, Hong Kong, the People's Republic of China, and Australia), and "yuppies" on the domestic scene. Among the company's most immediate concerns are product liability lawsuits that have been brought against the firm—despite the favorable 1986 ruling toward U.S. Tobacco in the Oklahoma City-Marsee trial. Current evidence suggests that one of the industry's main challenges is to decrease the nitrosamine levels in various brands of chewing tobacco and snuff.

Another of our fourteen that is less concerned with specific industry competitors than with certain environmental threats is Deluxe Check. Although some concern is directed toward competitors becoming larger and more aggressive, Deluxe is still four times larger than its nearest rival, the John H. Harland Company. What is more disturbing are several developments in the fields of banking and consumer credit:

Automated teller machines (ATMs), which are becoming more prevalent, eliminating the need for checks to be used for withdrawal transactions;

Point-of-purchase debit cards;

Banking by personal computer in the home and the use of phone transfers of funds between banks and accounts;

Banks that pass higher check-handling costs direct to its customers;

Large banks and financial institutions producing their own checks for depositors.

Although each of the above developments might represent small inroads into Deluxe's main product line, the potential exists for more serious damage in the future.

Deluxe has hedged these developments to a certain extent by purchasing a 44 percent interest in Data Card Corporation, a manufacturer of credit card printing and embossing equipment and by extending a $2 million loan to Signature Guarantee System, the manufacturer of an electronic device that debits an individual's checking account at the point of sale by reading and automatically cancelling the personal check. Other efforts that may benefit Deluxe's position are:

More types of financial institutions that extend check-writing privileges to customers such as savings and loans, money-market funds, insurance companies, and brokerage firms.

Price boosts on packets of checks and more expensive check options (such as elaborate artistic designs) being made available.

An increase in the number of checking accounts being maintained in households in which both spouses are employed.

Remarked one Deluxe executive, "The industry keeps changing; but so do we. We try to stay a step or two ahead of developments. Not a mile out front, because that can kill you; but certainly not behind."

One company that actually welcomed competition is Tambrands during the period when the corporate name was still Tampax. Thomas Casey frequently made the point, during his leadership of the company, that the entry of Procter and Gamble, Kimberley-Clark, and Johnson and Johnson probably did more to expand the total market for catamenial devices than Tampax might have been able to accomplish alone because of its relatively small advertising-expenditure base. True, Tampax's share of the market eroded during the competitive invasion, but its sales volume and after-tax profits soared. The company's greatest fears, during the late 1970s, lay in the blitz ad campaigns of Procter and Gamble, to which the far smaller Tambrands felt almost powerless to respond. "Fortunately," recalls a Tambrands veteran manager, "the Cincinnati giant didn't pull that stunt too frequently in our primary product line."

Betz Labs has learned much from the mistakes of its major competitors. One company placed a cap on salary-commissions so that no sales engineer could earn above a specific amount—that maximum being the president's salary. A top-level executive at Betz remarked that "most of their good salespeople left almost immediately—of which we were fortunate to recruit the best for our stable." The same manager believes that many of its competitors fail to understand the subtleties of the business they are in. "To repeat," said one spokesperson, "service is the absolute first priority item. Whenever they (or we) fail to remember that fact, troubles magnify. Never promise too much. But always deliver what is promised."

Recently, a relatively few of these fourteen firms have had to deal with industrial espionage. Kellogg has certainly been concerned with the increasing market share that generic R-T-E cereals have captured—and the formidable threat that General Foods might present to both R-T-E and convenience food segments, now that it has joined Philip Morris, has yet to unfold. But having to deal with one's competitors as spies is something for which even Kellogg was unprepared. Apparently two of its foreign competitors obtained valuable production and processing information while disguised as ordinary visitors during daily public tours. Kellogg's response was to close the Battle Creek plant, in April 1986, to all future public tour parties. "We know that many of our customers will be gravely disappointed because of our action," reflected a corporate spokesperson. "But in light of the significant threat to our future business position, we felt that the action we took was the only satisfactory and sure way to proceed. This remedy unfortunately brings to a close our long history of openness with respect to our production facilities."

Merck is not overly concerned with new entrants in its industry, again mainly because of the high entry costs, distribution networks, plant investments, and research facilities that are required to be successful. One aspect of the competitive environment it is deeply concerned about, however, is the number of trade secrets that have been stolen from its research labs and production facilities. "We've tightened security measures to prevent such things occurring in the future," said one research scientist. "But, of course, so long as ideas and techniques remain in our employees' minds overnight or over the weekend, security will never be airtight. It's just one more item that enters the corporate performance picture."

Another of our pharmaceuticals, SmithKline Beckman, also confronted an espionage episode recently, but in reverse fashion. For a couple of years, SKB has been seriously concerned with the prime competitor of its drug Tagamet, Glaxo Holdings, which manufactures and markets Zantac, making serious inroads into Tagamet's market share. In early 1986, SKB was approached by one of Glaxo's plant security supervisors to sell the Zantac formula to SKB. SKB immediately tipped off the Federal Bureau of Investigation, which was able to bring the matter to an abrupt close. Such instances will undoubtedly emerge in the industry in the future. Remarked one pharmaceutical president in an interview, "The stakes are so high that completely eradicating such events is likely to be a utopian dream."

International Flavors and Fragrances is in a position in which it can normally ignore the cut-throat price competition that exists in its industry—largely because it maintains a superior edge, with emphasis on quality, reliability, and assured delivery. In contrast to several other industrial segments represented among our fourteen companies, the cost of entering flavor and scent enhancers is relatively low. In fact, many loft-sized operations exist in the industry today, and most of these can function without expensive state-of-the-art technology, but the costs of remaining viable in the industry beyond two or three years is enormous. "It takes considerable investment in human resources and experience to maintain a continuity of performance," emphasized one of IFF's research directors. At one time, a threat seemed to be developing among some large marketers of consumer nondurables—such as Colgate-Palmolive, Avon Products, and Procter and Gamble—to create their own in-house fragrance and flavor production capabilities, rather than purchase those ingredients from outside. But most of these companies have discovered that the cost to establish and maintain that expertise in-house at the cutting edge of today's technology is exceedingly high. Hence at this point, that potential threat to flavor and fragrance manufacturers—IFF included—seems not overly critical.

Another of our organizations that is more concerned with existing competitors than with new entrants is Philip Morris. The entry fee into cigarette manufacturing and nationally distributed beer and food products is extremely high—so high, at least in cigarettes, that the current three-to-four member oligopoly will probably continue for many more years. For example, an entrant would need about a billion dollars worth of tobacco leaf storage, a huge manufacturing plant, a massive distribution machine, plus $50 to $100 million to launch each new brand. Such commitments of resources to enter the national scene seem remote in today's environment.

Its is interesting that PM does not take a belligerent or destructive attitude toward its competitors. Said a PM senior vice-president, "We never or rarely speak publicly of ourselves as being '#1' in the industry. It's an in-house taboo. In fact, we have great respect for a company like R.J. Reynolds. They are an extremely strong competitor; and we're constantly trying to win market share from them. But we don't bad-mouth them. They're much too sharp for us to try to destroy or gain a temporary advantage with such tactics."

On balance, most of our fourteen evidence some concern with their competition, but the primary stimulus for improvement, dominance, progress, and superiority derives from in-born drives, rather than from attempts to beat one's rivals. One executive among our elite summed it up fairly concisely: "Competition doesn't drive this organization. We supply our own motivation."

Forcing Competitive Advantages to Occur

While carrying out research into the political and economic strategies employed by a large number of business enterprises, Ian MacMillan (then of Columbia University) identified one particularly intriguing tactic that may partially account for the extraordinary performance of many of our fourteen.[2] That tactic is forcing a competitive advantage to occur—not waiting on the sidelines for circumstances to develop before exploiting an opportunity, but instead, forcing events and situations to unfold that work for the benefit of the organization.

Dover maintains constant contact with an array of investment bankers and industry analysts to flush out and identify potential acquisition candidates that could complement the existing network of subsidiaries and divisions. Executives at headquarters do not sit idly in their offices awaiting "the right one" to come through the door with an offer to be acquired. Rather, the strategy is to continuously probe the pool of potential candidates until a correct fit is identified.

Likewise, American Home Products actively searches out companies and products for acquisition. Clearly defined criteria are already developed by which to measure candidates—which include products that are easy to make, package, and merchandise, but that will prove difficult for competitors to match. Ideal nominees are products that (1) people keep buying even when the economy tightens up; (2) are habit-forming brand name items; and (3) can command "unconscionable profits," as one financial analyst calls it. Like Dover, when a likely candidate does appear, AHP pounces with deliberate speed.

One of the central tactics used by Kellogg to force competitive leverage is to keep pouring in massive doses of advertising until the desired breakthrough occurs. Merck's variation on this theme substitutes research for advertising dollars until either existing barriers are destroyed or new niches are developed, but the process requires time. In Merck's case, the company is exerting a growing presence in Japan's prescription drug market—the second largest (next to the U.S. market) ethical drug market in the world. However, according to one company officer, "It takes an incredibly long time to establish a base of operations in that country, let alone begin to reap rewards. Seems like the Japanese need to see your face for half a century before they start to trust your product and believe that you'll be around tomorrow to back it up. Involvement in that culture demands a *long-term commitment.*"

The cigarette industry's innovator, Philip Morris, continually probes to make something new and different happen. Those at its New York headquarters admit that actively generating new market segments and "personalities" entails enormous downside risks—but they are simultaneously viewed as containing the seeds for considerable upside rewards. The level of confidence with which SmithKline Beckman pursues new thrusts is expressed in one of its principal credos: "Stick to it long enough and we'll eventually come through in first-class style with a winner."

Both Deluxe Check and Dow Jones fully intend to remain atop their respective fields—not through their established momentum so much as by actively seeking new challenges and opportunities for product improvement. Deluxe believes that maintaining close ties with financial institutions through better approaches, plus staying at the sharp edge of production technology, will ensure continued success. On the other hand, Betz Labs exerts that extra measure of effort to service its clients even beyond a client's expectations. Said one Betz sales engineer: "We like very much to surprise a customer with a new unexpected addition in the area of service."

In only one instance was I able to pinpoint a case in which one of our companies appeared to have waited on the sidelines for a competitive advantage to occur. Tambrands, under Casey's regime, allowed its market share to erode to the betterment of its competition. Even in this situation, which was mentioned briefly above, the company seemed to have developed a purposeful strategy to snatch victory from defeat. One veteran Tambrands vice-president expressed it this way: "We hadn't the advertising muscle to enlarge the market. But competitors such as P&G did. Hence, we purposely let them cultivate demand with *their* promotional dollars. So long as our volume and profits grew at a good clip, we could afford to let some of our market share slide"—a somewhat perverse way of forcing a competitive advantage to occur, but very effective and rational under the circumstances prevailing at that time.

Economists frequently recast this tactic of forcing competitive advantages to occur in terms of creating barriers to entry. Alan Shapiro, at the University of California, Los Angeles, has done some investigative work into the role that this barriers concept plays in corporate strategy.[3] He asserts that the organization that (1) becomes the lowest delivered cost producer and (2) achieves an acceptable level of service and quality in its product or service creates an overwhelming competitive advantage that serves as an effective entry barrier. A similar end result can be achieved by the firm's (1) achieving a superior level of service and quality and (2) becoming a relatively low-delivered-cost producer. In either event, the two critical factors are low delivered cost coupled with high service and quality. Those organizations that are able to link the two together, and to maintain that linkage, earn higher ROIs, according to Shapiro.

This coupling can be achieved in a number of ways, at least one of which has been demonstrated by each of our fourteen organizations. One avenue that can erect almost impenetrable barriers to entry is the achievement of economies of scale on the marketing side—for instance, developing a large, well-trained, and effective sales force that competitors find exceedingly difficult to duplicate. Six of our fourteen have achieved this feat exceptionally well: Betz Labs, Commerce Clearing House, Deluxe Check, International Flavors & Fragrances, Lilly, and Philip Morris. A second vehicle is effective mass advertising, as evidenced by eight firms: American Home Products, Dow Jones (primarily in *The Wall Street Journal*), Kellogg, Philip Morris, U.S. Tobacco, and the three pharmaceuticals (with their medical practitioner clientele). Superb promotional and marketing skills that are attained and subsequently honed and adapted to the marketplace is a tough combination to attack.

Providing customers with extraordinary service (such as the solving of problems for individual clients and reliable delivery) and quality for the price charged is a third mechanism through which almost insurmountable barriers can be erected. Six organizations accomplish this alternative exceedingly well:

Betz Labs, CCH, Deluxe Check, Dow Jones, IFF, and Tambrands. The three pharmaceuticals could also be included in this group.

State-of-the-art production and distribution facilities, that allow a low delivered manufactured cost per unit provides another option for attaining competitive advantage. Once low-cost production and distribution is achieved at one or more locations, the learning-curve phenomenon (combined with appropriate matching price decreases) can effectively fend off invaders for a considerable period of time—in some cases, forever. CCH, Deluxe Check, Dover, Dow Jones, Kellogg, and Philip Morris are outstanding examples of firms that have invested heavily in state-of-the-art technology, maintained their expertise at the cutting edge, and ridden the learning curve down. Prospective competitors often find such odds overwhelmingly difficult to better.

Carrying out effective R&D programs and taking advantage of rights conferred through patents, trademarks, exclusive licensing agreements, and even brand-name products provide a fifth form of barrier. Each pharmaceutical company in our study, and such brand-name product organizations as AHP, Kellogg, Philip Morris (recall Marlboro), Tambrands (Tampax), and U.S. Tobacco easily fall into this category.

In short, forcing a competitive advantage to occur and creating effective barriers to entry are really two sides of the same coin—namely, building and maintaining an edge that potential invaders find extremely difficult to overcome. Each of our fourteen, in one form or another, accomplishes this task superbly.

Being in the Right Place at the Right Time—and Luck

Seldom mentioned by investigators who search for clues to extraordinary and consistent business success is the matter of an organization's being in the right place at the right time, and luck. One reason for this oversight is that the two explanations do not have what academicians call "respectable theoretical underpinnings." Luck and being in the right place at the right time have no body of knowledge or extensive literature to relate to or build from. Another reason for the inattention probably lies in the area of consultative advice. How welcome is advice received from a management consultant (or anyone else) that suggests that corporate (or personal) success might hinge on fickle fingers of fate or preordained destiny? "So, what else is new and helpful in the way of advice," the client might ask? However, depending on one's personal creed, a substantial amount of human existence has been and is either relatively "chancy" or preordained.

But totally ignoring the ingredients of being in the right place at the right time and luck in any formula or explanation of success is both a disservice and unrealistic. The "name of the game" in most competitive business is risk—and risk entails chance, strangely shaped probability-distribution curves, and possibilities for enormous gains and losses. Admittedly, most players confront the same rules.

The real disservice in ignoring these two elements may lie elsewhere—namely, the distinct possibility of overlooking the critical role that a single individual or small group of persons plays in the chance-luck part of the success equation. Numerous inventions, insights, and discoveries have fallen on deaf ears or been allowed to lie fallow and rot for lack of initiative. Some person or group must possess the astuteness, intelligence, talent, and energy to know what to do with chance opportunity when it knocks. This observation ties directly back to an attribute of success that was mentioned in a previous chapter—namely, a visionary founder or influential executives in the corporation.

During the process of probing into the hows and whys that might underlie the consistently extraordinary pattern of success in each of these firms, either I or the executive being interviewed eventually arrived at a bedrock question. Who can put a finger on the essence of this organization's continued success? Henry Walter, then CEO of International Flavors and Fragrances, openly admitted that the firm and certain individuals happened to be in the right place at the right time and that a considerable amount of success arose from "just plain luck." When he was asked to elaborate further, his reply was, "Mr. van Ameringen and I both saw that demand for odor and taste enhancers was about to take off. The entire post–World War II market was on the verge of explosion in consumer nondurables, cosmetics, and household products. And we both believed that the IFF organization was well situated to take advantage of the opportunities that were likely to unfold. We simply moved!"

Lilly's breakthrough as a major force in the pharmaceutical industry occurred in October 1923, when the organization marketed insulin to treat diabetes. Considerable perseverance and a certain degree of luck played a significant role in that process, then and since, but, most important, according to a Lilly economist, "It was the meshing and matching of several organizational attributes and individuals in the company at that time which made—and still make—it happen." Even in 1923, Lilly possessed well-trained research and sales forces, plus a team-oriented culture that could take advantage of opportunity when it arose. The organization was strong on the quality and R&D sides. In addition, the health care and prescription drug field was just on the threshold of a major takeoff. "We were there—at the right time with the right ingredients, the right people, and the right leadership," recalled the economist. "Fortuitous luck did play a role; but so also did an appropriate mix of things and people that enabled us to capitalize on events taking place. And that same process operates today—every day."

One example after another could be presented from among our fourteen that illustrate the reality of circumstances propitiously coalescing in the right place at the right time. The passage of the sixteenth amendment to the Constitution, in 1913, and Oakleigh Thorne's conviction that something was bound to happen with the new income tax legislation that could benefit Commerce Clearing House; Hotchkiss's innovative production process and the beginning explosion of a check-writing society in the United States enabled Deluxe Check to move in on the ground floor and establish an entirely new industry are examples. Tagamet at SmithKline Beckman and Dow Jones' *The Wall Street Journal* could both have foundered, had not sufficient astuteness been present in each organization to know what to do and when. As John Drew Betz summed it up: "I'll bet most of these fourteen organizations, including our own, were lucky to have been at 'some correct place' when something began to evolve which augured success. But continued performance at a high level of achievement requires some other added dimension—like perhaps perseverance, solidity, dedication, stamina—or maybe just more luck."

Notes

1. Robert H. Miles, *Coffin Nails and Corporate Strategies* (Englewood Cliffs, N.J.: Prentice-Hall, 1982).

2. Ian MacMillan, remarks made during a seminar for faculty and graduate students at Lehigh University, Bethlehem, Pennsylvania, on September 24, 1984.

3. Alan C. Shapiro, "Corporate Strategy and the Capital Budgeting Decision," *Financial Management Collection* (Winter 1986).

7
Some Overall Perceptions and Insights

> You do not disclose the game that makes money for you.
> —Jack A. Barbanel[1]

> Staying power is an attitude.
> —Isaac Asimov[2]

We have covered a considerable number of topics and touched on a substantial amount of detailed information in the previous six chapters with respect to our elite group of fourteen organizations. In bringing this investigation to a close, it might be appropriate to draw together several key points that emerged from the study. As with any book or report, its principal justification is to organize great masses of information into some semblance of sanity. We shall attempt to comply with this objective. Specifically addressed in this wrap-up segment are the following topics:

A recap of significant highlights and insights that were presented in the foregoing chapters will be compressed to form a composite picture of our fourteen organizations.

A brief discussion is warranted concerning some precautions that the reader may wish to consider before hastily or arbitrarily applying and extending these findings to other organizations, whether they be business or not-for-profit.

Of particular interest to several readers may be a summary of recent stock market performance of these fourteen corporations compared to the Standard and Poor's 500.

Finally, there are some predictions concerning possible arrivals to and departures from this elite group of business enterprises.

Composite Portrait of the Fourteen Organizations

Presenting some of the common attributes and characteristics that we identified among these fourteen most consistently and highly successful American corporations in the format of a composite picture of "our average organization" will help focus attention on several principal findings that emerged during the investigation, which may, at least in part, account for this group's consistent record of outstanding performance. Significant deviations from the average will be noted at appropriate points.

Clarity of Mission and Operating Protocols

A fundamental characteristic that was detected in each of our fourteen enterprises is a well-defined philosophy and perspective. Each firm has a crystal clear idea of its mission and central thrust. It knows precisely what its business is about. Rarely is this focal point allowed to become cluttered or fractionated with peripheral projects or tangential activities that erode energy and resources from that central task. For example, Kellogg's principal expertise has, since its founding in 1906, been ready-to-eat cereals—a focus that was only recently extended to include a very narrow slice of other convenience foods. Only once in its eighty-year history did "Big K" allow its focus to become fractionated. During 1980 through 1982, top management directed excessive attention to battling the Federal Trade Commission's suit, which charged that Kellogg (plus General Foods and General Mills) had amassed excessive control in the R-T-E cereal market, causing prices to be unfairly high and making it difficult for new competitors to enter the industry. Recall that Kellogg's market share dropped from over 40 percent to below 35 percent during that two-year period. But, immediately after the FTC dropped the suit, Kellogg attacked its erosion problem and relentlessly redirected total corporate effort to recoup its five percentage-point loss in market share. In short, each enterprise sticks to its knitting with an almost undivided attention and religious zeal.

A long-run view is deeply engrained in each of these organizations—as opposed to the short-run, quick-fix, "make it big now and to hell with the future" syndrome so prevalent today in many American enterprises. A well-measured pace, continuity, perseverance, and stamina characterize the mode of operations in virtually all of these firms. Even American Home Products, which stresses improvements in quarterly performance, consistently pursues that goal year after year—with the result being an unbroken superior record of accomplishment decade after decade. These companies rarely relax in their steady quest of top performance.

Those among the fourteen that have acquired or intend to acquire other companies and products have established well-defined guidelines for identifying potential acquisition candidates. Most subscribe to the proposition that unchanneled diversification is an extremely risky and usually unprofitable experience. Candidates that will supplement and reinforce the company's existing product lines are usually carefully screened, analyzed, and evaluated prior to—not after—the announcement of an acquisition. Once such an acquisition has been formalized, considerable energy is expended to carefully integrate and assimilate the new member into the parent company's organizational arrangements. Philip Morris, for example, labors patiently at this integrative process over a period of three to five years, during which time new operations are continuously monitored to detect weak spots and identify achievements warranting corporate applause.

Extensive planning activity plays a central role in all of these enterprises—a process that involves the entire swath of operations from R&D and product development programs to territorial reorganizations, personnel realignments, and marketing research and promotional campaigns. Merck exemplifies the critical role that planning plays in the success formula of these enterprises.

Well-defined and clearly articulated financial performance objectives are integral parts of this planning dimension. Priorities are carefully laid out and communicated to each link in the chain, from front office to production floor. All relevant personnel are tuned to the same channel. One interesting aspect of the financial dimension that emerged during this investigation is the relatively consistent pattern of financial ratios that are experienced in each of these companies. Once established in a particular company, each of the several key liquidity, profitability, and leverage ratios tends to fluctuate within a relatively narrow range—which is another reflection of the stability and steadiness of purpose so engrained in these firms.

Along with extensive planning and clearly defined financial objectives is an intense monitoring of organizational activities. Constant intelligence gathering and control of daily operations is normal routine in these organizations, but seldom are these control procedures viewed by personnel as "Big Brother" tactics. An inbred sense of self-criticism and self-appraisal also permeates these organizations. For example, a hallmark of Deluxe Check Printers is its forty-eight–hour turnaround (from receipt of customer's order to its completion and delivery to the postal system) objective. The slightest interruption in attaining that schedule triggers immediate concern and correction by plant supervision and department pesonnel. Yet, despite intensive control devices, there is still considerable latitude in most of these companies to facilitate entrepreneurial and off-the-record excursions—a squirreling away of financial resources apart from regularly budgeted items for a pet R&D project that looks promising is tolerated by most of these systems.

Forceful visionary founders and notably influential chief executive officers are another characteristic common to these organizations. Leadership with creative foresight—such as those by John Drew Betz at Betz Labs, Bernard Kilgore at Dow Jones, and Joseph Cullman at Philip Morris—provided stimulus and left enduring legacies in each enterprise. Even the occasional iron-fisted autocrat served the organization quite well, leaving the company larger, better, and more profitable than it was before that particular styled individual assumed the CEO post.

Succession into positions at or near the top in most of these organizations is a well-planned, well-orchestrated process. Effective managerial and executive training programs are in place in one form or another in the majority of organizations—and promotion from within seems to be the rule of thumb. Rarely are individuals recruited directly from the outside into key top management positions, particularly at the CEO and chief operating officer slots. In lesser organizations, such inbreeding might be considered a fault, but little evidence was discovered among our fourteen to suggest that promotion from within resulted in selections that proved poor or mediocre. Detected in several firms was the fact that a particular type of individual would very likely gravitate into the top echelon—for example, chemical engineers at Betz Labs, personnel with strong marketing backgrounds at Philip Morris, those connected with the reporting and editorial side of Dow Jones, and liberal arts and science generalists in SmithKline Beckman.

All of the fourteen run very tight ships with respect to maintaining a lean staff at headquaters and central offices. In fact, a few firms take considerable pride in operating their complex organizations with a very small cadre of personnel in the front offices and in executing their missions without lavish accouterments or furnishings in those central facilities. Conspicuous show and elaborate hype are not typical ingredients that make the vast majority of this elite group function so well.

On the other hand, no clear consensus emerged to suggest which organizational form was better—centralization or decentralization. A few corporations have been, at one time in their history, operated quite successfully under very centralized or autocratic leadership. Most, however, have experienced some degree of decentralization. But which of the two basic forms is better in specific instances remains quite debatable.

One facet of corporate life that is currently receiving close attention is the hostile takeover threat. All of the firms in this study evidenced sensitivity to this issue—several to the point of taking specific protective steps through stockholder action to alleviate, if not completely eliminate, future external challenges to control of the organization.

Cultural Characteristics

Not too surprising was the detection in each of these enterprises of a unique culture. However, the degree of conscious, explicit attention directed to the development of an organizational culture ranges from considerable through moderate and low key, to almost benign neglect. Some, such as SmithKline Beckman, Lilly, and Deluxe Check, direct substantial effort to developing various training seminars and companywide programs for all levels of personnel. Others, as Dow Jones, encourage the emergence of unique cultural attributes without devoting large resources or blocks of time to those endeavors. In two firms, some semblance of organizational culture has arisen almost in spite of little to no conscious attention having been directed toward its cultivation.

Specific behavioral characteristics that are quite actively nourished in each of these corporations include: (1) a sincere give-a-damn attitude on the part of officers, middle management, and rank-and-file employees; (2) a strong esprit de corps that permeates the entire enterprise; (3) a willingness to "go the extra mile"—evidenced by numerous examples of attending to the smallest details to improve the product or service; and (4) a mutual regard and concern among most of the employees and managers for the personal welfare of each other—as reflected in supportive interdepartmental arrangements and liberal fringe benefit packages. Perhaps the most pervasive cultural trait that became apparent to this investigator was the unvarnished enthusiasm that prevailed in each organization—a certain drive, sense of mission, desire to accomplish—call it what one will. Each firm exudes movement, progressive improvement, and eagerness to accept a challenge and implement changes.

Most of these organizations are relatively free of internecine warfare and internal politics—the sort that has destroyed more than one business venture before it reached its full potential. Even in the minority of enterprises in which unions exist, each level in the organization seems to have learned to accommodate organized labor. In fact, the presence of unions in these firms seems to make little or no restriction on their successful performance.

In brief, the internal organizational workings of each of these enterprises is tight, active, and replete with an enthusiasm that spreads and provides its own impetus to improve product and service.

Relations with Customers and the Competition

Organizations comprising this elite group are universally obsessed with providing customers with top quality, superior performance, and outstanding service. Each is dedicated to seeking ways to improve the mainstay of its business, including correction of minute details that lesser institutions frequently overlook or ignore. Marketing strategies and promotional programs are well articulated, and when a particular advertising expertise is unavailable within the corporation, outside competence is sought. None of our group allows its light to be hidden under a bushel, and all are aggressive go-getters in the best sense of the word.

Most are involved in extensive research and development activities and devote considerable effort and funding to maintaining the organization at the state of the art particularly in production capability. Several of these firms are the trend setters, the innovators, and high risk-taking prospectors in their industrial niche. Without exception, each of our fourteen enterprises represents the top in their respective fields.

Except for one or two entities, all of these firms deal in brand-name products or services, and those exceptions (International Flavors and Fragrances and Betz Labs) so closely cultivate relationships with their clientele as to render their products and services tantamount to being trademarked or tightly licensed. Most are expert in segmenting their markets into discrete compartments and in clearly distinguishing between specific clienteles and the needs of each, without encroaching on or alienating other segments. These latter concerns are most deftly handled by our four pharmaceutical firms and two of the enterprises in the publishing industry.

One rather surprising insight that emerged from this study was the degree to which these fourteen are inner-directed or internally driven. Their quest for steady successful performance and constant improvement does not, for the most part, seem to be motivated by concern about the competition. Instead, and almost without exception, these enterprises have developed an innate internal motivation to excel—whether their competition is close or distant. In fact, several are so far in front of rivals as to be placed in an almost unique industrial position without peers. Yet they continue to drive themselves to improve on their already outstanding performance.

For the most part, these firms force a competitive advantage to occur in their favor. And these competitive advantages are usually sought through a continual process of incremental improvements and patient step-by-step amendments, rather than through the development of some grandiose strategic leap. Their successful momentum comes more from a steady rhythmic pace than from sudden noisy breakthroughs.

Spokespersons in most of these organizations quite candidly admit that a considerable amount of their corporate success may be due to being in the right place at the right time and with luck, yet, while owning up to the role played by fortuitous circumstances, all emphasize that a combination of astute individuals, adequate resources, appropriate visionaries, and an aggressive willingness to assume risks must be present for the organization to take advantage of opportunity when it does knock. As most quickly point out, progress does not just occur. It must be made to happen with a ready cadre of sensitive, sharp individuals.

Overall View

Jack Barbanel, Gruntal and Company's director of futures trading, opened this chapter with an unwritten law of Wall Street—if not the entire business community—which states essentially: Never disclose a winning strategy to your opponents. To categorically state that this study has identified specific strategic secrets or the reasons for successful corporate performance would be most presumptuous.

One particular item kept gnawing at this investigator throughout this project that may well account for a significant portion of the consistently superior success records of these fourteen, and Isaac Asimov has, I think, accurately put his finger on it: "Staying power is an attitude"—of individual mind, of group behavior, and of organizational culture.

Many of the ingredients that were discovered in common among this collection of business enterprises undoubtedly contribute to corporate success to some degree. Crystal-clear mission, visionary leadership, give-a-damn perspective, and being in the right place at the right time—each plays a role, yet, the thread that seems to weave the structure together is an organizational attitude, of some mysterious origin, that stimulates individuals and groups in the company to persevere over adversity, take advantage of opportunity, and look within themselves for strength to excel. One of the CEO's interviewed during this investigation expressed the phenomenon well: "It may sound trite, but frame of mind and attitude are the critical, bedrock ingredients for continued success—whether business or personal."

These companies have developed a rhythmic attitude of steady commitment to superior performance. They are in the game for the long pull—not for the temporary success of today. Each has laid out a grand plan that is continually being renewed, that is guided by steadiness of purpose. It is a frame of mind that has its roots in the pioneering spirit of the Pilgrim and the persistence of the Midwestern settler.

Of course, any organization or person is free to adopt this attitude and perspective—and to abide by the demands. The odd reality is that so few elect to do so. If this study proves anything, it is that dedicated adherence to these so-called ancient truths does pay off—extremely well!

Some Caveats

In academic circles, no piece of research is complete without appending the standard litany of limitations and cautions that underlie the study. Those unimpressed with such ritual can ignore the following segment—with time and interest being better served by moving directly to the next section, which deals with recent stock market performance of our fourteen. However, for those who derive pleasure in the exposure of investigatory frailties, we shall take this brief detour.

Precautions surrounding this study concern five areas:

Sample size.

Comparative tests.

Cause-effect relationships.

Applicability to other organiztions.

Assurance of sustained extraordinary performance.

First, the sample size of this study is extremely small in relation to the universe of some fifteen million American business establishments. As noted previously, fourteen of that number represents .0001 percent—quite a small number. Also, only manufacturing industrials in a relatively narrow spectrum of Standard Industrial Classification codes are included—not by design, but simply because no banks, stock life insurance, agricultural, mining, construction, diversified financial, retailing, transportation, or utility enterprises were able to satisfy the rigorous criteria established for inclusion in this study. Conglomerates also did not meet those prerequisites. With the exception of Betz Labs and Dover, all of our organizations reside in or are closely allied with the consumer nondurables segment of the economy. With the possible exception of International Flavors and Fragrances and Betz, the group includes firms with highly visible brand-name products or services.

Second, no elaborate statistical tests or scientifically controlled experiments were conducted comparing these fourteen corporations with other less successful enterprises to verify or validate the findings presented here. Such comparisons or experiments for this type of study would be extremely cumbersome, time-consuming, and expensive to carry out (assuming that it were even possible to design and execute them). This investigation, as stated up front, is an exploratory study—not an hypotheses-testing project of the type that normally requires tightly codified parameters. A subsequent study of that type might well build on findings uncovered in this exploration.

Third, with respect to cause-effect relationships, no pretense can be made, on the basis of this study, that all ingredients prerequisite to extraordinary successful performance (defined in terms of return on sales and return on owners' equity) have been identified. Factors other than those identified may well play a significant part in the success equation. For that matter, no assertion can be made that all of the several characteristics found common among these fourteen enterprises are vital to continued success. Simply because a firm makes and markets only top quality riding crops and buggy whips to a select clientele, has a lean headquarters staff, and promotes personnel only from within the organization to its top positions, may not assure a sufficiently high sales volume and a continuously superior ROS and ROI.

However, this investigator is sufficiently comfortable with the proposition that the factors pinpointed in this study do contribute to generating the continuous record of outstanding accomplishment achieved by these particular firms. Furthermore, I see no obvious reason why many of these attributes are not applicable to a broad range of organizations, business related or otherwise. Such ingredients as astute promotional campaigns and aggressive, visionary leadership can contribute to the success of not-for-profit as well as profit-seeking entities.

Although reasonably confident that integration of many of these several findings into less successful companies might well enhance their financial and operating performances, I am far less sanguine with respect to suggesting precisely how they should be implemented into existing organizational arrangements. All corporate cultures contain an intricate network of complex parts and persons, the slightest alteration of any dimension of which can create unanticipated reactions in other segments. Still, aside from these caveats, the several commonalities identified here do strongly suggest that they contribute to successful performance, and those managers who choose to ignore their existence or relevance do so at some risk.

Finally, steadfast adherence to a number of the attributes and traits that are presented in this book will probably never ensure sustained extraordinary performance—perhaps even if they are continuously implemented in these fourteen organizations. Guarantees of success that last a lifetime are seldom available—as will be verified shortly—and luck will probably always be a key part of the U.S. business landscape. Nonetheless, in the final segment of this chapter, some predictions are advanced concerning which of the fourteen may "fall from grace" in the near future, and some candidates who could well find their way onto this exclusive list within three to five years.

Stock Market Performance

In chapter 1, we pointed out why shareholder wealth creation—defined as dividends plus price appreciation of a specific stock over a particular period, divided by the original cost of that stock to the investor—was rejected as a criterion for selecting corporations to be included in this study. Nonetheless, sufficient curiosity usually emerges concerning how well a portfolio of stocks performed in the market. Would you have bettered, matched, or suffered a shortfall with respect to the overall market performance had you purchased a portfolio comprised of some or all of these fourteen stocks? It is an intriguing question, and one that deserves at least one response before we bring this investigation to a close.

Displayed in table 7–1 is a summary of the performance of each of our fourteen corporate common stocks compared to the Standard and Poor 500 index over the ten year period, January 1, 1976 through December 31, 1985. The performance of each individual stock has been adjusted to eliminate its systematic (or market-related) risk. (In technical language, each stock has been adjusted for its beta coefficient factor.) The three columns reflect the

Table 7-1
Individual Stock Performance Compared to the Standard and Poor 500 Index, 1 January 1976 through 31 December 1985
(percentage of time a specific stock bettered the index)

	On Upswings	On Downturns	Overall
American Home Products	42	60	50
Betz Labs	30	71	50
Commerce Clearing House	61	82	69
Deluxe Check Printers	66	87	75
Dover	63	80	70
Dow Jones	65	78	69
International Flav & Frag	35	59	46
Kellogg	63	54	60
Lilly	58	48	52
Merck	59	39	50
Philip Morris	55	70	61
SmithKline Beckman	64	68	66
Tambrands	81	82	79
U.S. Tobacco	71	66	69
Average of the fourteen	58	67	62
Average of the top seven performers	67	78	71

Source: Bridge Data Company

specific stock's performance with respect to its frequency of bettering the Standard and Poor 500 index: (1) when the general market is increasing (on the upswing); (2) when it is decreasing (on the downturn); and (3) overall. The exhibit does not reveal the extent that each stock bettered the Standard and Poor index, merely the frequency with which the respective stock exceeded the index.

American Home Products, for example, outperformed the Standard and Poor index 42 percent of the time during market upswings, 60 percent during market downturns, and 50 percent overall. Restated, AHP stock during this period proved more favorable (less costly) to hold in market downturns than during upswings. In short, it proved to be a better defensive (or conservative) than offensive stock. On the other hand, Deluxe Check Printers bettered the index 66 percent of the time during market upswings, 87 percent during downturns, and 75 percent overall.

During this ten-year period, these fourteen stocks as a group outperformed the Standard and Poor 500 index 58 percent of the time on market upswings, 67 percent during market downturns, and 62 percent overall. In other words, this portfolio bettered the index irrespective of the directional swing in the market, although it did reflect somewhat better results during downturns than on upswings or overall. Restated, the portfolio was a slightly better performer in bear markets than in bull markets or overall. Proceeding a step further, a portfolio composed of the seven top performers (CCH, Deluxe Check, Dow Jones, Dover, SKB, Tambrands, and U.S. Tobacco) bettered the index 67 percent of the time on upswings, 78 percent on downturns, and 71 percent overall.

To summarize, actual past performance with this portfolio reflects a rather impressive record of success. Not the best, if one were greedy—but quite respectable. Of course, performance of these fourteen compared to other indices might yield substantially different results, and predicting future performance of specific stocks by extrapolating historical performance is always risky.

Some Predictions of Future Arrivals and Departures

Before unveiling the likely departures from and arrivals to this group of most consistently highly successful large publicly held American corporations that this investigator foresees in the near future, I would like to share the list of firms that made this elite group for ten or more consecutive years in prior periods. They have since been displaced. The period and consecutive years that each of the thirty organizations made the list are indicated in table 7–2.

Although many of these firms continue to reflect quite respectable records of financial and operating performance, an investigation to identify specific reasons why each disappeared from among the elite has yet to be undertaken. Discovering the extent to which each of the above organizations did or did not share characteristics that the current fourteen hold in common might prove both interesting and instructive. Likewise, pinpointing circumstances that might account for these enterprises falling from the list could also be of considerable value. For example, one of the reasons that partially explains why Hershey Foods "fell from grace" after 1966, was the incursion of steadily increasing advertising and promotional expenditures. Until 1967, Hershey made almost no use of mass media advertising, relying instead on point-of-purchase promotional devices, such as its classic dark brown and silver candy-bar wrapper. Particularly intriguing would be uncovering the various shortcomings experienced by several corporations that appeared among the elite group for twenty or more years: Avon, Eastman Kodak, Reynolds, Schering-Plough, and Square D.

Possible Departures

Pinpointing explanations for past successes and shortfalls is fraught with difficulties, but substantially less so than accurately forecasting which of our

Table 7-2
Past Members of the Most Consistently Highly Successful Companies

	Period	Consecutive Years
AMP	1965–74	10
Amerada Hess	1960–71	12
Avon Products	1956–81	26
Champion Spark Plugs	1958–75	18
Chesebrough-Pond's	1967–77	11
Coca-Cola	1958–79	22
Corning Glass Works	1956–67	12
Dr. Pepper	1970–81[a]	12
Du Pont (E.I.) de Nemours	1956–65	10
Eastman Kodak	1956–75	20
Emerson Electric	1969–78	10
Gillette	1956–73	18
Hershey Foods	1957–66	10
Ingersoll-Rand	1956–71	16
International Business Machines	1967–80	14
Louisiana Land & Exploration	1971–80	10
Lubrizol	1968–81	14
Masco	1969–79	11
Maytag	1968–79	12
Minnesota Mining & Manufacturing	1956–74	19
Pacific Lumber	1969–81	13
Panhandle Eastern	1961–72	12
Polaroid	1958–69	12
Reynolds (R.J.) Industries	1958–77	20
Schering-Plough	1957–80	24
Square D	1956–81	26
Sterling Drug	1956–73	18
Union Carbide	1956–65	10
Warner-Lambert	1957–72	16
Xerox	1962–74	13

[a] Financial data no longer made public.

current fourteen will be displaced from this group, or which firms from among the thousands out there will find their way onto the list. But I shall venture some opinions.

Both Dover and International Flavors and Fragrances appear to be candidates for departure in the near future. Dover may be becoming overly diversified and fractionated into too many industrial niches, for even the current adept executive group at headquarters to manage. In addition, several of its divisions are confronting serious downturns in the domestic petroleum industry with no immediate recovery in sight.

IFF is beginning to encounter increasingly aggressive competition from other relatively solidly entrenched fragrance and flavor manufacturers. In addition, the transition from the lengthy Walter-Spitz era to new leadership may prove to be a traumatic adjustment process. The development of a cadre of managerial talent that might have been able to provide continuity of leadership was not given high priority under the prior administration. The results of that negligence may emerge in the near future.

Potential Arrivals

Somewhat easier to predict are those organizations that may arrive among the elite during the next three years. The following three corporations have met the criteria established in chapter 1 for seven or more consecutive years:

	Period	Consecutive years
Abbott Laboratories	1977–85	9
Gannett	1977–85	9
Nalco Chemical	1979–85	7

Abbot Labs is a manufacturer and marketer of pharmaceuticals; Gannett is a newspaper publishing chain; and Nalco Chemical is a major competitor of Betz Labs.

Five former members of the select group could well reappear on the list within the next four or five years: Coca-Cola, Emerson Electric, IBM, Maytag, and R.J. Reynolds. In addition, Bristol-Myers, McGraw-Hill, and Tandy could be emerging candidates for inclusion within four or five years.

An Ending Note

Considerable commentary and criticism have emerged among business experts and observers during the past ten to fifteen years, concerning what is right and wrong with the U.S. industrial machine. Particular attention has focused on the philospy, perspective, and performance of counterparts in such diverse countries as Japan and West Germany. In several respects, the most successful business enterprises in each of these societies have discovered and stuck to tried and tested ways of achieving outstanding performance. Very briefly, three of these ways justify some closing words.

First, James C. Abegglen and George Stalk, Jr. in their book, *Kaisha: The Japanese Corporation*, point out that price increases in a particular Japanese company's stock scarcely makes the list of priorities among managements of those companies.[3] In sharp contrast, movement in a corporation's stock is often of first or second priority on the list of a great many top U.S. executives. It is not so among our fourteen organizations. Most top managers in these enterprises, like their Japanese counterparts, place a very low order of importance on how well or poorly the firm's stock is doing at a particular moment. Emphasis is primarily directed toward serving customers, developing innovations, and striving to improve organizational performance. As a top executive in American Home Products summed up, "We concern ourselves with far more important matters than the current market price of our stock. That will take care of itself. Our primary tasks lie elsewhere."

Second, top management both in Japanese enterprises and in our elite group have long since learned to be patient with capital. Financial and human resources in both sectors are invested for the long haul—not for an immediate short-term payoff. Capital infusions nurture these companies through extended periods of low returns, adversity, even losses in some departments—with the overall objective of proving out over an extended period of time. Short-term profitability is not of top concern in most of our fourteen, nor in most successful Japanese enterprises. These managers have learned the lesson that immediate satisfaction and gratification can be deferred for longer-term payoffs.

Finally, these fourteen and many successful Japanese organizations appear to understand that no single attribute or characteristic makes for long-run success. As a Lilly spokesman stressed, "Any extraordinary success we've had has come about through a propitious blend of a lot of variables—including astute CEOs, good timing, hard work, risky innovations, dedicated and concerned employees, excellent promotional activities, and a bit of luck." What emerges from this study is clear evidence that considerable truth lies in two old saws: (1) Few short-cuts exist for arriving at long-term success; and (2) Everything is connected to everything else, especially in complex organizations. Those that appear among this august group have learned these lessons extremely well.

Notes

1. Jack A. Barbanel, "Those Big Swings on Wall Street," *Business Week* (April 7, 1986), pp. 33, 35.

2. Isaac Asimov, "On Staying Power," *The Wall Street Journal* (May 21, 1986), p. 18.

3. James C. Abegglen and George Stalk, Jr., *Kaisha: The Japanese Corporation* (New York: Basic Books, 1986).

Appendix A: ROS and ROI of Firms in the *Fortune* 500

Reflected here are the return on sales (ROS) and return on owners' investment (ROI) for two categories of firms in the *Fortune* 500 directories during the thirty-two-year period, 1954–85:

The average ROS and ROI generated by firms in the top 500.

The minimum ROS and ROI cutoffs for firms in the top 20 percent of the top 500, in other words, the top quintile of the top 500.

A graphic display of this data is shown on page 5.

148 • *Corporate Staying Power*

Return on Sales (ROS) and Return on Owners' Investment (ROI) of Firms in the *Fortune* 500 Directories, 1954–85

| | Percentages ||||
| | Top 500 Average || Top 20% Cutoff Points ||
Fiscal year	ROS	ROI	ROS	ROI
1954	6.0	N/A[a]	N/A	N/A
1955	6.9	N/A	N/A	N/A
1956	6.6	13.2	8.8	17.4
1957	6.2	12.3	8.1	15.5
1958	5.4	9.5	7.4	13.2
1959	6.1	11.0	8.3	14.8
1960	5.7	10.1	7.7	13.3
1961	5.6	9.6	7.5	12.7
1962	5.9	10.6	7.3	13.4
1963	6.1	11.1	7.3	13.2
1964	6.5	12.1	7.8	14.7
1965	6.7	13.0	8.4	16.1
1966	6.6	13.2	8.7	16.9
1967	6.0	11.8	7.8	15.3
1968	6.0	12.2	7.7	15.4
1969	5.5	11.5	7.3	14.9
1970	4.7	9.5	6.5	13.6
1971	4.7	9.8	6.3	13.1
1972	5.0	10.9	6.6	14.1
1973	5.8	13.7	7.5	16.1
1974	5.2	14.1	7.1	17.2
1975	4.4	11.4	6.7	15.6
1976	5.1	13.5	7.2	16.7
1977	4.8	13.3	7.1	16.7
1978	5.1	14.2	7.4	18.2
1979	5.4	16.1	8.1	19.9
1980	4.9	15.0	7.5	19.2
1981	4.7	14.3	7.1	18.5
1982	3.7	10.2	6.5	16.9
1983	4.1	10.9	6.5	16.4
1984	4.9	13.6	7.4	18.5
1985	3.8	10.4	6.6	17.4

[a] Not available

Appendix B: Financial Statement Analysis of Profitability, Liquidity, Leverage

Substantial financial data was digested from some 275 annual reports that were issued by the fourteen organizations in the study. A summary of several significant ratios gleaned during that review is displayed for each of the fourteen for each year it was a member of this elite group during the thirty-year period 1956–85:

> The two key *profitability* ratios are shown: ROS and ROI, in this case return on average owners' investment. (Return on average owners' investment is determined by dividing the average of the beginning and end-of-year total owners' investment into the net profit after taxes that was earned during the year).
>
> *Liquidity*—the ability to meet financial obligations when they fall due—is reflected in terms of the current ratio (current assets divided by current liabilities) and the cash cycle (the number of days required to convert inventory into cash collected from sold merchandise).
>
> The degree of financial risk—*leverage*—is reflected in terms of two measures: percentage of overall leverage (total liabilities divided by total assets), and interest-bearing debt as a percentage of total assets.

American Home Products

Fiscal year	Profitability ROS[a]	Profitability ROI[b]	Liquidity CR[c]	Liquidity CC[d]	Leverage O/A[e]	Leverage IBD[f]
1956	10.6%	34.3%	2.3	151	42.7%	6.3%
1957	11.1	36.8	2.3	158	41.0	5.5
1958	11.3	35.4	2.3	168	38.2	4.9
1959	11.1	34.4	2.3	171	36.9	4.9
1960	10.9	31.5	2.2	172	36.1	4.7
1961	10.7	29.2	2.3	164	34.1	4.3
1962	10.6	28.3	2.2	169	34.9	4.0
1963	10.7	27.6	2.2	158	33.8	4.0
1964	10.8	27.5	2.3	155	32.9	1.7
1965	10.2	29.0	2.4	142	36.9	4.6
1966	10.3	28.3	2.7	144	34.1	3.5
1967	10.5	26.6	3.2	145	31.1	4.1
1968	10.3	26.1	2.7	143	35.2	3.9
1969	10.3	27.1	2.6	147	35.2	3.4
1970	10.5	27.2	2.7	152	34.7	3.0
1971	11.2	28.5	2.9	146	35.1	2.5
1972	11.1	27.7	2.9	143	36.0	2.1
1973	11.2	29.0	2.9	141	37.2	1.4
1974	11.0	29.9	3.1	144	35.5	1.1
1975	11.1	29.5	3.1	149	35.4	.6
1976	11.2	29.4	3.3	143	34.4	.5
1977	11.4	30.2	3.1	148	35.6	.6
1978	11.4	31.4	3.0	147	36.7	.7
1979	11.6	31.7	3.1	151	36.8	.5+
1980	11.7	31.9	3.0	151	37.9	.6+
1981	12.0	31.8	3.2	154	36.1	.6+
1982	12.2	32.0	2.7	148	34.9	.4+
1983	12.9	32.2	3.0	155	33.6	1.7
1984	15.2	33.0	3.9	171	31.1	1.6
1985	15.3	32.7	3.4	163	32.5	1.4

[a]ROS = Return on Sales = Net profit after tax ÷ Sales (%)
[b]ROI = Return on Owners' Investment = Net profit after tax ÷ Average owners' investment (%)
[c]CR = Current Ratio = Current assets ÷ Current liabilities (times)
[d]CC = Cash Cycle = (365.25 ÷ Average accounts receivable turnover) + (365.25 ÷ Average inventory turnover) (days)
[e]O/A = Overall leverage = Total liabilities ÷ Total assets (%)
[f]IBD = Interest-Bearing Debt = Total interest-bearing debt ÷ Total assets (%)

Betz Laboratories

| Fiscal | Profitability | | Liquidity | | Leverage | |
year	ROS	ROI	CR	CC	O/A	IBD
1974	8.1%	20.0%	2.2	206	33.7%	5.7%
1975	8.3	20.5	2.3	174	31.8	4.0
1976	9.1	21.4	2.7	165	26.4	2.7
1977	10.7	23.2	2.6	159	24.8	1.1
1978	13.6	26.4	3.1	137	22.6	.8
1979	11.0	22.0	3.2	116	20.9	.7
1980	11.0	23.2	3.3	109	21.5	1.1
1981	11.4	24.4	2.9	104	23.0	.8
1982	12.0	22.6	2.1	106	23.0	2.7
1983	12.4	21.7	2.3	103	20.8	.4
1984	12.1	22.1	2.3	95	22.7	.2
1985	11.5	20.1	2.3	96	23.2	—

Commerce Clearing House

| Fiscal | Profitability | | Liquidity | | Leverage | |
year	ROS	ROI	CR	CC	O/A	IBD
1975	8.7%	20.2%	5.3	140	59.4%	.7%
1976	8.2	22.0	5.6	118	59.9	.4
1977	8.5	21.8	5.4	126	60.8	.3
1978	9.2	31.7	4.4	130	75.2	.2
1979	9.5	59.3	3.7	130	81.8	.2
1980	9.1	63.1	3.9	130	78.8	1.4
1981	9.2	55.4	3.8	130	76.0	1.0
1982	9.0	45.6	3.6	130	71.5	.9
1983	6.6	30.3	3.6	118	71.3	1.5
1984	9.7	40.9	4.3	107	67.7	1.3
1985	9.9	36.6	4.1	107	66.0	1.0

Deluxe Check Printers

Fiscal year	Profitability ROS	Profitability ROI	Liquidity CR	Liquidity CC	Leverage O/A	Leverage IBD
1969	8.6%	22.0%	2.1	69	28.9%	5.6%
1970	9.5	24.2	2.1	69	26.7	4.7
1971	9.7	23.9	2.3	67	25.2	3.8
1972	9.7	23.3	2.4	66	24.0	3.0
1973	9.3	22.4	2.2	67	25.0	2.4
1974	8.9	22.1	1.9	67	26.1	2.4
1975	11.0	27.8	1.9	66	27.9	2.6
1976	10.1	24.2	2.3	66	25.9	2.2
1977	9.6	23.5	2.0	64	26.9	2.6
1978	10.2	25.5	1.9	62	27.0	2.2
1979	10.5	26.6	1.8	64	27.8	1.7
1980	10.4	26.2	2.0	62	29.3	3.7
1981	10.6	26.6	2.2	60	28.5	3.0
1982	11.8	27.2	2.6	59	26.4	2.3
1983	12.4	28.2	2.6	57	29.3	1.9
1984	12.9	30.1	2.6	58	31.8	2.0
1985	13.6	31.9	2.7	60	32.0	2.6

Dover

Fiscal year	Profitability ROS	Profitability ROI	Liquidity CR	Liquidity CC	Leverage O/A	Leverage IBD
1975	7.5%	19.7%	4.9	171	29.6%	15.5%
1976	8.6	21.4	4.3	148	29.1	12.2
1977	9.1	21.8	4.1	142	28.4	11.7
1978	8.5	22.2	3.8	131	28.9	10.6
1979	8.6	23.9	2.4	147	37.0	17.0
1980	8.8	25.3	2.8	148	33.0	10.9
1981	9.4	27.1	2.9	138	30.4	6.5
1982	8.7	21.4	3.4	137	26.6	5.6
1983	7.7	16.3[g]	2.7	139	28.6	5.0
1984	7.8	18.9	2.2	139	39.1	14.4
1985	6.9	16.8[h]	2.3	143	38.5	13.3

[g] .1 percentage point below cutoff.
[h] .6 percentage points below cutoff.

Dow-Jones

Fiscal year	Profitability ROS	Profitability ROI	Liquidity CR	Liquidity CC	Leverage O/A	Leverage IBD
1969	16.9%	34.0%	1.8	27	32.1%	-0-%
1970	13.0	25.3	1.5	28	35.2	6.8
1971	12.5	23.8	1.5	28	35.3	5.8
1972	12.1	24.7	1.4	27	36.2	4.6
1973	12.9	27.6	1.1	29	36.0	2.9
1974	11.1	23.9	1.4	31	41.1	9.2
1975	11.1	25.9	1.5	30	40.2	6.8
1976	11.0	25.4	1.5	34	42.6	10.1
1977	12.3	30.3	1.2	34	40.7	3.0
1978	12.2	30.8	1.0	35	41.6	4.6
1979	11.6	29.9	1.0	36	44.7	7.4
1980	11.1	28.9	1.0	37	44.2	4.0
1981	11.1	29.1	.8	38	49.3	10.3
1982	12.1	29.2	.8	38	46.4	6.8
1983	13.2	30.4	1.0	35	40.5	2.9
1984	13.4	28.0	.9	36	37.1	3.2
1985	13.3	25.1	.7	35	49.0	21.4

International Flavors & Fragrances

Fiscal year	Profitability ROS	Profitability ROI	Liquidity CR	Liquidity CC	Leverage O/A	Leverage IBD
1969	14.3%	20.1%	3.7	244	21.6%	5.9%
1970	14.7	19.7	3.2	250	23.8	8.9
1971	15.0	19.4	3.5	255	21.0	6.3
1972	15.6	21.4	2.9	241	26.0	8.9
1973	15.5	22.9	2.6	242	31.6	12.6
1974	14.4	22.9	2.3	278	35.5	17.3
1975	11.0	15.2[1]	2.9	300	27.4	10.8
1976	13.7	21.0	2.7	256	30.9	9.1
1977	14.5	22.2	3.3	271	28.4	7.2
1978	15.4	23.8	3.5	257	26.8	4.1
1979	15.0	22.9	3.6	249	26.4	4.1
1980	14.1	21.0	3.9	249	24.0	4.7
1981	14.7	20.5	3.9	260	23.4	4.7
1982	14.1	19.0	4.2	260	22.2	4.3
1983	14.8	20.1	3.5	250	24.9	3.7
1984	14.5	19.9	4.4	260	22.4	3.5
1985	13.9	17.9	4.2	262	23.7	3.4

[1] .4 percentage points below cutoff.

Kellogg

Fiscal year	Profitability ROS	Profitability ROI	Liquidity CR	Liquidity CC	Leverage O/A	Leverage IBD
1960	8.4%	22.2%	2.3	67	23.7%	-0-%
1961	8.2	21.0	2.2	68	22.8	-0-%
1962	8.5	21.2	2.2	69	23.1	-0-
1963	8.8	22.5	2.0	68	24.9	1.4
1964	9.3	23.8	1.9	70	27.7	4.5
1965	9.6	23.3	2.1	72	23.5	3.4
1966	9.0	23.0	2.2	76	25.2	6.0
1967	9.1	22.1	2.3	80	22.9	4.6
1968	9.1	21.1	2.3	81	27.1	4.6
1969	8.2	20.6	1.9	82	29.4	4.6
1970	8.1	21.0	2.0	84	28.7	5.0
1971	8.1	21.4	2.0	82	29.2	5.9
1972	8.7	21.6	2.2	85	27.5	4.7
1973	7.8	21.3	2.0	82	31.6	6.9
1974	7.1	21.4	2.0	84	30.7	7.2
1975	8.5	27.2	2.2	81	40.7	14.4
1976	9.4	29.2	2.4	78	36.1	13.4
1977	9.0	26.7	2.3	84	35.1	12.8
1978	8.6	25.4	2.2	87	36.6	11.6
1979	8.8	25.9	2.2	92	37.0	10.7
1980	8.6	26.3	2.0	92	37.1	8.5
1981	8.8	26.4	1.9	86	36.7	8.2
1982	9.6	26.9	1.8	81	31.8	1.4
1983	10.2	26.1	1.8	80	33.3	2.6
1984	9.6	34.2	1.1	78	70.8	42.3
1985	9.6	48.0	1.4	77	60.4	24.8

Lilly

Fiscal year	Profitability ROS	Profitability ROI	Liquidity CR	Liquidity CC	Leverage O/A	Leverage IBD
1962	12.0%	13.6%	3.8	N/A[1]	16.1%	.8%
1963	10.7	13.5	3.1	264	18.5	1.8
1964	12.0	15.9	3.0	268	19.7	2.1
1965	13.2	19.4	2.9	253	22.7	2.1
1966	13.6	21.2	2.7	252	23.9	2.2
1967	13.1	20.5	2.8	241	24.8	4.4
1968	14.7	23.0	2.7	222	26.7	3.0
1969	15.5	22.8	2.7	231	26.4	2.7
1970	15.9	22.2	1.9	255	32.6	11.5
1971	13.3	19.8	2.0	257	34.8	14.0
1972	15.4	22.3	2.4	263	28.8	8.0
1973	16.0	23.1	2.5	266	28.4	7.0
1974	16.1	22.7	2.2	303	32.9	12.5
1975	14.7	20.1	2.2	323	33.2	15.4
1976	14.9	19.7	2.4	304	31.9	12.6
1977	14.4	19.1	2.5	317	31.0	12.8
1978	15.0	21.3	2.2	311	32.5	9.9
1979	14.9	22.3	2.5	312	27.9	4.8
1980	13.4	20.7	2.1	303	33.4	8.3
1981	13.5	20.7	2.0	308	34.9	9.1
1982	13.9	20.9	1.9	291	34.9	9.3
1983	15.1	21.9	1.9	288	37.9	11.6
1984	15.8	18.0	1.7	276	39.0	12.6
1985	15.8	22.5	1.9	276	39.6	13.7

[1]Not available

Merck

Fiscal year	Profitability ROS	Profitability ROI	Liquidity CR	Liquidity CC	Leverage O/A	Leverage IBD
1957	12.4%	16.1%	3.4	198	18.9%	.3%
1958	13.4	17.9	3.3	198	19.5	.3
1959	13.8	17.8	3.8	199	17.8	.3
1960	12.7	15.3	4.2	206	16.4	.3
1961	11.9	14.1	3.8	199	18.5	.2
1962	12.1	14.6	3.5	193	19.5	.2
1963	13.5	17.1	3.7	184	20.2	.2
1964	15.7	20.2	3.3	183	24.0	-0-
1965	18.0	24.7	3.1	171	24.8	-0-
1966	18.1	28.6	2.6	162	25.0	-0-
1967	16.9	28.3	3.0	144	23.0	2.3
1968	15.9	25.3	3.2	150	21.7	2.2
1969	15.6	25.0	2.9	147	23.5	2.7
1970	15.2	25.5	2.6	146	25.8	2.8
1971	15.4	25.7	2.7	220	26.6	8.3
1972	15.4	26.1	2.7	277	25.8	7.0
1973	16.0	27.4	2.4	266	28.4	8.2
1974	15.8	27.7	2.0	308	33.8	9.0
1975	15.4	25.8	2.4	326	39.6	18.9
1976	15.4	24.9	2.3	292	38.5	17.7
1977	16.9	24.4	2.5	300	35.9	15.0
1978	15.5	22.5	2.4	303	35.4	12.6
1979	16.0	24.5	2.2	285	36.3	13.6
1980	15.2	23.5	2.3	271	35.0	11.0
1981	13.6	20.6	1.9	264	39.5	15.5
1982	13.6	19.7	2.1	267	39.6	16.5
1983	13.9	19.4	1.7	250	42.2	17.9
1984	13.8	19.8	2.0	224	44.6	12.8
1985	15.2	20.9	1.9	246	46.3	10.2

Philip Morris

Fiscal year	Profitability ROS	Profitability ROI	Liquidity CR	Liquidity CC	Leverage O/A	Leverage IBD
1969	7.6%	17.4%	2.2	401	63.6%	50.2%
1970	7.8	19.2	1.9	366	63.5	45.0
1971	8.4	19.7	2.0	363	58.4	39.8
1972	8.8	19.5	2.1	362	59.1	40.0
1973	8.7	19.7	1.7	336	61.3	44.9
1974	8.6	19.6	1.9	367	63.3	46.0
1975	8.3	19.2	2.0	338	60.8	46.0
1976	8.5	20.0	2.5	311	60.1	42.6
1977	8.7	21.5	2.8	289	58.2	38.6
1978	8.2	21.5	2.4	273	62.3	42.3
1979	8.3	22.2	2.5	246	61.3	39.4
1980	7.9	21.7	2.2	233	61.3	38.0
1981	8.1	22.0	2.0	233	64.3	41.2
1982	8.6	22.7	2.4	244	62.2	38.7
1983	9.5	23.5	1.5	221	58.3	31.8
1984	8.8	21.9	1.5	203	57.2	27.7
1985	10.3	28.4	1.5	222	72.8	46.0

SmithKline, Beckman

Fiscal year	Profitability ROS	Profitability ROI	Liquidity CR	Liquidity CC	Leverage O/A	Leverage IBD
1956	18.1%	46.2%	3.6	125	19.0%	-0-%
1957	17.8	41.4	2.1	156	33.1	-0-
1958	16.8	35.4	2.1	151	28.8	-0-
1959	18.5	37.5	2.2	155	26.8	-0-
1960	16.5	32.8	2.3	153	26.1	+[k]
1961	16.8	32.7	2.3	143	27.0	+
1962	16.9	32.9	2.4	148	27.6	+
1963	16.8	32.7	2.5	159	28.1	+
1964	17.7	33.0	2.6	159	26.6	+
1965	17.3	32.7	2.3	159	26.4	+
1966	16.4	29.8	2.5	193	23.0	+
1967	16.2	28.0	2.7	209	21.9	+
1968	14.9	25.9	2.5	212	23.8	4.0
1969	12.8	23.4	2.2	218	27.5	5.8
1970	12.6	23.7	2.1	222	27.2	5.7
1971	12.6	22.4	2.3	230	29.9	11.2
1972	12.2	22.1	2.2	218	34.0	13.5
1973	11.9	21.7	2.0	217	38.4	20.2
1974	11.2	21.7	3.1	227	44.9	27.1
1975	10.8	21.3	2.6	222	45.3	29.6
1976	10.7	21.3	2.5	206	45.8	28.6
1977	11.4	22.8	2.4	211	43.6	22.8
1978	14.8	33.8	2.5	201	41.6	14.5
1979	17.3	37.1	2.3	240	40.4	13.0
1980	17.4	36.2	2.5	237	36.5	11.4
1981	18.6	33.4	2.4	250	34.9	10.1
1982	15.3	29.7	2.3	195	35.6	13.6
1983	17.3	25.1	1.9	267	35.2	12.5
1984	17.1	24.4	2.1	239	35.2	6.8
1985	15.8	23.7	1.9	218	39.2	7.7

[k]Positive but not determinable

Tambrands

Fiscal year	Profitability ROS	Profitability ROI	Liquidity CR	Liquidity CC	Leverage O/A	Leverage IBD
1969	22.1%	36.8%	3.9	166	22.4%	-0-%
1970	24.3	39.5	4.3	167	21.3	-0-
1971	25.0	40.8	4.2	156	21.3	-0-
1972	24.6	39.8	4.2	146	20.8	-0-
1973	24.3	36.7	4.1	158	20.3	-0-
1974	24.1	33.2	4.6	196	18.8	-0-
1975	22.8	31.1	5.5	189	16.4	-0-
1976	21.8	28.9	6.9	173	13.8	-0-
1977	21.8	29.1	5.5	188	16.7	-0-
1978	19.7	25.5	6.8	199	13.9	-0-
1979	22.3	30.5	5.6	197	17.1	-0-
1980	18.2	24.2	5.1	204	14.8	-0-
1981	18.1	25.9	4.3	183	17.8	-0-
1982	15.1	25.2	5.4	140	15.8	-0-
1983	14.8	29.0	2.8	124	27.0	-0-
1984	15.1	31.3	3.2	118	26.5	-0-
1985	13.8	27.3	2.2	128	31.0	-0-

U.S. Tobacco

Fiscal year	Profitability ROS	Profitability ROI	Liquidity CR	Liquidity CC	Leverage O/A	Leverage IBD
1969	9.1%	15.3%	2.3	284	37.6%	28.1%
1970	9.1	17.3	2.2	254	37.4	27.3
1971	10.2	19.1	4.4	243	33.6	21.7
1972	11.2	18.7	4.1	258	31.7	19.6
1973	11.3	18.4	2.8	256	34.4	23.8
1974	10.8	19.5	2.1	270	39.7	26.4
1975	11.1	20.0	2.3	306	38.3	25.9
1976	11.7	21.6	4.2	300	38.7	26.7
1977	13.4	23.7	3.6	322	38.0	26.2
1978	13.5	23.7	2.5	348	42.8	31.5
1979	13.7	24.0	2.4	349	41.5	28.6
1980	14.2	24.8	2.4	351	38.4	23.4
1981	15.3	24.7	2.9	352	33.9	19.0
1982	17.3	27.4	2.6	351	34.3	19.8
1983	18.4	29.5	3.3	352	30.3	14.4
1984	18.9	30.9	2.8	351	31.2	16.4
1985	19.5	30.9	4.0	384	30.9	13.1

Appendix C:
Interview Schedule Outline

Focal Point
    Mission pinpointed and communicated throughout the organization?
    Niche(s) identified and pursued?
    Willingness/reluctance to fractionate or compromise a central thrust?
    Common thread running through the entire organization?

Culture
    Presence of "a culture" in the form of tacit understandings, esprit de corps, camaraderie? Its composition?
    Conscious efforts to alter or manipulate "culture?"
    Time-frame anticipated to modify a culture?
    Concensus versus an individualistic atmosphere?
    Cultivation and transmittal of specific traditions, values?

Key Executives
    Impact on the organization?
    Legacies, enduring impressions, major contributions of specific key executives and/or founders?
    Change of direction attempted or instituted by key individuals?
    Leadership/managerial styles?

Organizational Structure
    Elaborateness? Flat/multi-layered?
    Degree of decentralization/centralization of activities within functional areas and/or divisions?
    Flexibility-smallness versus bureaucratic hugeness?
    Communication pathways?

Innovation and Risk-Taking
    Attitude toward uncertainty and ambiguity?
    Degree of commitment to searching?
    Willingness to tolerate, perhaps encourage, failure?
    Entrepreneurial atmosphere and its cultivation?
    Criticalness of R&D activities?
    Attitude toward leadership in innovation—at the cutting edge of the art, or a follower?
    Criticalness of patents, licenses, franchises, trademarks, or brand-names?

Incentives
    Reward and recognition structures?
    Promotion from within or from external sources?
    Type individuals/functional specializations likely to rise or be represented in the top echelon?

Unique compensation schemes?

Marketing and Sales
Nurturing customers/clientele?
Caretaking of channels of distribution?
Role of marketing research? Integration with engineering, product development?
Promotional strategies and devices?

Operations
Product line proliferation/narrowing/concentration?
Productivity measures?
Approach to analysis of problems and opportunities? Highly structured, quantitative, subjective, or "do it and get on with it" orientation?
Degree of strategic/tactical planning?

Personnel
Executive development activities?
Rank-and-file development programs?
Job enrichment and job enlargement schemes?
Labor relations? Extent of unionization and those relationships?

Financial and Accounting
Budget/measurement review process?
Planning and control mechanisms?
Attitude and policies toward leverage, liquidity, profitability?
Specific critical financial ratios? Benchmarks/objectives?

Acquisitions/Spin-Offs/Mergers
Deliberateness of planning with respect to acquisition, diversification, spin-off, merger ventures?
Investigatory policies toward acquisition or merger candidates?

Multinational and Foreign Operations
Degree of integration with or separateness from domestic operations?

Overall
Perceived uniqueness or singular contribution of the organization within the industrial grouping and/or in the American/international arena?
Insights into why the organization is so extraordinarily successful?

Appendix D:
International Involvement

Each of our fourteen organizations is involved in overseas operations, varying from less than 10 percent of 1985 revenues to almost 60 percent. Those deriving more than 10 percent of their revenue and/or operating income during fiscal 1985 from foreign operations are displayed in the following table. IFF, for example, generated 57 percent of its total revenue and 69 percent of its before-tax operating income from overseas activities.

	Percentage derived from foreign operations during fiscal 1985	
	Revenue	Operating income (or derivative)
International Flavors & Fragrances	57%	69% (before-tax operating income)
Merck	45	25 (before-tax profit)
Lilly	32	25 (before-tax profit)
Kellogg	29	21 (after-tax profit)
SmithKline Beckman	28	25 (before-tax profit)
Tambrands	26	22 (after-tax profit)
American Home Products	22	17 (before-tax operating income)
Philip Morris	22	5 (before-tax profit)
Dover	16	12 (before-tax operating income)
Betz Laboratories	14	18 (after-tax profit)

Bibliography

General references are listed first; they are followed by articles and books pertaining to each of the fourteen corporations that comprise this study, in alphabetical order.

General

Abegglen, James C., and George Stalk, Jr. *Kaisha: The Japanese Corporation.* New York: Basic Books, 1986. 309 pp.
Bolman, Lee G., and Terrence E. Deal. *Modern Approaches to Understanding and Managing Organizations.* San Francisco: Jossey-Bass, 1984. 325 pp.
Byrne, John A. "Business Fads: What's In—and Out." *Business Week* (20 January, 1986): 52–61.
Carroll, Daniel T. "A Disappointing Search for Excellence." *Harvard Business Review,* vol. 61, no. 6, (November–December 1983): 78–88.
"CML Group, Inc." In C.R. Christenson, N.A. Berg, and M.S. Salter, *Policy Formulation and Administration,* 7th ed. (Homewood, Ill.: R.D. Irwin, 1976), pp. 571–603.
Cook, James. "Bring on the Wild and Crazy People." *Forbes* (28 April 1986): 54–56.
Drucker, Peter F. *Innovation and Entrepreneurship.* New York: Harper & Row, 1985. 268 pp.
Drucker, Peter F. *Management: Tasks, Responsibilities, Practices.* New York: Harper & Row, 1974. 839 pp.
Drucker, Peter F. *The Practice of Management.* New York: Harper & Row, 1954. 404 pp.
Hutton, Cynthia. "America's Most Admired Corporations." *Fortune* (6 January 1986): 16–27.
Johnson, W. Bruce, Ashok Natarajan, and Alfred Rappaport. "Shareholder Returns and Corporate Excellence." *The Journal of Business Strategy* (Fall 1985): 52–62.
Kanter, Rosabeth Moss. *The Change Masters: Innovation for Productivity in the American Corporation.* New York: Simon & Schuster, 1983. 432 pp.

Levering, Robert, Milton Moskowitz, and Michael Katz. *The 100 Best Companies to Work for in America.* Reading, Mass.: Addison-Wesley, 1984. 372 pp.

Levinson, Harry, and Stuart Rosenthal. *CEO: Corporate Leadership in Action.* New York: Basic Books, 1984. 308 pp.

Marshall, Joseph R. "America's Best Managed." *Dun's Review and Modern Industry* (September 1960): 38–40.

Measday, Walter S. "The Pharmaceutical Industry." In Walter Adams, ed., *The Structure of American Industry.* New York: MacMillan, 1971, pp. 156–88.

Miles, Gregory L. "Information Thieves are Now Corporate Enemy No. 1." *Business Week* (5 May 1986): 120–124.

Pennar, Karen. "Is the Financial System Shortsighted?" *Business Week* (3 March 1986): 82.

Perry, Nancy J. "America's Most Admired Corporations." *Fortune* (9 January 1984): 50–62.

Peters, Thomas J., and Nancy Austin. *A Passion for Excellence.* New York: Random House, 1985. 437 pp.

Peters, Thomas J., and Nancy Austin. "A Passion for Excellence." *Fortune* (13 May 1985): 20–32.

Peters, Thomas J., and Robert H. Waterman, Jr. *In Search of Excellence: Lessons from America's Best-Run Companies.* New York: Harper & Row, 1982. 360 pp.

Prokesh, Steven E. "*Excellence* Spawns a Too-Similar Sequel." *Business Week* (3 September 1985): 14–15.

Roethlisberger, F.J. and William J. Dickson. *Management and the Worker: An Account of a Research Program Conducted by the Western Electric Company, Hawthorne Works, Chicago.* Cambridge: Harvard University Press, 1947. 615 pp.

Sellers, Patricia. "America's Most Admired Corporations." *Fortune* (7 January 1985): 18–29.

Selznick, Philip. *Leadership in Administration: A Sociological Interpretation.* New York: Harper & Row, 1957. 162 pp.

Shapiro, Alan C. "Corporate Strategy and the Capital Budgeting Decision." *Financial Management Collection* (Winter, 1986): 1–14.

Smith, Geoffrey, and Paul B. Brown. "Emerging Growth Stocks—Why So Many Peak So Early." *Forbes* (28 January 1985): 69–75.

Uttal Bro. "The Corporate Culture Vultures." *Fortune* (17 October 1983): 66–72.

Waterman, Robert H., Jr. "Nobody Said Excellence Was Forever." *Business Week* (26 November 1984): 9.

"OOPS!: Who's Excellent Now?" *Business Week* (5 November 1984): 76–88.

American Home Products Corporation

Fraker, Susan. "American Home Products Battles the Doubters." *Fortune* (25 July 1983): 59–64.

Giges, Nancy. "AHP Shows New Face to Analysts." *Advertising Age* (24 October 1983): 3, 94.
O'Gara, Jim. "Inside Story of American Home Products." *Advertising Age* (20 November 1972): 25, 41–44.
Waldholz, Michael. "Pill Promoters: Marketing Often Is the Key to Success of Prescription Drugs." *The Wall Street Journal*, (28 December 1981): 1.
"Alvin Brush's Specialty House." *Fortune* (April 1958): 141–146.
"American Home: A Reticent Giant." *Business Week* (21 March 1970): 76–82.
"American Home: Low-Keyed Success." *Financial World* (9 April 1975): 15.
"American Home—Marketing Wizard." *Financial World* (9 September 1970): 10.
"American Home Products." *Barron's* (15 February 1971): 27.
"American Home Products: Can William Laporte Keep Those Profits Growing?" *Business Week* (20 October 1980): 80–88.
"Growth at American Home." *Financial World* (26 February 1964): 14.
"The Nearly Invisible Money Machine." *Forbes* (15 October 1965): 28, 31.
"Where Do We Go from Here?" *Forbes* (1 September 1968): 37.

Betz Laboratories, Inc.

Dannen, Fredric. "Nalco and Betz: Is Their Rapid Growth a Thing of the Past?" *Barron's* (6 February 1984): 34, 36.

Commerce Clearing House, Inc.

Sherman, Stratford P. "The Company that Loves the U.S. Tax Code." *Fortune* (26 November 1984): 58–65.
Sloan, Allan. "The Thornes' Sharp Deal." *Forbes* (29 October 1979): 125, 127.

Deluxe Check Printers, Inc.

Blyskal, Jeff. "Cancel that Complacency." *Forbes* (23 May 1983): 139.
Ling, Flora. "10 Billion Checks Can't Be Bad." *Forbes* (3 April 1978): p. 74.
Zemke, Ron. "Deluxe Check Printers, Inc.: Keeping Corporate Culture Alive." *Training* (November 1983): 24–30.
"Deluxe Check Printers: Electronic Banking Pushes It into Business Forms." *Business Week* (6 September 1982):103–104.
"Deluxe Check Printers: Facing the Age of Electronic Banking" *Business Week* (28 August 1978): 110–111.

Dover Corporation

"Big Man in the Elevator Trade." *Financial World* (31 March 1983): 30–31.
"Dover Corp.: A Game Plan that Keeps Succeeding." *Dun's Review* (March 1980): 33–34.

Dow Jones & Company, Inc.

Dorfman, John. "Two Little Old Ladies." *Forbes* (10 May 1982): 94–95.
Emmrich, Stuart. " 'WSJ' Not-So-Quietly Changing Its Ways." *Advertising Age* (30 January 1984): 3, 70.
Fisher, Anne B. "Dow Jones is Still Better than Average." *Fortune* (24 December 1984): 38–51.
Hall, Peter. "Inside Dow Jones: The Boom in Business News." *Financial World* (30 May–12 June 1984): 12–17.
Kerby, William F. *A Proud Profession: Memoirs of a Wall Street Journal Reporter, Editor, and Publisher.* Homewood, Ill.: Dow Jones-Irwin, 1981. 214 pp.
Phillips, Warren H. "A Report to *The Wall Street Journal's* Readers," *The Wall Street Journal,* (11 January 1983): 35.
Royster, Vernon T. "End of a Chapter." *The Wall Street Journal* (5 March 1986): 32.
Schardt, Arlie. "The Best-Selling U.S. Daily." *Newsweek* (21 April 1980): 64, 67.
Silberman, H. Lee. "Will Success Spoil Dow Jones?" *Finance* (April 1973): 58–62, 84.
Wendt, Lloyd. *The Wall Street Journal: The Story of Dow Jones and the Nation's Business Newspaper,* Chicago: Rand McNally, 1982. 448 pp.
"Dow Jones & Co., Inc." *The Wall Street Transcript* (11 April 1983): 69, 440.
"Dow Jones Joins the Media Conglomerates." *Business Week* (13 November 1978): 60–61,67–72.
"Dow Jones Moves to Insure Family Control." *Editor and Publisher* (28 January 1984): 57.
"Dow Jones Puts Latin America on the Back Burner until 1987." *Advertising Age* (2 December 1985): 46.
"New Book Details History of *The Wall Street Journal*." *The Wall Street Journal* (5 October 1982): 34.

International Flavors & Fragrances, Inc.

Bass, Don. "IFF the Market Leader: More Market Winners in Every Category." *Cosmetic World News* (April 1979): 12–14.
Hall, Trish. "Scientists Working to Develop Products That Make Food Tastier for the Elderly." *The Wall Street Journal* (7 November 1985): 33.
Hughes, Merideth. "International Flavors & Fragrances: Company with a Nose for New Markets." *Industrial Marketing* (September 1970): 52–55.

Karp, Richard. "The Big 'If' at IFF: How Much Longer Can Hank Walter Keep Swinging his Axe?" *Dun's Review* (March 1974): 52–55, 112.
von Koschembahr, John C. "International Flavors & Fragrances Inc.: New Styles in Corporate Management." *Finance* (March 1974): 11–15.
"Chief Executives Who Won't Let Go." *Business Week* (8 October 1984): p. 39.
"IFF Tastes the Recession." *Financial World* (23 April 1975): 18.
"IFF: The Sweet Smell of Success." *Forbes* (15 October 1973): 34–43.
"International Flavors: Funding Far-Out Ideas for Future Growth." *Business Week* (12 November 1984): 129, 133.
"International Flavors Looks for Growth, Despite Inflation, Raw Material Shortage" *Chemical Marketing Reporter* (20 May 1974): 4, 16.
"What Lies behind the Sweet Smell of Success." *Business Week* (27 February 1984): 139–141.

Kellogg Company

Blyskal, Jeff. "Beyond the Breakfast Table." *Forbes* (20 July 1981): 65.
Breckenfeld, Gurney. "Kellogg's Battle of Battle Creek." *Fortune* (29 November 1982): 122–124.
Eastman, Roy O. "The W.K. Kellogg Story: How to be Successful although Self-Effacing." *Advertising Age* (6 March 1967): 102–104.
Franz, Julie. "Agency Pours It on for Kellogg." *Advertising Age* (1 August 1985): 40–44.
Meyers, William. "The Word for Today is Health." *Madison Avenue* (April 1985): 63–65.
Willoughby, Jack. "The Snap, Crackle, Pop Defense." *Forbes* (25 March 1985): 82, 86.
"GM of the Breakfast Table." *Forbes* (15 November 1963): 35–36.
"Kellogg Looks Beyond Breakfast." *Business Week* (6 December 1982): 66–69.
"Kellogg: Still the Cereal People." *Business Week* (26 November 1979): 80–93.
"Kellogg: Target for Today." *Forbes* (1 June 1973): 24–31.
"Less Snap, a Little Crackle–Any Pop?" *Forbes* (4 September 1978): 35–36.

Eli Lilly and Company

Burke, W. Warner. "Conversation with Richard D. Wood." *Organizational Dynamics* (Spring 1981): 22–35.
DeBoest, Henry F. "Lilly: The Train Trip that Was a Turning Point.: *Nation's Business* (January 1971): 72–73.
Jaffe, Thomas. "Lilly on the Offensive." *Forbes* (15 February 1982): 58,61.
Kahn, E.J., Jr. *All in a Century: The First 100 Years of Eli Lilly Company*. Indianapolis: Eli Lilly and Co., 1976. 211 pp.
Lilly, Eli. "The First One Hundred Years: Eli Lilly and Company." *Medical Marketing and Media* (July 1976): 17–22.

Newcomb, Richard F. "Drugstore Fortunes: Case Studies." *Drug Topics* (19 April 1982): 31–37.
Wilcke, Gerd. "Prescription for Growth at Lilly." *The New York Times* (27 May 1973): F7.
"Charges against Lilly." *Business Week* (23 August 1982): 33
"Coming up Lilly's." *Forbes* (15 July 1968): 47.
"Eli Lilly & Co.: A Living Testimonial." *Drug Topics* (5 April 1982): 50–51.
"Eli Lilly: New Life in the Drug Industry." *Business Week* (29 October 1979): 134–145.
"Eli Lilly: Weakness Behind the Facade?" *Forbes* (15 April 1971): 26–34.
"The Miracle Drug that Became a Nightmare for Eli Lilly." *Business Week* (30 April 1984): 104.
"The Transition to Professional Management is Complete." *American Druggist Merchandising* (15 June 1973): 31–35.

Merck & Co., Inc.

Eklund, Christopher S., and Judith H. Dobrzynski. "Merck: Pouring Money into Basic Research to Replace an Aging Product Line." *Business Week* (26 November 1984): 114, 118.
Gibson, Paul. "Being Good Isn't Enough Anymore." *Forbes* (26 November 1979): 40–41.
Goldstein, Jeffrey M. "Putting Employees in the Picture." *Public Relations Journal* (March 1983): 26–27.
Robertson, Wyndham. "Merck Strains to Keep the Pots Aboiling." *Fortune* (March 1976): 134–139, 168–170.
Smith, Lee. "Merck has an Ache in Japan." *Fortune* (18 March 1985): 42–48.
"Merck: The Redoubtable Researcher." *Dun's Review* (December 1974): 52–54.
"Ready, Aim: Merck Got Shot Down Once in Diversifying." *Forbes* (15 May 1968): 29.
"The Prescription for Profits: More R&D." *Business Week* (9 January 1984): 72.
"TWST Names Horan Best Chief Executive Ethical Drug Industry." *The Wall Street Transcript* (25 February 1985): 76, 999.

Philip Morris, Inc.

Gibson, Paul. "The George Weissman Road Show." *Forbes* (10 November 1980): 179–188.
Gloede, William F. "Agency Execs Feel at Home in Marlboro Country." *Advertising Age* (1 August 1985): 46.
McGeehan, Pat. "Cowboys Image Connects." *Advertising Age* (1 August 1985): 46.
Meyers, William "Philip Morris Tries to Regain Its Footing." *Madison Avenue* (May 1985): 44–50.

Miles, Robert H. *Coffin nails and corporate strategies.* Englewood Cliffs, N.J.: Prentice-Hall, 1982. 298 pp.
Nulty, Peter. "Living with the Limits of Marlboro Magic." *Fortune* (18 March 1985): 24–33.
Sasseen, Jane. "The General Foods Deal May Not Be So Sweet." *Business Week* (14 October 1985): 40–41.
"A Call for Philip Morris." *Management Today* (May 1976): 77–80.
"At Philip Morris, Soda and Beer Are Still Falling Flat." *Business Week* (17 December 1984): 61–62.
Everybody's Business: An Almanac. M. Moskowwitz, M. Katz, and R. Levering, eds. New York: Harper & Row, 1980, pp. 229–232.
"Innovative Segmentation Distinguishes Philip Morris Firms." *Marketing News* (4 February 1983): 11.
"Jim Thompson Tells How Philip Morris Hit the Top." *Marketing and Media Decisions* (January 1984): 62–63, 123.
"Joseph F. Cullman III." *Financial World* (15 March 1977): 30–31.
"Joseph F. Cullman III." *Financial World* (15 March 1976): 42.
"Joseph F. Cullman III: Leaving Philip Morris with a Rich Legacy." *Financial World* (15 March 1979): 31.
"Marketing Strategy at Philip Morris Involves More Than Spending Money." *Management Accounting* (January 1980): 12–16.
"Notable and Quotable." *The Wall Street Journal* (9 February 1984): 26.
"Philip Morris for Steady Growth." *Financial World* (6 August 1969): 4.
"Philip Morris Gallops to the Top." *Financial Times* (9 March 1977): 19.
"Philip Morris, Inc." *The Wall Street Transcript* (30 May 1983): 70, 070.
"Philip Morris Lays Off 175 at Cigarette Plant." *The Wall Street Journal* (5 March 1984): 18.
"Reynolds vs. Philip Morris: Dramatic Moves in Different Directions." *Business Week* (11 July 1983): 101, 104.
"The Marvelous Marketer." *Dun's Review* (December 1976): 42–44.
"Why Philip Morris Thrives." *Business Week* (27 January 1973): 48–54.

SmithKline Beckman Corporation

Koenig, Richard. "SmithKline's Beckman Unit Gets Slow Start." *The Wall Street Journal* (23 December 1983): 11, 17.
Louis, Arthur M. "SmithKline Finds Rich Is Better." *Fortune* (30 June 1980): 63–66.
Seneker, Harold. "Life after Cost-Plus." *Forbes* (25 March 1985): 66, 70.
Weinberger, Thomas R. "SmithKline Corporation: A profile." *Medical Marketing and Media* (March 1981): 23–31.
"A Painful Time for SmithKline." *Financial World* (22 February–6 March 1984): 31–33.
"SK&F Seeks a Cure for Tired Margins." *Business Week* (26 October 1968): 170–174.

"SmithKline & French Labs." *Commercial and Financial Chronicle* (24 July 1969): 4, 304.
"SmithKline Joins the Health-Care Giants." *Business Week* (14 December 1981): 31–32.
"SmithKline: Reducing Its Dependence on Drugs." *Business Week,* (14 November 1983): 211, 215.
"The Prescription for Profits: More R&D." *Business Week* (9 January 1984): 72.
"The Product that Made SmithKline Red Hot." *Forbes* (15 December 1976): 30–31.

Tambrands, Inc.

Abrams, Bill. "Tampax, Facing Mounting Competition, Plans Changes in its Marketing Strategy." *The Wall Street Journal* (9 May 1980): 30.
Rotbart, Dean. "State of Alarm: Tampon Industry Is in Throes of Change after Toxic Shock." *The Wall Street Journal* (26 February 1981): 1, 23.
Seneker, Harold. "Test Time for Ed Shutt." *Forbes* (16 December 1985): 114.
Siegel, Sherry. "Tambrands Survives in Market 'Jungle'." *Advertising Age* (5 November 1984): 4, 74.
Yaeger, Deborah Sue. "Rising Rivalry: Tampax is Challenged by New Competition in the Tampon Market." *The Wall Street Journal* (21 August 1978): 1, 16.
"Is Tampax's Glamour Gone for Good?" *Financial World* (6 August 1975): 15.
"Sitting duck?" *Forbes* (1 March 1974): 54.
"Specialized Agency Reports." *Harvard Business Review* 52, no. 2 (March/April 1974): 83–84.
"Tampax Faces Life." *Forbes* (29 May 1978): 61.
"Turnabout at Tampax." *Barron's* (15 November 1982): 59–60.

United States Tobacco Company

Harris, Marilyn A. "What Could Burn the King of Smokeless Tobacco." *Business Week* (17 March 1985): 86.
Lappen, Alyssa. "Just a Pinch." *Forbes* 136, no. 6 (9 September 1985): 134–136.
Rhein, Reginald. "Now Smokeless Tobacco Comes under Fire." *Business Week* (26 November 1984): 61.
"Smokers Are Starting to Choke on Soaring Prices." *Business Week* (19 December 1983): 62–63.

Index

Abbott Laboratories, 145
Abegglen, James C., 145
Acquisitions strategies, 32–41, 134–135
Advertising strategies. *See* Marketing, promotion, and advertising strategies
Advil, 37
Aldomet, 109
Amerada Hess, 144
American Cyanamid, 39
American Demographics, 34
American Home Products Corporation, 1, 8, 10, 31, 146; acquisition strategy, 36–40, 63–64; barriers to entry, 129–130; centralization, 80; corporate anonymity, 63–64, 115; cultural characteristics, 88, 93–94; financial objectives and performance, 52–54, 142, 150; forcing competitive advantage to occur, 128; innovation and R&D activity, 63–64, 78, 110; international involvement, 163; lean headquarters, 79; long-term perspective, 42–43, 53, 134; managerial succession and training, 74; marketing, promotion, and advertising strategies, 115–118; mission, 23–24; monitoring activity, 56; planning, 49–50, 64; product quality, performance, and service, 105; unionization, 101; visionary founders and influential CEOs, 62–64
American Safety Razor, 40
AMP Corporation, 144
Anacin, 23, 37, 63, 115; compared to aspirin, 115–116
Annual stockholder reports, 15
Anonymity, 63–64, 115
Ansolysen, 117
Applicability of results of study, 140–141
Arden, Elizabeth, 35, 117
Attitude, 139
Autocratic leadership, 73, 135–136
Avon Products, 17, 126, 143–144

Bancroft, Jane, 85
Bancroft family, 15, 85
Barbanel, Jack, 138
Barriers to entry, 129–130

Barron, Clarence Walker, 29, 64–65, 85
Barron, Jessie Waldron, 85
Barron's, 29, 106, 111
Beatrice Company, 63
Beckman Industries, 31, 36, 91–92
Benedict, Ruth, 87
Bergstresser, Charles M., 64
Betz, John Drew, 67–69, 74, 80–84, 88, 112, 132, 135
Betz Laboratories, Inc., 7–8, 10, 14, 78, 140, 145; acquisition strategy, 32, 40; attitude toward competition, 125; barriers to entry, 129–130; centralization/decentralization, 80–81; cultural characteristics, 88–89, 96; financial objectives and performance, 51, 54, 142, 151; forcing competitive advantage to occur, 128; give-a-damn attitude, 98; innovation and R&D activity, 112; international involvement, 163; lean headquarters, 79; long-term perspective, 42; managerial succession and training, 68–69, 74, 76–77, 136; mission, 26–27; marketing, promotion, and advertising strategies, 119–120, 138; monitoring activity, 56; operating philosophies, 67–68, 83, 88; planning, 47, 51; right place/right time and luck, 132; transition from entrepreneuial to professional management, 81–84; unionization, 100; visionary founders and influential CEOs, 67–69, 135
Biotechnology research (at Kellogg), 112–113
Board of directors (mini), 56, 74, 89
Book Digest, 34
Brach candies, 23
Brand name loyalty, 116
Brand names, 39, 63, 116, 138
Bristol-Myers, 145
Brush, Alvin, 39, 62–64
Burnett, Leo agency, 114, 122
Bush, Vannevar, 70–71
Business Week, 123

Carmichael, James, 28, 66

174 • *Corporate Staying Power*

Carnegie, Andrew, 23
Casey, Thomas F., 49, 72–74, 80, 94, 120, 125
Cash cycle, 149–159
Cause-effect relationships, 140
Central thrust. *See* Mission, clarity of
Centralization/decentralization, 73, 79–81, 86, 136
Champion Spark Plugs, 144
Chef-Boy-ar-dee foods, 23
Chesebrough-Pond's, 144
Clapp baby foods, 39
Clark gum, 40
Clinoril, 109
CML Group, 25–26
Coca-Cola, 144–145
Coffee clatch communication, 57
Colgate-Palmolive, 126
Commerce Clearing House, Inc., 7–8, 10, 14–15, 78; acquisition strategy, 32; attitude toward competition, 123; barriers to entry, 129–130; compensation packages, 100; cultural characteristics, 88, 92, 95–96; decentralization, 81, 89; financial objectives and performance, 51–52, 84, 142–143, 151; give-a-damn attitude, 98; innovation and R&D activity, 112; lean headquarters, 78; long-term perspective, 42; managerial succession and training, 76; marketing, promotion, and advertising strategies, 119; mission, 26–27; product quality, performance, and service, 104; right place/right time and luck, 132; stock repurchase, 84; unionization, 100; visionary founder and influential CEOs, 71
Communication: coffee clatch, 57; internal, 90–92
Compensation packages, 99–101
Competition, attitude towards, 122–127, 138
Concentration decision, 23, 27, 32
Concern for employees, 99–100, 137
Conflict resolution styles, 91
Conglomerates, 10, 140
Connelly, John F., 67, 94
Continuity, 73–74, 141
Control. *See* Stockholder control
Controlling. *See* Monitoring activity
Cordiner, Ralph, 79
Corning Glass Works, 144
Corporate Products Committee (Philip Morris), 49
Cross-fertilization, 68–69, 88
Crown Cork and Seal Company, 67, 94
Cullman, Joseph F., III, 72, 75, 135
Cultivation of culture, 88–95
Cultural characteristics, 87–101, 136–137
Cultural differences, 36, 72, 90–92

Current ratio, 149–159
Customer loyalty, 116
Customers targeted, 118–119

Data Card Corporation, 124
Decentralization. *See* Centralization/decentralization
Dee, Robert, 81
Delegation, 63
Delivered cost-level of service as a barrier to entry, 129
Delivery system, 111–112
Deluxe Check Printers, Inc., 8, 10, 78; acquisition strategy, 33; attitude toward competition, 124–125; barriers to entry, 129–130; compensation, 100; cultural characteristics, 88–89, 92, 96, 136–137; decentralization, 81; financial objectives and performance, 52, 142–143, 152; forcing competitive advantage to occur, 128; give-a-damn attitude, 98; innovation and R&D activity, 111; lean headquarters, 78; long-term perspective, 42; marketing, promotion, and advertising strategies, 118; managerial succession and training, 74–76; mission, 29; monitoring activity, 58, 135; part-time employees, 100; planning, 47, 49; product quality, performance, and service, 105; right place/right time and luck, 132; unionization, 100; visionary founder and influential CEOs, 66–67
Dickson, William, 95
Dover Corporation, 7–8, 10, 15, 140, 144; acquisition strategy, 38–39; attitude toward competition, 123; barriers to entry, 130; cultural characteristics, 88, 94; decentralization, 81; financial objectives and performance, 54–55, 142–143, 152; forcing competitive advantage to occur, 127–128; innovation and R&D activity, 112; international involvement, 163; lean headquarters, 78; long-term perspective, 43; managerial succession and training, 75; mission, 24–26; monitoring activity, 56–58; planning, 47; stock repurchase, 84; unionization, 101
Dow, Charles H., 64
Dow Jones & Co., Inc., 7–8, 10, 15; acquisition strategy, 34; attitude toward competition, 123; barriers to entry, 129–130; compensation packages, 100; cultural characteristics, 88, 95–96, 137; decentralization, 81; financial objectives and performance, 54, 142, 153; forcing competitive advantage to occur, 128; innovation and R&D activity, 111–112; lean headquarters, 79; long-term perspective, 43; managerial succession and

training, 69, 76–77, 136; marketing, promotion, and advertising strategies, 118; mission, 29; monitoring activity, 57; new stock issue, 85; planning, 47; product quality, performance, and service, 105; right place/right time and luck, 132; stockholder control, 85; unionization, 100–101; visionary founders and influential CEOs, 64–65, 135
Dristan, 23
Drucker, Peter F., 2, 32, 70–71
Duffy-Mott, 39
DuPont (E.I.) de Nemours, 144
Duval, Betty A., 76

Earnings per share (EPS) measure, 4, 6
Eastman Kodak, 143–144
Eggo dressings, 35
Ekco Products, 24, 40
Emerson Electric, 144–145
Enthusiasm, 137
Espionage, industrial, 125–126, 138–139
Esprit de corps, 95–97, 101, 137
Ethical drugs, 36, 116–117
Exxon, 37

Federal Bureau of Investigation, 126
Federal Drug Administration, 108
Federal Register, 26
Federal Trade Commission, 31, 114, 134
Ferst, Monie, 28
Ferst, Robert H., 66
Financial objectives and performance, 50–55, 135, 149–159
Financial performance and ratio analysis, 52, 135, 149–159
Forbes, 123
Forcing competitive advantage to occur, 1, 127–130, 138
Fortune, 123
Fortune Directory, 2, 3
Free advertising, 121
Fringe benefit programs, 99

Gadsen, Henry W., 38, 70
Gannett, 145
General Electric Company, 50
General Foods, 30, 41, 76, 114, 125, 134
General Mills, 114, 134
Generalists, 75, 91, 136
Gillette, 40, 144
Give-a-damn attitude, 1, 97–99, 101, 137
Glaxo Holdings, 126
Griswold, Earle, 73, 80
Goodrich, B.F., 39
Gulf & Western Industries, 10, 24

Harland, John H. Company, 29, 124
Harmon Color Works, 39

Harris, Arthur, 66
Harvard University, 37
Hawthorne experiments, 95
Head, Howard, 73, 81
Hershey Foods, 143–144
Hirsch, Harold, 28, 66
Horan, John J., 71
Howitt, Richard, 29
Hutton, Cynthia, 6–7
Hypotheses testing, 140

Image creation, 121–122
Inderal, 23, 110
Indocin, 109
Indonesia, 113
Industrial classification, 7, 10
Ingersoll-Rand, 144
Innovation and R&D activity, 106–113, 137–138
Insulin, 110, 131
Intercollegiate Case Clearing House, 37
Interest-bearing debt (as percent of total assets), 149–159
International Business Machines (IBM), 10, 37, 144
International Flavors and Fragrances, Inc., 7–8, 10, 15, 78, 140, 144–145; acquisition strategy, 33; attitude toward compensation, 126–127; barriers to entry, 129–130; centralization, 80; cultural characteristics, 88, 94, 97; financial objectives and performance, 52, 55, 142, 153; give-a-damn attitude, 98; innovation and R&D activity, 113; international involvement, 120–121, 163; lean headquarters, 78; long-term perspective, 43; managerial succession, 74; marketing, promotion, and advertising strategies, 118–120, 138; mission, 29; monitoring activity, 57; planning, 47–48, 54; product quality, performance, and service, 105–106; right place/right time and luck, 131–132; unionization, 100; visionary founders and influential CEOs, 71–72
International involvement, 120–121, 163
International Telephone and Telegraph (ITT), 10, 24
Internecine warfare and internal politics, 95–97, 137
Interview schedule, 161–162
Irwin, Richard D., Incorporated, 29, 34, 81, 118

Japan, 97, 111, 128, 145–146
Johnnie (Philip Morris), 30
Johnson, Bruce, 6
Johnson and Johnson, 125
Jones, Edward D., 64

Jones, Reginald, 11

Kefauver Commission, 11
Kellogg, John Harvey (W.K.'s brother), 71
Kellogg, William Keith, 71, 114
Kellogg, W.K. Foundation Trust, 53, 84
Kellogg Company, 9–10, 78; acquisition strategy, 34–35; barriers to entry, 129–130; cultural characteristics, 88, 92; Federal Trade Commission suit, 114; financial objectives and performance, 142, 154; forcing competitive advantage to occur, 128; industrial espionage, 125–126; innovation and R&D activity, 112; international involvement, 115, 163; lean headquarters, 78; long-term perspective, 42; managerial succession and training, 77; marketing, promotion, and advertising strategies, 114–116; mission, 31, 134; product quality, performance, and service, 104; stock repurchase, 84–85; visionary founders and influential CEOs, 71
Kerby, William F., 34, 65
Kilgore, Bernard (Barney), 34, 65, 96, 135
Kimberley-Clark, 125
K-Mart, 89

LaPorte, William F., 50, 56, 62–64, 74, 110, 116
Lean headquarters and central staff, 78–79, 86, 136
Lear, William, 73, 81
Leighton, Charles M., 25
Leverage, degree of overall, 4, 149–159
Lilly, Colonel Eli (founder), 70, 105
Lilly, Eli (brother of Josiah, Jr.), 70
Lilly, Eli and Company, 8, 10; acquisition strategy, 35–36; barriers to entry, 129–130; compensation, 100; cultural characteristics, 88–90, 92, 101, 136–137; financial objectives and performance, 142, 155; innovation and R&D activity, 107, 109–110; international involvement, 163; long-term perspective, 42–43, 138; managerial succession and training, 75–77; marketing, promotion, and advertising strategies, 117–118; mission, 31; monitoring activity, 57–58; planning, 47, 49; product quality, performance, and service, 105; right place/right time, 131; stockholder control, 84; unionization, 100; visionary founders and influential CEOs, 69–70
Lilly, Josiah (founder's son), 70, 75
Lilly, Josiah, Jr., 70
Litton Industries, 24
Long-run perspective, 1, 41–43, 128, 134, 139, 146

Louisiana Land and Exploration, 14
Lubrizol, 144
Luck, 130–132, 138

McGraw-Hill, 145
MacMillan, Ian, 127
Magnetic Ink Character Recognition (MICR), 111, 118
Management development, 50
Management Development Executive Institute, 91
Managerial succession, 49, 68–69, 72–76, 86, 136
Mann, Ellery, 73
Marietta Dyestuffs, 39
Market share versus profitability, 64, 116
Marketing, promotion, and advertising strategies, 114–122
Marlboro, 30, 122, 130
Masco Corporation, 144
Mass advertising, 129
Maxithins, 120
Mayo, Elton, 95
Maytag, 144
MBA: graduates, 75; programs, 42
Measday, Walter S., 37
Merck, George W., 70
Merck and Company, Inc., 7–8, 10, 17; acquisition strategy, 37–38, 40; barriers to entry, 130; compensation package, 100; cultural characteristics, 88, 92; financial objectives and performance, 142, 156; forcing competitive advantage to occur, 128; industrial espionage, 126; innovation and R&D activity, 107–109; international involvement, 128, 163; long-term perspective, 43; managerial succession and training, 76; marketing, promotion, and advertising strategies, 117–118; mission, 31; planning, 46, 49, 135; product quality, performance, and service, 105; stockholder control, 84; unionization, 101; visionary founder and influential CEOs, 70–71
Mexican entry (Kellogg), 115
Midwestern work ethic, 42, 89, 139
Miles, Robert H., 30, 106
Miller Brewing Company, 30, 41, 55, 107
Minnesota, Mining and Manufacturing Company, 77, 144
Mission, clarity of, 1, 11, 21–32, 134
Mission Viejo Realty, 41
Monitoring activity, 55–59, 135
Murray, John F., agency, 116

Nalco Chemical, 145
National Observer, 34
New York Stock Exchange, 7
New York Times, The, 123

Northeastern Food, 37–38, 48

Odor Evaluation Board (OEB), 57
Oraflex, 90, 117
Ottaway, James, Sr., 34
Ottaway newspapers, 34
Over-the-counter, 7, 116–117

Pacific Lumber, 144
Panhandle Eastern, 144
Parkinson, C. Northcote, 1, 2, 78
Participative management, 91
Patents, 11, 108, 113
Patience. See Long-run perspective
Per inquiry commercial, 111
Performance. See Product quality, performance, and service
Perseverance, 1, 43
Peters, Thomas J. and Robert H. Waterman, Jr.: In Search of Excellence, 3, 27, 32, 87; comparisons with this study, 16–18; criteria used, 17; skunk works, 59, 87, 135
Peterson, Richard L., 72
Pfizer, 11
Pharmaceutical industry: rates of return, 31
Pharmaceutical research: revolution in, 78, 109
Philip Morris Incorporated, 9–10, 78; acquisition strategy, 38, 40–41, 125, 135; attitude toward competition, 127; barriers to entry, 129–130; compensation and fringe benefit programs, 99–100; cultural characteristics, 88, 92, 96–97; decentralization, 81; financial objectives and performance, 55, 142, 157; forcing competitive advantage to occur, 128; innovation and R&D activity, 106–107; international involvement, 163; lean headquarters, 78–79; long-term perspective, 42–43; managerial succession and training, 75–78, 136; marketing, promotion, and advertising strategies, 119, 121–122; mission, 30; monitoring activity, 58; planning, 48–49; visionary founder and influential CEOs, 72, 135
Phillips, Warren H., 29, 65
Planning, motivating, organizing, controlling (P.M.O.C.), 45
Planning activity, 45–50, 135
Polaroid, 144
Pope, Liston, 42
Precautions, 19–20, 139–140
Predictions of arrivals and departures, 143–145
Preparation H, 23, 37, 116
Prentice-Hall, 27, 123
Proctor and Gamble Company, 73, 77, 116, 125–126, 129

Product quality, performance, and service, 104–106, 137
Production and distribution facilities, 130
Promotion from within, 76–77
Promotion of ethical drugs, 117
Proprietary drugs, 36
Prospector organizations, 30, 106
Pulitzer prizes, 65, 96

Quick-fix orientation, 1, 41, 134, 146

Rauch, Thomas M., 79, 108–109
Reciprocal commercial time, 111
Repackaging information, 111
Research and development: barriers to entry, 130; impact on ROI and ROS, 11, 31, 41–42; monitoring activity, 58–59; planning, 46, 71. See also Innovation and R&D activity
Return on owners' investment (ROI): average of Fortune 500, 4–5, 148; average of fourteen companies, 4; averages graphed, 5, 13; defined, 3, 4; each of fourteen companies, 149–159
Return on sales (ROS): average of Fortune 500, 4–5, 148; average of fourteen companies, 4; average of U.S. enterprises, 4; averages graphed, 5, 12; defined, 3, 4; each of fourteen commpanies, 8–9, 149–159
Return on total assets, 4
Reynolds, R.J., Industries, 127, 143–145
Right place/right time, 130–132, 138
Roethlisberger, Fritz, 95
Rogers, E.P., 66
Roper agency, 122
Roubos, Gary L., 57, 67, 75
Routes to the top, 77–78
Royster, Vermont, 65
Ruger, William, 73

Ste. Michelle wines, 33
Sales force, 119–120, 129
Sales volume, by company, 8
Sams, Herbert "Bo", 66
Satellites, 111
Schering-Plough, 11, 143–144
Scientifically controlled academic research experiments, 140
Scripto Incorporated, 27–29, 37, 66
Searle, G.D., 11
Securities and Exchange Commission, 7
Seibert, Peter W., 72, 90
Selznick, Philip, 32
Seven-Up, 30, 40, 55, 107
Shapiro, Alan, 129
Shareholder wealth creation measure, 6
Sharp and Dohme, 37, 117
Shutt, Edwin H., Jr., 73, 76–77, 80

Signature Guarantee System, 124
Silicon industry, 37–38
Singer, Carl, 28, 66
Skunk works, 59, 87, 135
Sledge-hammer advertising, 116
Sloan, Alfred, 79
Smith, Adam, 27
SmithKline Beckman Corporation, 1, 9–10; acquisition strategy, 36; barriers to entry, 130; cultural characteristics, 88, 90, 136–137; decentralization, 81; financial objectives and performance, 54–55, 142–143, 158; forcing competitive advantage to occur, 128; give-a-damn attitude, 98–99; industrial espionage, 126; innovation and R&D activity, 108–110; international involvement, 163; lean headquarters, 79; long-term perspective, 43; managerial succession and training, 75–76, 136; marketing, promotion, and advertising strategies, 118; mission, 31; planning, 49; product quality, performance, and service, 105; right place/right time and luck, 132; Tagamet, 23, 31, 36, 54, 103, 109, 132
Smith's, Mrs., pies, 31, 35
Snake dance, 75, 81
Spitz, S.J., 57, 74, 80, 145
Sprague, E. Russell, 80
Square D, 143–144
Stalk, George, Jr., 145
Sterling Drug, 11, 144
Stern, Eugene, 66
Stick to knitting, 27, 134
Stock market performance as a priority, 145–146
Stock market performance of the fourteen, compared to Standard & Poor 500 index, 141–143
Stockholder control, 84–85, 136
Strategic planning. *See* Planning activity
Sturm, Ruger, and Company, 73–74
Success: criteria, 3, 7; measures of, 2–3, 7
Succession to top management. *See* Managerial succession
Sutton, Thomas C., 67

Tagamet, 23, 31, 36, 54, 103, 109, 132
Tambrands, Inc., 9–10, 14–15; acquisition strategy, 33; attitude toward competition, 125; barriers to entry, 130; centralization/decentralization, 80; compensation, 100; cultural characteristics, 88, 93–94; financial objectives and performance, 53–54, 142–143, 159; forcing competitive advantage to occur, 128–129; give-a-damn attitude, 99; international involvement, 163; lean headquarters, 79; managerial succession and training, 74, 76; marketing, promotion, and advertising strategies, 120; mission, 23–24, 26; planning, 49; product quality, performance, and service, 104–105; unionization, 100; visionary founders and influential CEOs, 72–73
Tampax, 120, 125, 130
Tampax Incorporated. *See* Tambrands, Inc.
Tandy, 145
Textron, 10
Thorne, Oakleigh L., 71, 132; estate, 15
Timoptic, 31, 109
Training programs, 49, 68–69, 74–75
Transition to professional management, 81–84
2 + 2 + 2 formula (SmithKline Bechman), 75–76

Union Carbide, 144
Unionization, 100–101, 137
United States Tobacco Company, 7, 9–10, 14, 78; acquisition strategy, 33; attitude toward competition, 123–124; barriers to entry, 129; cultural characteristics, 88, 97; financial objectives and performance, 55, 142–143, 159; innovation and R&D activity, 112; international involvement, 124; marketing, promotion, and advertising strategies, 121; mission, 30–31

Vagelos, P. Roy, 71, 107
Vail Associates, 72, 90, 92
van Amerigen, A.L., 71–72, 131
Virginia Slims, 30, 122
Visionary founders, 62–73, 86, 135–136

Wall Street Journal, The, 29, 43, 64–65, 74, 77, 92, 105, 111, 121, 123, 129, 132
Walter, Henry G., Jr., 30, 72, 80, 94, 113, 131, 145
Warner-Lambert, 11, 114
Waterman, Robert H., Jr. *See* Peters, Thomas J. and Robert H. Waterman, Jr.
Wendt, Henry, 81
West Germany, 97, 145
Western Electric Company, 95
Whitney yogurt, 31
Wholesalers, 31, 117
Wood, Richard, 47
Woolite, 23, 116
Wrigley, 40
Wyeth Laboratories, 117

Xerox, 144

Youth Garde, 116

Zantac, 126

About the Author

James B. Hobbs is the Frank L. Magee Professor of Business Administration at Lehigh University, where he specializes in business policy, strategic decision making, and accounting. He received the A.B. degree from Harvard in 1952, an MBA from the University of Kansas in 1957, and the Doctor of Business Administration at Indiana University in Bloomington in 1962. Hobbs has taught and conducted seminars at the undergraduate, graduate, and executive levels at Kansas State University, Lehigh University, the University of Edinburgh in Scotland, and the University of Canterbury in Christchurch, New Zealand. He has served as associate dean, department chairman, and director of MBA programs at two universities. He has acted as a consultant to several major U.S. corporations, small business enterprises, the National Academy of Sciences, and American and international universities. Prior to entering academe, Hobbs was a financial analyst, cost specialist, and internal auditor at General Electric Company in Chicago.

Dr. Hobbs is senior author of three editions of the textbook *Financial Accounting*, several articles in professional journals, and a recent reference work entitled *Homophones and Homographs: An American Dictionary*. Included in *Who's Who in America*, he has been cited several times for outstanding teaching awards, and is a member of seven honorary scholastic societies.